IN THE LAND

of

BLUE BURQAS

IN THE LAND

of

BLUE BURQAS

KATE MCCORD

A Protective Pseudonym

MOODY PUBLISHERS
CHICAGO

Scripture quotations are taken from *The Holy Bible, English Standard Version.* Copyright © 2000; 2001 by Crossway Bibles, a division of Good News Publishers. Used by permission. All rights reserved.

Edited by Annette LaPlace
Interior design: Rose DeBoer
Cover design: Kirk DouPonce, DogEared Design
Cover photo: Amy Jacobsen (protective pseudonym)

Library of Congress Cataloging-in-Publication Data

McCord, Kate.
    In the land of blue burqas / Kate McCord.
        p. cm.
    Includes bibliographical references.
    ISBN 978-0-8024-0814-3
    1. Missions--Afghanistan. 2. Missionaries--Afghanistan. I. Title.
BV3225.M336 2012
266.009581--dc23

                                                    2011048186

We wish to protect those who graciously shared their stories and their lives in the pages of this book, so all of the locations and names have been changed to ensure their anonymity.

We hope you enjoy this book from Moody Publishers. Our goal is to provide high-quality, thought-provoking books and products that connect truth to your real needs and challenges. For more information on other books and products written and produced from a biblical perspective, go to www.moodypublishers.com or write to:

Moody Publishers
820 N. LaSalle Boulevard
Chicago, IL 60610

7 9 10 8 6

Printed in the United States of America

For Miss Lillian Stevens,
who shared her love, her faith, and her memories with me
through the gentle but life-changing medium of simple stories

contents

1. Become One of Us, Foreigner 9
2. Where It All Starts.. 31
3. Whose Example Do We Follow? 47
4. Facing Hatred 65
5. Choosing Love 83
6. Who Is God?.. 103
7. How Do We Respond to Evil Done to Us?......... 121
8. How Do We Respond to Insult? 145
9. Who Can Judge?.. 163
10. Who Protects Us from Temptation? 181
11. Understanding the Journey 201
12. How Do We Learn to Live Our Faith?.............. 217
13. How Should We Pray? 237
14. How Should We Fast?...................................... 257
15. How Do We Live with Open Hands?................. 277
16. Saying Good-bye.. 299

    Scripture Notes 307
    Acknowledgments.. 311

Become one of us, foreigner

I climbed into the rickshaw, a 125cc motorcycle with a pickup truck bed welded over shock-less back tires. The rickshaw had metal sidewalls and a burgundy canvas roof stretched over metal rails and trimmed with fat, swinging, red tassels. Plastic sheets covered the space between the walls and roof making a sort of blurry window just below eye level. The back was open, allowing entrance and a view to the street behind. In the truck bed, two narrow metal benches covered with thin red cushions provided just enough space for four people to sit hip-to-hip on each side, knees interlocking with four facing passengers on the opposite bench.

Inside the rickshaw were two men, one with a gray beard and the other with a long black one. As soon as they saw me, the black-bearded man shifted beside the other, making space for me to sit alone on one side of the rickshaw. It was the right thing to do, and I was pleased that they had adjusted. The rules in Afghanistan are clear, and all must follow them.

I lifted my long coat with one hand, pulled myself up with the other, and climbed in, careful not to brush against the men's knees as I sat. I wedged my hand between one of the metal roof rails and the stretched canvas it supported, locked on, lowered my head, and watched the street outside the back. The boy rickshaw operator popped into gear and bounced down one of the few paved roads in the Afghan town in which I lived.

I had muttered a soft "Salaam" as I climbed inside. It's polite, although a woman hidden under the all-encompassing blue burqa probably wouldn't have done it. The two men eyed me. That was rude, and they certainly wouldn't have stared if my face had been hidden. I was used to it. Virtually all Afghan men, completely unashamed, stared at me wherever I went—another price of being a foreign woman in Afghanistan.

It was early winter, the season of cold, intermittent rain and mud. I wore a long, dark blue coat made of a gabardine-like fabric. Draped around my head was a thin, burgundy scarf, loosely wound, my brown bangs resting against the edge of my sunglasses. I had a small, black leather purse across one shoulder with a bright yellow telephone pouch and a bunch of keys clipped on with a carabiner. Often, well-intentioned Afghan men told me that I should put my telephone and keys away where they wouldn't be stolen: "You can't trust anyone here." They had no idea how strong that carabiner was.

I had my own objectives. The phone was security. I had to be able to hear it and reach it quickly. In Afghanistan, I lived without armed guards or concertina wire. My body armor was a cotton scarf and gabardine coat; my combat boots, sandals, or slip-on shoes; my phone, a lifeline—literally.

In America, people carry their cell phones because they're emotionally attached to them. They wouldn't dream of being out of touch. In Afghanistan, I carry mine because I must. Suppose one of my coworkers is kidnapped or there's a bomb threat in town. How would I know? If I were lucky, I would get a phone call or text message. Or suppose someone tried to kidnap me? I had to keep my cell phone near at all times.

The keys were another matter. I had a habit of collecting swirling clouds of children around me whenever I walked down my street. They all knew me and loved to draw close. I certainly couldn't be digging through my purse to find anything with such an entourage. Everything the foreigner has or does is fascinating. I wanted my gate key handy.

I wore dark sunglasses, even in overcast weather, and women in sunglasses were always an unusual sight. I had found wearing the glasses easier than exposing my shockingly blue eyes. Afghans said it was good that I hid my eyes behind the sunglasses. They told me it was good that I dressed conservatively, even if I didn't dress exactly like an Afghan woman. Often people thought I was a Muslim because I wore the long coat and headscarf. Misrepresenting myself was never my intention; avoiding stones thrown in rage was.

The two men, the gray-beard and the black-beard, studied me carefully. I hung on to the roof rail, pulled my knees close, and watched the paved road behind me. I suspected they would break the silence and hoped they wouldn't. I waited and thought of other trips I had taken in the company of other random men.

Once, in a different town, an Afghan taxi driver had asked me to take him to America. I had told him I couldn't; it wasn't possible.

"Why not?"

"Because you're not my relative."

"No problem. I will marry you. Then you can take me to America." I remembered watching him smile in the rearview mirror. He had been delighted with his own cleverness.

I can't count the number of Afghan men who have offered to marry me. Afghan women have even asked me to marry their sons or their brothers. At first I thought it was just because I'm exotic, a crazy blue-eyed foreigner with a quick smile. Eventually, though, I figured it out. I was far too "other" to be safe or even comprehensible. If I was going to live there, among Afghans, they needed me to become one of them, to fit in their social construct. There's no place in Afghanistan for an independent, unmarried adult woman. I didn't make sense. And anyway, in Afghanistan, marriage is a legal, practical arrangement. It isn't meant to be the deep, romantic companionship we prize in the West.

With that taxi driver from the other city, I had taken a guess. "You know, not everyone in America is a Muslim. Very few women wear headscarves."

At that, he shot me a wide-eyed glance in his rearview mirror. "But you do."

I smiled and responded, "Not in America."

He arched his back, stretched his neck, and completely abandoned the road for the rearview. "You walk around with your head naked?"

I narrowed my eyes and grinned. "Yep." I wanted to add, "You'd better believe it, buddy" but figured I'd expressed enough.

His response had been classic Afghan male. He lowered his eyebrows, tilted his head downward, and lectured me through the rearview: "You should be ashamed of yourself. And if America is like that, I don't want to go."

I figured his marriage proposal had just vanished. Ah, me, another opportunity lost. I smiled, grateful, and gently told the driver, "I know, you are not American." For him, the other, the stranger, the one who is not like us is simply incomprehensible.

I remembered that driver as the two men in the cabin of the metal rickshaw studied my clothes. They could see the edge of my calf-length navy skirt and the bottoms of my lightweight black tambon pants sticking out from underneath. They looked at my foreign shoes, ankle-high, flat-heeled, slip-on leather boots with Velcro closures. Certainly not the typical, shiny black plastic slip-ons or high-heeled, long-pointed shoes Afghan women favor. I think they even looked at my socks. In the winter, I always wore thick, brown, smart wool socks that someone had sent me from America. They were the best for the ice and cold. I only wished they were black so they'd disappear under my tambons.

All the while our little metal rickshaw with its boy driver bounced and braked and jerked along the main street through our little town. I clung to the metal roof bar and kept my eyes on the street behind us. It would only take a few minutes to reach the center of town where I'd jump down, pay a few Afghan coins, and go about my business. I wondered if I'd make it without conversation, but that wasn't to be.

I could see the gray-beard out of the corner of my eye, stroking his beard, considering his question. Finally, he found one. "Where are you from?" A simple question, but like any interaction in Afghanistan, full of potential danger or gracious welcome.

I didn't take my eyes off the street behind us. "America," I said, without apology, arrogance, or pride. I simply answered his question.

In my part of Afghanistan, Germany is more popular than America. For the most part, locals don't like America and have, on many occasions, made that very clear to me. Once, a bearded man in another rickshaw told me Americans were black-hearted, evil, and cruel. Germans were good. I had been very polite and had asked, "Do you believe I'm black-hearted, evil, and cruel?" I'd put him on the spot. I knew there was no way he could insult me. I was his guest.

That man had responded quickly, almost stammering, "No, no. You are our guest. Obviously, you are a good person. You must be here to help us. Do you work for an NGO? Which one? What kind of projects does your NGO do? Ah, that's very good. See, you are here to help us. You are good."

That day I had ignored offense and sidestepped confrontation. Before I had climbed out of that rickshaw, I had spoken a blessing over the man. It was a small blessing, but still generous: "May God bless you and your family." He'd been delighted.

This day, though, I was with two different men in the back of a rickshaw who were studying me closely. I waited, held on to the roof rail, and wondered where the conversation would go.

On some trips to the town center, I caught rickshaws full of women and children, uncomfortably packed, but I could climb inside without any trouble or fear. Sometimes I caught rickshaws with men, and they made space for me. I've stood on the street and waited until they all shifted and were satisfied that they had created an appropriate place for me to sit. They always did. The rules are clear.

Once I climbed into an old Russian taxi with space for three in the back and two on the passenger seat in the front. When I climbed in, there had been only a single male passenger in the front seat, plus the driver. I sat in the empty backseat. We drove from one to another small village outside of town. That vehicle was a linie, a taxi that drives the same route over and over, back and forth. It picks up whoever wants a ride. Everyone shares the space. If there's no room in the vehicle, the children sit on the roof and the women in the trunk. It's dirt cheap and easy to catch. That particular line cost something like ten cents for a twenty-minute trip.

I had been alone in the backseat of that vehicle. It was a nice ride. When the vehicle stopped to pick up another man, he immediately climbed onto the passenger seat in the front, jamming in next to the other passenger who already had that seat. I still had the entire backseat to myself. Then the driver stopped to pick up another man. That rider slid into the wide backseat next to me, and I immediately got out of the vehicle. I told the two men in the front seat to move into the back and they did. They smiled, sheepishly, but they did it. I slipped into the front passenger seat. There are rules, and they're important. They must be obeyed.

Once I even moved passengers on an airplane. I was flying from Istanbul to Kabul on a late-night flight. There was one other woman in the waiting lounge, a French aid worker living in Kabul. I asked her to sit with me, and she agreed. The plane was packed. About half the passengers arrived in the departure lounge in handcuffs. They were illegal refugees evicted by the German government. Their warders removed their shackles just before the illegal refugees boarded the plane. The French woman's assigned seat was in the center of a row of three. Mine was by the window in a row of two. I stood in the aisle next to my assigned seatmate, a young man newly freed from his German chains, and loudly ordered him to move and take the place of my companion. He hesitated. The flight attendant told me to take my seat, but I refused. "It's not appropriate. He must move." The other Afghan men seated nearby laughed at the youth and commanded him to yield. My French companion and I took our seats and slept peacefully all the way to Kabul. There are rules—rules about what to wear, where to sit, when to marry, and more. They must be obeyed.

The gray-bearded man in the back of the rickshaw with me knew the rules too. He could talk to me but not touch me. I could talk to him but should not look directly into his eyes. Instead, I studied the broken, potholed road behind us and waited.

Finally, the gray-beard leaned his relaxed face just slightly toward me, cocked his head sideways, and asked me honestly if there were mosques in America.

I breathed. It wasn't a threatening question. I have a stock response and gave it without looking at the man: "Yes, there are mosques in America. America is a free country, and people can worship God as they choose."

The gray-bearded man nodded thoughtfully. He stroked his long beard. Then he asked the expected question: "Are you a Muslim?"

I hesitated. His was a common question and I'd faced it many times. No matter what I said, my response wouldn't please him. I considered my options, the situation, and the rickshaw that both carried and trapped me.

The man hadn't asked if I went to the mosque in America. In Afghanistan, women don't go to mosques. There are a few exceptions, but so rare you can count them. Most of the women I know in Afghanistan, literally hundreds, have never walked into a mosque in their adult lives.

In Afghanistan, the culture, the rules are synonymous with the Holy Quran and the Hadith. A Muslim is a person who submits to these rules. The Quran, of course, is the holiest book of Islam, considered to be the very words of Allah spoken in Arabic, the language of Allah. The Hadith, and there are many, are written collections of the teachings and examples of the Prophet Mohammed. Most of Sharia law, the law of Islam, is drawn from the Hadith.

In Afghanistan, women wear burqas, the blue chadaris with the screen woven over the eyes. Burqas are required by the Holy Quran and the Hadith. Women cannot allow a male doctor or nurse even to take their blood pressure, let alone listen to their hearts, because it's the commandment of the Holy Quran or the Hadith. Women must ask their husbands' permission before they can leave the walls of their compound. These are all commandments.

Whether the Muslim holy books record these as true commandments or not isn't relevant in Afghanistan. If the local mullah, the neighborhood religious leader, says this is what the Prophet Mohammed taught, then that's all there is to it. There's nothing to debate. There are rules, and they must be followed without question.

I lived in Afghanistan for five years. I learned the rules. I had to.

The gray-beard and black-beard in the back of the rickshaw eyed me. The gray-beard had asked me, "Are you a Muslim?" For him, the word *Muslim* had a very clear definition. He did not just mean, "Are you submitted to God?" To which I could have said, "Yes, of course." He meant something much more precise: "Do you submit to the laws of the Prophet Mohammed as recorded in the Holy Quran and Hadith and as taught by the mullahs?"

Whatever true response I could give would not be welcome. Still, I could only give a true response. I answered the gray-bearded man's question softly and again without arrogance or apology. "No, I am not a Muslim. I am a follower of the Honorable Jesus Messiah."

I didn't look directly at either man. That would be rude. I kept my eyes down on the gray-beard's gnarled hands resting loosely on his knees. They didn't flinch, and I relaxed. He had accepted my answer.

I flicked my eyes across him and then looked down again. He was wearing a light-brown wool blanket called a *pathu* that wrapped around his shoulders and hung down to just above his knees. Beneath it, he had a khaki *Shalwar kameez*, the knee-length, cotton blend, long-sleeved shirt and matching oversized pajama bottoms. He wore rubber boots like English wellies but cheaper. He had a light gray, fairly small turban wrapped around his head. The color of his turban indicated that he was not a mullah. In our area, most mullahs wore white turbans. Some wore black, but that's the Taliban style. The size of his turban indicated he was probably Tajik. Most Pashto men wear larger turbans if they wear turbans at all. I took all this in with the slightest glance but kept my eyes downward.

I caught the measure of the black-bearded man in the same brief flicker. He wore a black turban, slightly smaller, in the northern style. He would be conservative and perhaps a mullah. His beard was chest long, like his Prophet's. Beneath that, he wore a brown *pathu*, similar to the older man's and a light brown *Shalwar kameez*. I caught his

17

face just briefly and stiffened; I was not out of danger.

The black-bearded man scowled, brows furrowed, mouth tight as one might scowl at a hated child or a loose dog. He leaned too close to my face and glared directly into my averted eyes. His words came out as a command, short and abrupt: "You should become a Muslim. It would be better for you in this life and the next."

My body shivered.

It was not unusual for Afghans to press me to convert. I doubt if a week went by when someone didn't try. Usually, they just encouraged me to say the Shahada in Arabic, the Muslim statement of faith. I knew better than to say it. If I recite the phrase, I am automatically Muslim. My conversion would be irrevocable.

This black-turbaned, black-bearded man wasn't at all unique in trying to get me to convert. However, his intensity and barely contained fury were not the norm. I had lived in Afghanistan for five years and had run into other men like this one. It was a dangerous situation, and I weighed my response.

I looked directly at the man. I sat straight in my seat, nodded, and said simply, "Thank you." Then I looked away. My action was combative but my words conciliatory.

The man was not satisfied. He leaned even closer to my averted face and repeated, "You should become a Muslim. It would be better for you in this life and the next."

His words ricocheted in my heart and pressed my blood pressure upward. "Your life would be better in this world and the next." I had just left the house of an Afghan woman friend who had recounted yet another horrible Afghan woman story. I've heard hundreds of these—heart-crushing accounts of abuse, oppression, and violation. I thought, "My life would be better in this world? Do you know anything at all about the lives of Afghan women? Have you ever even considered them?"

Afghanistan, during the years I lived there, was certainly a dangerous place. I've heard the explosions of bombs and seen the glass on my house tremble. I've evacuated my home under personal kidnapping threat. I've sneaked out of the country through an active war zone hidden under the protective cover of an all-encompassing blue burqa. Still, my greatest fear in the country has always been that I would be kidnapped and sold to some warlord as a fourth or fifth wife, relegated to household and sexual slavery behind a twelve-foot, mud-brick wall and locked gate. Even the mildest stories of Afghan women's lives haunt me.

I thought of the black-beard's challenge, his confidence, and his ignorance. I recalled the stories of other Afghan women, returnees from decades or more in Iran, Muslim women who had learned the bitter challenges of life in Afghanistan. Often their stories began with hope and excitement. They talked of the hardness of life in Iran, of how they weren't accepted by the Iranian community. There they were called "Afghani-gaks" with a sneer: Little Afghans. They were regularly denied education while their Iranian neighbors went to school. Their fathers and brothers, if they worked at all, labored at heavy, load-bearing, unskilled jobs for low pay. Their language was similar enough. Dari and Hazaragi are both related to the Farsi language of Iran. Their religion, Shiite Islam, was the same as their Iranian neighbors. Still, in Iran, they were outsiders, and no one wants to be an outsider.

Most of these women dreamed of returning to Afghanistan, a home they either had never seen or had fled as small children. They had grown up in a country not their own. When the ruling Taliban were finally ousted, many returned "home" full of hope and false promises.

One group of sisters and sisters-in-law told me their story in great detail. They returned to live with a brother who had bragged that he had a shoe factory in Afghanistan. A factory owner, ah, that must be a great man! They packed everything they owned, things they had acquired in Iran and some they had brought with them when their family fled one of the many regional wars in Afghanistan. They had clothes, bridal-gift carpets and gold bangles, hand-cranked sewing machines, pots, pans, teakettles, cups, plates, and all the other things that make up a modest Afghan household.

This family was promised a home to move into, and they had expectations for what that would look like. In Iran, they had hot and cold running water right inside their houses, indoor kitchens with counters and sinks, gas heating systems, and 24-7 electricity. They had refrigerators and gas ovens. They had no idea how good they had it.

The family, some eight men and women plus a few small children, hired a line taxi to take them across the border from Iran into Afghanistan near the ancient city of Herat. They were excited, full of hope. They were going home—finally. They were going home. They expected their lives to be better.

But their joy vanished as soon as they crossed the border into Afghanistan. First they were robbed, not by Iranians who despised them, but by their own countrymen, Afghans wielding Kalashnikovs (Soviet assault rifles). Shuddering with sadness, disappointment, and a dull fear about how they would establish themselves with nearly nothing, they continued their journey. There was no turning back. When they agreed to leave Iran, they lost their right to stay or even to return. That was the deal Iran made with its Afghan refugees—a bargain not fully understood when refugees accepted Iranian assistance.

The family traveled on, catching one vehicle after another. Finally they reached "home," the city of their future promised by their affluent factory-owning brother. They still had hope. They'd made it. Everything would be all right. But it wasn't what they had expected.

The brother's compound was a collection of small, mud-brick

houses behind the standard twelve-foot matching mud-brick wall. The floors were bare dirt. They didn't recognize the wooden doors and glass windows as an unusual benefit for refugee returnees. They had them, but nothing else.

The yard of the compound didn't have a blade or sprout of vegetation. The bathroom was a pit toilet behind a canvas curtain in the yard. In the heat, its stench filled the entire compound. The kitchen was a mud shed with a mud oven built low into the wall and fueled by a fire pit. There was no electricity. The water pump was two blocks away, out on the street.

The women cried. They had thought their lives would be better. That had been the promise, and they had believed it.

They discovered that the affluent brother with the shoe factory was actually the owner of only a single, hand-cranked shoemaking machine. Each day he sat on a blanket on the sidewalk in the center of the city stitching, gluing, and repairing shoes. If he had customers, he bought lunch from a street vendor in town. If there was anything left, he brought it home to his wife and children. There wasn't much. In those days, the city was full of returning refugees. Some came back from Pakistan, most from Iran. The Westerners provided temporary work for many of the men, but after the first year of the newly freed Afghanistan, most of that work dried up. In the meantime, the population continued to swell.

For the sisters, the first summer was brutal. There were no trees in their refugee returnee neighborhood, no fans or electricity to power them, and the wind, when it did blow, covered everything with a thick carpet of fine Afghan dust. They closed their windows against the dust and slept out on their roofs, rising before dawn to escape the eyes of neighbors who were all doing the same.

Winter was worse. Each day, even in the coldest of the winter, they squatted on the frozen dirt, filled their pots with rice and icy water, built a small fire, and cooked their family's food. If they had tomatoes or onions or cucumbers, they sliced them with stiff, aching hands. They had no counters, no cutting boards, and no running water. Inside their dark home, kerosene lamps provided dim circles of illumination through the long evenings. Wood coal fires built under a table covered with blankets provided their household warmth.

But the worst for the sisters was the culture, the rules of this country they called their own. When they recounted their story, the women had looked at me earnestly, nodding in agreement as one sister said, "Iran was free—modern and free."

It took me a long time to understand their perspective. I'm an American. To me, Iran is anything but free—modern perhaps, but free? I look at the world through my American eyes. I come from a land of tolerance with a level of diversity incomprehensible to even the most modern-thinking Afghan.

When the sisters arrived in Afghanistan, they had brought the small, white headscarves they pinned or tied under their chins. They had brought ankle-length black cloaks they draped over their heads. In Iran, a land of small headscarves and long coats, they had been conservative. They were accustomed to walking Iranian neighborhoods and streets with their faces open. They could ride buses and shop without harassment. Women in Iran had faces. That's what they grew up with, what they understood.

In Afghanistan, they were called "Irani-gaks" with a sneer: Little Iranians. Men walked past them on the streets and called them "naked" because their faces were not hidden. The younger sisters quickly acquired burqas and learned to live their very limited public lives under them.

And they cried. All that first year, they cried. Their lives were certainly not better.

Each sister told me her story. Each told me of her tears. The filth, the poverty, the ignorance broke their hearts. This was not the country they had dreamed of, the life they had wanted, the future they had hoped for. Yet it was theirs. They had become Afghan women.

The man in the rickshaw with the black turban and black beard had said, "It would be better for you in this life." I wondered if he was cruel. Did he have any idea how good my life was? Had he thought about how harsh and difficult the lives of Afghan women are? Did he even see these strong, beautiful women who hid their faces and voices in public but knew how to laugh when the doors were closed? My heart and mind were filled with their faces, the sounds of their voices and their stories, too many stories of poverty, war, ignorance, and oppression.

The man in the rickshaw had said, "Become a Muslim . . . It would be better for you in this life," and my heart railed. I held on to the rickshaw and kept my eyes on the road. I would have to find another response, a calm but true word, but first I would have to sift through my emotions.

I thought of heaven. After all, he had said, "Your life would be better in this world and the next."

Many Afghan men have told me exactly what heaven is like, in stunningly great detail. Men will get their wives back as well as, if they've been very good, seventy virgins who regain their virginity each time it's taken. There will be wonderful food, even meat. Ah, the good life. What every Afghan man dreams.

Once, after a male Afghan friend had detailed his understanding of Muslim heaven and derided me for my very incomplete understanding of what heaven looks like according to Jesus, I had privately asked an Afghan woman what she expected to find in heaven. Was there anything for her? Her response was jarring.

She was carrying a restaurant-wide, round aluminum tray of dirty dishes into the yard, and I had followed with her baby in my arms.

"Is there anything for you in heaven?"

She looked down, shrugged her shoulders, and said in perfect Afghan slang, *"Machem,"* meaning, "How should I know?" She slid the tray onto the ground and retrieved her baby. If there was any soft ray of sweet heaven's hope, I missed it.

I looked straight at the black-turbaned, black-bearded man just long enough to speak my response. I smiled, nodded my head, and said again, "Thank you." He had given his advice, and I had heard it. That would have to be enough. I didn't want to enter into an argument or any kind of spiritual discussion with the man. No matter what, I would lose, and my loss could be great. I was quite aware that I was riding in the back of a metal rickshaw in a small city in Afghanistan with only a headscarf and a cell phone to protect me. I would not provoke this man.

The man wasn't satisfied. He leaned even closer and growled, "You should become a Muslim now." It was not advice. It was a command, the third time he had given the same command. There are rules. Afghanistan is a Muslim country. The stranger in our midst must become one of us.

I glanced quickly at the gray-bearded man. Would he rescue me? Would he defuse this wrath? But he was still, his hands folded, his eyes downward. He would not speak. The black-bearded man was a mullah. His black turban outranked even the gray in his companion's beard. I was on my own.

I caught my breath, sat up even straighter, pressed the back of my head into the canvas roof behind me, and responded in the gentlest voice I could find: "I am a follower of the Honorable Jesus Messiah. He is my Savior and my Lord. I believe I have chosen the right path. Thank you for your counsel."

The black-turbaned, black-bearded man leaned back, perhaps considering his next challenge. I took the space he'd left in front of me to signal to the driver-boy to stop. I was several blocks from where I needed to get off, but walking would be safer.

I jumped down, paid the rickshaw driver the equivalent of fifteen cents for a ten-cent ride, and stepped up onto the sidewalk. I had escaped.

Relieved, I turned toward the center of town. To one side was a large park surrounded by a low concrete wall. The park, as always, was full of men; some lounged, some clustered in groups, others played soccer. Those who saw me turned to stare.

On the sidewalk in front of the wall, vendors squatted on blankets, selling used fabric, spices, and random electronic gear. On the street, rows of wooden carts called *karachis* displayed fruits and vegetables, makeup, combs and brushes, cell phone covers, and portable chargers. Each man and each boy stopped talking to stare at me. Some nudged their neighbors. "A foreigner. Look."

I walked slowly, picking my way around clusters of men and boys, *karachis*, and blankets stacked with wares. I stood as tall as I could and at five-foot-seven inches, that's tall enough to be dramatic. I kept my eyes straight ahead. I passed young staring men and didn't acknowledge their existence. I passed old bent white-bearded men, placed my right hand on my heart, and whispered a respectful *"Salaam."* I ignored the teenage boys who tried out their English or spoke openly to their companions about me.

I thought about the black-bearded man in the rickshaw. "You should become a Muslim. It would be better for you in this life and the next." His framework, his experience, his faith and practice could not be further from my own.

My eyes flicked across the men squatting on their vendor blankets and leaning against their *karachis*. I thought about them, Afghan men living in a gender-segregated society.

I thought about the Afghan women I'd spoken with over the years. I knew without a doubt that I had engaged in long and deep conversations with far more Afghan women than these Afghan men had ever seen the faces of, let alone talked to. The black-bearded man, so confident, couldn't possibly know. The hearts and minds of Afghan women are completely invisible to him. Yes, he sees his mother or his wife and his daughters cooking in the yard, sweeping the house, laying out the floor-cloth, and serving his tea and his meals. But that's the way it's always been. That's the rule. For him, the lives of women are nothing to question. The Islam he knows, expressed in his culture, simply must be the best way to live. I had to believe he thought he was offering me a better life. He just didn't know the life he was demanding I embrace. And he certainly didn't know the life he was asking me to trade.

And what about God? What about Jesus? What about the faith that infuses every aspect of my life, my thoughts, and my actions? What about the promise of heaven, eternal life spent in the presence of the God I love, the God I see as astoundingly good and beautiful? What does the black-turbaned, black-bearded man know of my God, my faith, my hope?

How could I respond? What could I possibly say that would make any sense in the framework of his worldview? Any alternatives I could show him would simply seem to be the ramblings of the profane—nothing worth considering, and perhaps, even, an attack on Islam itself.

Could I assure him, "No, my life would not be better in your world as an Afghan woman"? The idea is horrifying even without considering my faith in a God who loves and a prophet who saves. As for Jesus, the prophet who saves, there's no way I could trade Him for the Prophet of Islam.

Throughout my years in Afghanistan, I've thought about the Prophet Mohammed, Islam, and especially the brand of Islam practiced in Afghanistan. Almost every day in the country, Afghans showed me or told me the stories and teachings of their religion.

Sometimes they did it because they wanted me to understand. Sometimes they did it because I'd asked a specific question, and virtually every question of culture or faith goes back to their Prophet, the Holy Quran, or the Hadith. Often they explained things because they wanted me to see that their Prophet is the true and final Prophet of God and that their religion is the true and final religion.

I have met the Prophet Mohammed through his people in Afghanistan. I have learned about his life through what I've read and through the stories my Afghan neighbors have told me. I've come to know Islam through their lives, their culture, and the teachings they've explained to me.

Throughout my five years in the country, Afghans asked me, "We believe this . . . What do you believe?" A great many Afghans have questioned me closely about what I believe, how I practice my faith, and why. It's always the second great conversation. The first is different for men and women. For men, the most interesting conversation is about government and war. For women, the first most interesting conversation is marriage and family. But the second great conversation is always about our faith and our practice.

From my Afghan neighbors, I've learned about the Prophet Mohammed and Islam. From me, they've learned about Jesus and what it means to follow Him. We've traded our stories.

Imagine sitting at a lunch table with a group of American coworkers. Perhaps you are sitting on plastic chairs at a plastic table. One of your coworkers looks across the table, focuses hard on your face, and asks, "Do you pray?" Everyone at the table goes still and wide-eyed. We simply don't normally have these conversations in America, but we do in Afghanistan. We have them all the time.

"Do you pray?" "Really?" "How?" "Why don't you pray like we do?" "Do you fast?" "Really?" "How?" "Why don't you fast like we do?" "What do you do with your dead?" "Really?" "How do you do that?" "Why don't you bury your dead like we do?" "How do you expect to get to heaven?" "Really?"

Each time I entered a conversation, I was challenged to think through the answers. Afghans asked about America assuming that all of America is Christian and that all Christians do the same things. Their questions pressed me into clarifying what I believe as an American and what I believe as a follower of Christ. Those are not always the same things. After all, American culture is not a one-to-one expression of biblical teaching.

For example, Afghan women wear headscarves, usually even indoors. They do it because it's the commandment of the Holy Quran and is required by Islam. That's what they tell me. They ask me, "Do women wear headscarves in America?" And I must answer them. I might start by reminding them that America is a free nation and that the people of America practice all different religions or even no religion at all. I might tell them America does not pass laws dictating how people are to live or worship. Then I might go on to explain why I, as a follower of Jesus, don't wear a scarf in America.

They are often surprised by my answers, and sometimes I'm satisfied with what I've said. Other times, I walk away and think, "Why didn't I tell them this?" or "I should have said that." Sometimes I forget to differentiate between what I believe as an American woman and what I believe the Bible teaches. America is my culture, and Jesus is my Savior and Lord. Sometimes it's hard to untangle the two. Afghans challenged me to try.

This book is a journey into Afghanistan, into some of those conversations. I invite you. Come with me. Join me in the rickshaws and taxis, the bazaars, offices, and Afghan homes. You will be our guest. Listen in to our conversations as we share our lives and our faith with one another.

It's a privilege to live in such a different society, immersed in a different culture. Sharing stories with Afghans has helped me consider and clarify who I am and what I believe. My faith has grown clearer and stronger through the journey. Perhaps, as you sit with me in Afghan homes or ride with me in Afghan taxis or walk along Afghan streets, you too will grow deeper in your understanding of what you believe, why, and what it means to live out your faith. Along the way, you'll meet Afghans, real people with real troubles, hopes, and dreams—people not unlike us, precious men and women who are also on a journey, their own journey of faith.

where it all starts

In Afghanistan, I lived within a walled compound. From the street, my home looked just like my neighbors'—a gate, a thick, mud-brick, six-foot wall, the smoke of cooking and heating fires drifting upward from various chimneys. Despite the outward similarities, my life could not be more different. I had my own room and slept alone in it. I ran a generator for electricity when I needed it. I had an indoor kitchen with a sink and a bathroom with a flush toilet. Most importantly, within my walled compound, I was an American. I walked, talked, and even breathed like an American, not an Afghan.

Afghan men and women live in two entirely different, gender-segregated worlds. Men live in the public sphere. They work outside the home, sit in the shops, herd flocks of sheep or goats, work as day laborers, tradesmen, or farmers. They do most of the shopping. The bazaar, the mosques, teahouses, and even street corners belong to them. When women appear, they're covered, often in the all-encompassing blue or white burqa. In a sense, Afghan women are visitors in the public sphere. They pass quietly, sometimes in groups with other women, often with a child in tow, rarely alone.

Women live in the domain of the family compound, called an *aouli*. Each *aouli* typically encloses a house or series of houses, an outdoor kitchen, and a separate pit latrine all within a twelve-foot-high, mud-brick wall. Often two or three families, each with multiple generations, live within the compound. An Afghan woman defines herself by her relationships. She is called the mother of so-and-so or the wife of such-and-such.

There are clear social rules governing the interactions of men and women, specific to the type of relationship. Closely related men and women may speak freely. A woman may speak to a shopkeeper to conduct business or to a taxi driver. The unrelated are separated. They pass each other silently on the streets, not even looking in each other's direction. Afghans know the rules and, for the most part, honor them.

The *aouli* is the women's sanctuary. There, Afghan women work, laugh, and talk. They may keep their heads covered, but their faces remain open. They may push their sleeves up above their elbows to expose what would be scandalous in public. They might even wear a short-sleeved, knee-length shirt. If a woman is washing clothes, she might tuck the front of her long shirt into the elastic waistband of her oversized pants.

She keeps her gate unlocked to enable children and neighbors to come in and out but does not expect any unrelated man to enter without warning and specific invitation. If a man or older boy does request entry or enters with a male relative, the women and older girls are warned, given time to hide. The man is invited into a sitting room, and a boy or a small girl will bring him his tea.

Women step inside their own or their neighbor's *aouli* quietly, unannounced, and then make their presence known. Friends and relatives will not only enter a compound unannounced but will walk straight into the homes. It's not unusual for a woman to simply appear in a neighbor's sitting room.

Children, both boys and girls, run in and out of the *aouli* freely. Smaller children and boys spend most of their days playing out on the street with other neighborhood children. Older girls learn to stay inside the walls and, early on, share the responsibility for maintaining the household. Older boys often take on apprentice roles in town or help their fathers and brothers herd flocks or farm land.

As a foreign woman, I occupy a space with less-defined rules. I'm accepted in both the public and professional domains of men, and in the *aoulis* of women. I am a stranger, an outsider, and a relative of no one. I had to adopt a cultural approach that honored the Afghan culture, established my identity within the community, and somehow enabled me to live an emotionally sustainable life.

I realized very quickly I would not be able to completely enculturate. I could not live as an Afghan woman. I am, without doubt to anyone, a middle-aged American woman with all the cultural markers and worldviews that brings. And of course I couldn't do my job as a humanitarian aid worker if I completely adopted the normative behavior of the vast majority of women in my community.

There are women who work outside of their *aouli,* but it's not the norm. Even in my small town, there were a few women doctors, lawyers, and NGO (non-government organization) project workers. There were teachers who worked at the large girls' schools in town. There were even women with the courage and family support to stand for Parliament. But I was not like these women, either. Each lived in the context and defined social structure of their immediate and extended families. Their place in the world was clearly defined and understood.

I was an oddity, a stranger who didn't fit properly into any category, and so I had to make my own rules. I watched Afghans, questioned them, and learned from them. I tried to understand the principles underneath the social rules and then adapted them. I worked hard to understand who had the social right to visit whom, how often, and when. When they did visit, how did they enter the *aouli*? Where did they sit in the visiting room? How much tea did they really drink? What treats did they eat? How long did they stay? How and when did they leave?

I watched, asked questions, and learned. Over time I developed a hybrid approach—a little oddly foreign and yet culturally honoring. Each time I stepped through my gate onto an Afghan street, I not only entered my neighbor's world, but I also clothed myself in a cultural role with rules and expectations that required constant conscious attention. The effort was wearying. I couldn't simply wander out of my house, jump into my car, and drive off. I had to stop, think, and prepare. I had to check my clothes, my keys and phone, my attitude. I hesitated before unlocking my gate and emerging from my sanctuary onto the Afghan street.

As soon as I stepped through my gate I became the center of attention. Children cried, "Foreigner! Foreigner!" and ran up to demand pens, pencils, candy, or anything they thought they could get from me. They gathered around like my own personal cloud and followed my path. Men stared, and sometimes younger men called out or attempted their few English words. Beggars reached out their hands. I walked slowly, with as much patience and grace as the situation warranted. Eventually I would reach my destination, the *aouli* of a friend or a family I wanted to meet.

I would ask a child on the street if his mother or grandmother were home. I would never call the woman by her own name. Instead, I would ask for the mother of so-and-so or the wife of such-and-such, giving only the name of a boy or a man. Sometimes, if the child was young enough, he would run inside ahead of me and announce my presence. If the child was older, he might just tell me to go in.

If I didn't find a family's child on the street, I would simply push the gate open and call out the traditional greeting, "Salaam." Once inside the gate, off the street, I might call to the woman by her own name. I knew that, as a woman, I had the right to enter virtually any *aouli* in the country. I also understood that as a foreigner, a perpetual guest, I needed to announce my presence and enable the family to decide how and where to receive me.

Often, I would enter the courtyard of an *aouli* and find a woman or a girl emerging from the house, the outdoor kitchen, or the area where the women were washing laundry. We would clasp hands, kiss cheeks, and trade the normal greetings without listening to one another's responses: "How are you? How is your family? How are your children? How is your health?" If the woman I was looking for was present, I would be ushered into a small, carpeted room with thick, raw-cotton sitting mats laid out on the floor against each wall. As a foreign guest, I would take a seat of honor, far from the door. I usually left the farthest seat, the position of highest honor, empty. That way, if someone of greater honor came in, perhaps a gray-haired mother-in-law or grandmother, she would be able to take that seat without anyone being shamed.

If I sat down at too low a seat, too close to the door, then my host's family and other guests would have to sit beneath me, leaving them clustered in the doorway without mats to sit on. They would never complain, but I understood.

The women of the *aouli*, often several wives, mothers-in-law, and older daughters would come and sit with me while a girl or the woman I was actually visiting fetched tea and trays of candy, nuts, and raisins for everyone in the room. Our conversation would begin.

With most Afghan women, the first conversation is always about family. That's how we get to know each other. "How many children do you have? Boys or girls? How old are they? How many grandchildren do you have? Is your husband here, or has he gone to a distant place to work? Are your parents still with us, or have they gone on?" The answers to these questions define a woman's identity and establish where she fits in the social structure.

Each time I entered an Afghan home for the first time, I surprised the family with my presence. I am a blue-eyed foreign woman, middle-aged, oddly but appropriately dressed. I speak Dari, the most common language, and have a fairly good understanding of the culture. I know how to sit on a toshak, the cotton floor mat, and can do so easily and gracefully. I know what to talk about and how to drink tea. I am both an exotic and simultaneously normal creature. That is, until we arrive at my marital status. That becomes the second surprise. The conversation almost always starts the same way.

"How many children do you have?"

"I have none." I smile, waiting for the next question.

The women look at me in confusion and wonder what to say. A woman without children is a sad thing in Afghanistan. It's a sign of shame and indication of deep loss and vulnerability. "You have no children?"

"No." I smile again. My life has been blessed with the presence of children, but none have been my own. I confess I'm grateful for that. I've walked on different journeys, but none that are comprehensible in Afghanistan.

"Why not?" Afghans tend to think that Americans can fix anything. If an Afghan woman can't have children, she assumes that if she could just see the right doctor, a good foreign doctor, the problem would be solved. So, clearly, if I am unable to have children, or if my children have all died, there must be a doctor in America who can fix me.

My next revelation is always startling: "I never married." I smile again, mischievously. I know where this conversation will go.

Most Afghan women in my area marry between fifteen and nineteen. In the villages near us, a girl is married between eleven and fourteen. Usually a girl is married against her desire. Most young brides don't know the men they're marrying nor the family situation they're marrying into. I've asked many Afghan men to tell me the story of the happiest day of their lives. Usually they tell me about the day they acquired their first wife. I've asked Afghan women the same question. Their answer never includes their wedding day. But when I ask women about the saddest day of their lives, their responses are similar. If the story doesn't include bombs and guns and dead children, it almost always starts with "The day I married my husband."

Women tell me stories of weeping for months after the engagement and before the wedding. They tell me about crying on their wedding day, not from joy, but from fear and grief. They tell me of the tears they shed as they made the journey with their new husband to his family's home. It's not that all of these marriages turn out bad; it's just that the girls aren't ready to enter into them. They're too young. Their new husbands and the family they'll join are strangers. They don't know anything about the sex that awaits them. They lose the company of their mothers and sisters and the known safety of their own *aouli* and instead fall into the hands of mothers-in-law who will treat them any way they choose. These young brides are simply afraid of what's to come and grieving what's being lost.

Then there's the work. When I asked men what their wives do for work, they usually said, *"Be-kar,"* meaning "without work." Some Afghan men joke that their wives sit around and gossip all the time and have nothing else to do. But when I visit women's homes, I find them squatting on the ground in all weather, washing clothes by hand or huddled in the kitchen-shed, cooking rice in a deep aluminum pot over an open fire, or reaching into the fiery heat of a buried *tandoor*, a cylindrical, clay pot, to pull out fresh baked loaves of flatbread. I hear them over the wall, dragging cotton mats outside to the porch and beating them with sticks.

I saw my Afghan women friends' exhaustion from taking care

of babies and children that they'd birthed *shir-ba-shir*, which literally means "milk by milk," or one after the other before the previous infant was weaned. I've watched them cry at the realization of yet another pregnancy and struggle with far too many small voices competing nonstop for their attention.

In Afghanistan, the lives of women are hard. The work is heavy and unremitting. The comforts are few. Yet despite the hardships, most Afghan women I met could see no other possibility. Few sat in their houses wishing they could go off to work in an office or a school. Some, of course, did dream such dreams, but most didn't. They accepted their situation as simply the way it was. As for marrying, what choice did they have? When I asked, "Why did you marry your husband?" The answer was almost always the same: "What could I do? My parents decided, and that was all."

So when I tell them, "I never married," with a mischievous smile, they're often intrigued and confused. The questions follow: "Why not? How were you able to do that? Is that really possible?" And then, of course, comes the conventional wisdom: "You should marry an Afghan man."

I often laughed at this advice. One of my foreign friends, a young woman by our standards, old by theirs, developed her own stock response: "I will, if he'll wash the dishes." To which everyone laughs because Afghan men don't do such work.

The truth is, our expectations of marriage are just completely different. In the West, we see marriage as lifelong companionship. In Afghanistan, it's a much more practical, economic arrangement.

Each time I entered this conversation, I measured my response depending on the situation. My real goal was to get past this subject mostly because I was bored with it. I knew how it would unfold. I wanted to get on to something more interesting. And I wanted to find laughter. I always wanted to find laughter. It's good for the soul, and I just loved to hear a group of Afghan women laugh, hard and deep.

"Ah, I'm too lazy to marry!" I feigned self-incrimination and added, "Men are a lot of work, and babies more. I'm way too lazy for all that!"

The women always laughed. They tossed looks at each other. They threw their heads back and howled or shook them in agreed disgust. Yes, men are a lot of work, helpless and demanding. Households are a lot of work—the dust, the filth, the cooking pot, the never-ending demands of babies and children. This crazy foreign lady's got that right.

The truth is, I never wanted them to think that the way I live as an ever-single professional woman is the solution to all of their heartaches. My life as an American woman is my context. Their marriages are theirs. The challenge for all of us, Afghan and American, is to find peace, love, and joy in whatever situation we find ourselves.

Eventually my new Afghan women friends and I would get to the end of this subject. If we were fortunate, we would have learned something about each other and we would have laughed.

Often women would ask me directly, on the heels of this conversation, how American men and women choose to marry each other. I always tried to explain something of our idea of personal choice and our practice of getting to know one another. I talked about how men and women consider the possibility of marrying and what it looks like to make that decision. I described the traditional, down-on-one-knee proposal and the classic church wedding service. I told them about our gender-integrated wedding receptions. Ah, and it all sounds so romantic, beautiful, and free.

If there's anything in American culture that Afghans, both young men and all women really admire it's this: that men and women decide who and when to marry. It touches on their greatest sorrow and their deepest dream. And yet I never wanted to present the American way as the ultimate model and solution to all of their problems. My American culture comes with its own baggage, its own failures, sorrows, and heartaches. I wanted to show my Afghan women friends that it's not marriage that's brutal for women, but rather, brutality expressed in marriage that's evil.

Many times I asked Afghan women to describe the characteristics of a good husband and have been amazed at the common responses. He works and makes good money; he doesn't marry more than one wife, or if he does, he supports them both well in separate households; he doesn't have a bad temper and definitely doesn't beat his wife more than just a little.

I've never met an Afghan woman who has said that her husband never hit her. Once I asked a recent widow if her husband had been a good man. She said, "Oh yes, absolutely. He only beat me a little the first few years we were married. After that, he stopped hitting me." I remember struggling to hide my shock and horror.

Marriage in Afghanistan is, for women, an absolute requirement. Like everything in Afghan culture, the commandment is believed to come from the Holy Quran. A woman must marry because the Prophet of Islam says she must. And yet marriage is fraught with dangers and hardship. A girl often enters it with tears and learns to adjust to whatever reality she encounters. She may dream of delaying her marriage until she's older and a good man is found, but she's not likely to want to live unmarried and childless. It's not marriage she scorns as much as the particular husband who never knew her well enough to choose her personally and who lives separate from her, visiting for meals and nights. For an Afghan woman, life, faith, and the practice of her faith all begin in her home.

I was never surprised to meet Afghan women who loved the Western approach of choosing one's spouse and being chosen by him. And yet I didn't want to leave a home with the illusion that the America way is the solution to their problems. Marriages aren't bad because they're arranged any more than they're good because they're chosen.

In Afghanistan, I learned to take the conversation back to the beginning, the very beginning, the first relationship. I would launch into the story of Father Adam and Mother Eve. Afghans know Adam and Eve and have their own variation of the creation story. They absolutely believe that Allah created the man and the woman—but not in his own image. That's too great. They believe the man and the woman have a human spirit, unique from the animal world. In their understanding of Muslim teaching, they believe Allah made Father Adam and Mother Eve and put them in his garden in heaven. Then Adam and Eve disobeyed Allah, and Allah threw them out of the garden onto the earth. These things are not ideas in Afghanistan; they are facts, accepted as one accepts air and water.

There's enough of this story that we share for me to feel comfortable reminding them of it and elaborating on it. Often our conversation went something like this: "Marriage isn't bad. Do you remember the story—how God created Father Adam?"

I never use the word "Allah" when I speak of God. In Dari, we have another word, *Khoda,* so I use that. No one has objected.

The women nod in agreement when I ask them if they remember Father Adam.

I go on. "God created Adam first, but Adam was alone and God said that wasn't good. Men really can't live alone, can they?"

At this, my women friends laugh. They know the men in their lives are helpless without them. Who would brew their tea, cook their meals, and wash their clothes? And then there are the other things that men need. Obviously, it's not good for men to live without women.

"So what did God do?"

Usually they tell me God created Eve. Mother Eve, that's what they call her.

"Yes, God created the beautiful Eve, and Adam loved her. God arranged the first marriage, and it was good."

At this, the conversation gets interesting. Yes, of course God arranged the first marriage. Neither Adam nor Eve had earthly parents to arrange the marriage for them. And of course, the marriage had to be good, didn't it? After all, God arranged it.

"God brought the beautiful Eve to the beautiful Adam, and they loved each other. They really loved each other."

The story becomes a romance, and romances are enchanting in any culture.

"Do you remember? Adam and Eve were naked . . ."

At this, the women laugh and the girls try to look shy. Nakedness is a thing that isn't discussed. Only very small children should ever be naked, and they ought to learn quickly that it's shameful. And yet I imagine that the women are also thinking about the pleasure a man and a woman find in each other's bodies and are embarrassed by the thought. So the laughter of the girls is closed in shyness and embarrassment while the laughter of the women is closed in knowledge and experience.

"But listen, they weren't ashamed! They were naked with each other, and they weren't ashamed."

By now, the story is the only thing happening in the room. Older children have been chased out. Small girls have been commanded to take their smaller siblings to the street or the yard of the *aouli*. Their interruptions are no longer welcome. A story is being told, and stories are wonderful.

"Adam and his wife, Eve, were together, and they weren't afraid of each other. They didn't fight or argue. They loved one another, and they treated one another with kindness and respect."

This is like a dream for most women—not only Afghan women, but women everywhere. Our stories are full of love, joy, and peace. Every culture has its romance stories. Every boy and every girl dreams it. Somehow, it's embedded in the human heart.

"This is what they were made for: Love. This is what we're all made for."

The women are drawn completely into the story. Father Adam, Mother Eve living in bliss in the garden of God. What a beautiful dream, what an ancient memory.

Then I say perhaps the most important thing. "That is the will of God, the desire of God. It's what He created us for. It's what He wants for us."

I don't know if my women friends began our conversation with this belief, or if they just dream it could be true. Regardless, the idea touches something deep inside them. They always nod in wistful agreement. It's important to know what the will of God is. It validates hope and chastises evil. It gives the human heart a place to breathe.

I go on. "But what happened?"

They know the story. Sometimes a woman will answer, "They disobeyed Allah, and Allah threw them out of his garden in paradise."

If they don't provide the answer, I do. And I add, "And ever since then, everywhere on earth, there have been problems between men and women. Everywhere, not just in Afghanistan, but in America too. Everywhere."

They know their own problems, the situations and challenges they face in their families, but everywhere? Isn't there someplace on earth where men and women live in love, joy, and peace? Isn't there some cultural model, economic context, or educated society where marriage is categorically good? How we define the source of our problems determines where we look for solutions. I don't want to encourage my Afghan friends to believe their lives would be perfect if they could just have better husbands or some Western approach to personal choice.

I continue, "Everywhere, men and women struggle to love each other and to live in peace and joy. Men oppress women with their strength, but we know how to fight back too, don't we?" I ask the last question slyly. I smile with a knowledge the women all recognize, and they laugh.

Women everywhere know we have power, and often we know how to use it. It's a guilty laughter, an admission. The women cut sidelong glances at one another, knowing glances. Nothing is hidden in the *aouli*. They've seen one another, heard one another. They've learned from one another.

"But this is not the will of God. It's God's will that we live like Father Adam and Mother Eve in God's garden. It's God's will that we live together with love, respect, joy, and peace. When we fight and argue and try to hurt people, we are not living under the governance of God, the kingdom of God, and we pay the price. We suffer. It's not God's will, and it's not what we're made for. God wants us to live His way and enjoy the benefits of the life He gives us. That's what it means to live submitted to God. That's His will."

These are revolutionary words, life-changing ideas. I've avoided the easy scapegoat, Afghan men. I've ignored the American solution, personal choice. I've introduced the goodness of God, illumined our own complicity, and redefined what it means to live submitted to God. I've changed the conversation, and I've done it where the lives of our faith begin.

For women in Afghanistan, and perhaps for women everywhere, the deepest and most fundamental human relationship is marriage. The next and fully intertwined relationship is the family. Likewise, often, the deepest well of pain and loss is experienced in those very relationships that were meant to be life-giving and life-affirming. The greatest tragedy for women in Afghanistan is not that they experience such loss and pain in their marriages, but that they believe and are constantly told that the pain they experience is the will and desire of the god they worship.

The kingdom, the rule and desire of God, is not synonymous with the government or religious rule of Afghanistan or America. It's not bound to a particular cultural expression. It's defined by God's will, and His will is defined by His goodness.

In Afghanistan, Allah's desire is not defined by goodness. Its source and motivation are not understood to be love. Allah's desire is defined by a code of laws written in the Holy Quran and Hadith, a collection of rules individuals and society must obey. Allah's will encompasses anything and everything that happens, both good and bad. When a girl is taken by force into marriage, it's the will of Allah. When a man beats his young wife, it's the will of Allah. When a baby succumbs to sickness and dies, it's the will of Allah. If you are the girl taken, the wife beaten, or the mother bereaved, you must understand that your loss is Allah's will. It's simply an expression of what Allah wanted for you.

I don't believe that. I believe God is good and when we do good, we are submitted to God. When we do evil, we are not. When God said, "You shall not murder," did He mean, "You shall not murder"? If He did, then when a person murders another person, shall we say that the murder is an act of the will of God when God has already expressly forbidden it?

Many Westerners have asked me if Allah and God are the same. I tell them I don't know Allah, and it isn't for me to interpret the God of Islam in the light of my own understanding. My responsibility is to follow Jesus and to share the faith I have. Jesus shows us who God is and what He desires for us.

I believe God made everyone to live in His kingdom, under His governance. I believe God is good, wholly and completely. I believe He made His kingdom for everyone, Afghan and American, women and men, Muslim and Christian. I believe wholeheartedly that God loves the people of Afghanistan just as He loves the people of America. I believe He created us to live in His kingdom and that within every human soul is not only the desire but also the need to live in the beautiful kingdom God created for us.

When I tell my Afghan friends about God's goodness and His will for us, my stories are like fresh air breathed into the dusty, stale air of their lives. Over the years, many Americans have asked how I can get away with telling such stories, as though the telling is dangerous. Perhaps it is dangerous, but I've found my stories more than welcome. I'm not surprised. These stories describe the life we're made for. For my Afghan friends, the notion that it's God's will for men and women to live in love and peace is revolutionary. It's also a dream buried in their deepest being.

Often Afghan women think that if they could just choose their own husbands, all would be well—or if their economy were stronger, or if the soldiers would stop fighting—as though a correction in some external contextual reality could make all things beautiful. How we define the source of our problems determines where we look for solutions.

I refuse to identify Afghan men or some external circumstance as the source of all evil nor the solution to all heartaches. Instead I invite my listeners back to the beginning; to the place where there was only one man, one woman, and the God who created us.

I remind my Afghan friends that we all have a part. I show them that the solution is not in money or government or even better men. My words provide not only a gentle rebuke, but also a glimmer of light. "Perhaps, just perhaps, God doesn't mean for me to be beaten, for my life to be so narrow and hard. Perhaps, just perhaps." And that "perhaps" is like an open door that allows hope, genuine hope to enter into the places where we are most vulnerable, where our lives begin.

How we understand God is, perhaps, the most important, most fundamental thing. Who is He? What does He want for us? How do we know Him?

3

whose example do we follow?

One day, while I was walking out of a meeting at a local NGO office, three women gathered around me and joined me as far as the gate that led from the compound out to the street. They each wore the common light blue burqa with the shorter front part folded back over their shoulders and the front hem balanced on the top of the embroidered cap that keeps the burqa bound to their heads. In the safety of the office *aouli*, they had left their faces open.

We chatted through the usual greetings and determined one another's family status. All three women were married with children. I had never seen them before, nor have I talked to them since. They gathered around me like small children, full of curiosity and questions. Before we had stepped off the concrete porch of the building, one woman asked, "Do men in America take multiple wives?"

It was a common question, so I'd already prayed and thought through possible responses. I'd developed some fairly stock answers and had learned the Dari vocabulary that would enable me to explain my thoughts clearly.

That day, I didn't have time to engage in a lengthy conversation, so I answered briefly, "No. A man in America cannot take more than one wife at the same time. It's against the law."

They all laughed and agreed that this was much better than the Afghan way.

As we walked toward the street, I asked why.

One woman responded, "Our husbands take second, third, and fourth wives. We hate it." There was finality in her statement. It was more a declaration than explanation: "We hate it."

By then we were halfway to the gate, and I knew I wouldn't have much time. As soon as we emerged onto the street, the women would pull the fronts of their burqas down over their faces and hurry off in another direction or settle into the silence Afghan women practice in public spaces. I was blunt. "You are followers of the Prophet Mohammed, aren't you?"

"Yes, yes. Of course, of course. We are Muslims."

I smiled and said, "Your Prophet had multiple wives. You must live like your Prophet. Therefore, your men take multiple wives. It's *Sunnah*."

Sunnah is the example of the Prophet of Islam. In Afghanistan, everyone tells me that they must follow the examples of their Prophet. I've listened to stories by numerous Afghan men of their experiences during the Taliban occupation. In some towns, they were required to grow long beards because the Prophet had a long beard. The Taliban considered facial hair *Sunnah* and enforced the rule.

Many aspects of *Sunnah* are recorded in the Hadith and are expected to be followed. But of course, not everyone in the Islamic world shares the same understanding of what aspects of *Sunnah* or even which collections of Hadiths must be followed. Different groups of Muslims recognize different collections of the

Hadiths. It's not a homogenous religion.

In Afghanistan, there are some who believe that because the Prophet had a long beard, every man should have a long beard, but others disagree. Likewise, a great many men in Afghanistan believe that because the Prophet had multiple wives simultaneously and said that Muslim men can have up to four wives at the same time, they are not only free but encouraged to take additional wives.

I've never met an Afghan woman who likes the idea of her husband taking a second, third, or fourth wife. They consider it a great loss. The husband is only supposed to take additional wives if he can provide for them all equally, but in practice that's rarely the case. Often a woman and her children, if she has them, lose when her husband takes a second or subsequent wife. In the area of Afghanistan where I lived, having multiple wives was the norm.

The women walking around me nodded and laughed. "Yes, yes it's *Sunnah*. We must do it."

Just before we reached the gate I said, "America was established primarily by men who believed in the goodness of the teachings of Jesus. Jesus did not have multiple wives, nor did He command or recommend His followers to do so, therefore we don't do that."

The women sighed, quickly agreed that having only one wife was better, but that since they were Muslims and followers of the Prophet, they couldn't live that way.

I pushed open the wooden gate. The women pulled their burqas down over their faces, said goodbye, and walked away, their blue burqas billowing behind them.

According to Muslim tradition, the Prophet Mohammed married his first wife, Khadija, before he received the revelation from the angel Gabriel and was called to be a prophet. Khadija was wealthy and perhaps educated. She was a widow for whom Mohammed worked as a caravan trader. In my part of Afghanistan, I've been surprised that most women didn't recognize the name Khadija. Most didn't know her story. In other parts of Afghanistan, among other groups, Khadija is a common name and her story is often referenced. Khadija believed her husband when he said the angel Gabriel had spoken to him and called him to be a prophet.

After Khadija died, the Prophet Mohammed remarried repeatedly. Apparently, one of his wives was a Jewish woman from a city the Prophet Mohammed later destroyed. No Afghan has ever told me a story about her. I found her through outside research.

Another one of the Prophet Mohammed's wives was considered to be his favorite, Aisha. According to tradition, Aisha was six or seven years old when engaged to the Prophet Mohammed, but the marriage wasn't actually consummated until she was nine or ten years old. Aisha and her descendents are key players in the development of Sunni Islam. She survived the Prophet by years and had a significant role in bringing together the scattered sayings of the Prophet Mohammed. Some of those sayings formed the Hadith collection of writings accepted by the Sunni branch of Islam. ShI'as developed a set of Hadiths but drew most of their text from other sources.

Another one of Mohammed's wives, Zaynab bint Jahsh, was said to have been the wife of the Prophet Mohammed's adopted son. Allah himself ordained that the woman's husband should divorce her so that she could marry the Prophet. Apparently, the Prophet had seen her and admired her beauty.

In total, the Prophet Mohammed is said to have had thirteen wives or concubines.

If one considers *Sunnah*, the examples of the Prophet Mohammed to be a guide for life, then several lessons must be drawn and applied from his model of the most precious relationship, marriage. First, multiple wives are good. Second, wives of different religious or ethnic backgrounds are fine. Third, it's good to marry a very young girl. Finally, marrying a divorced woman is fine. Each of these approaches is acceptable in Afghanistan. The one we follow defines how we live.

In Afghanistan, most girls in the villages are married while they're quite young, often between the ages of eleven and thirteen. Occasionally, especially during the wars, girls were married even younger. One woman told a foreign friend of mine that she had lost her milk teeth in her husband's house. My friend was appalled. It wasn't unusual for a woman to tell me that she had had her first period in her husband's home or even that she hadn't bled until after her firstborn or after her first lost pregnancy.

Once, while sitting in a mud-brick house with a group of women and a dozen or so children, one of the mothers pointed to her very young daughter and said, "She's engaged and will be married soon."

My foreign coworker and I were both deeply disturbed. The girl looked to be around twelve years old, still a child in our very Western eyes. We said that to the mother to see what she would say.

In response, she pointed to one of her other daughters, an old married woman of about twenty. The woman already had three children and had lost one in pregnancy. She was thin, and her cheeks were hollow. In stature and bone structure, she looked all of eighteen, but her face looked closer to thirty-five. The mother said, "Look how ugly she is. She's twenty years old. A girl is most beautiful at thirteen and should be married then."

The roughness of her words stunned me: "Look how ugly she is." The young mother didn't flinch. She merely pulled her squalling baby to her breast, drew down her shirt, and suckled him. Her two toddlers played, diaperless, upending trays of treats and knocking over teacups.

My foreign coworker said the young mother looked old because she had three children and had lost one. All the women in the room laughed and agreed, but it didn't matter. They told us that a Muslim girl's responsibility is to marry, procreate, and maintain a household.

That's her purpose in life. When she's physically ready, she must do it.

We asked the younger girl if she wanted to marry. Again, everyone in the room laughed. The girl shrugged as if to say, "What difference does it make?"

One of the other women in the room explained that no girl wants to get married, but she must. It's the law.

One day, while I was having tea with an Afghan woman friend, her teenaged son brought his English-language exercise book to show me. He was quite proud of his work. He turned to the page that listed family relationships, and I read the corresponding English text he had written beside each Dari word. On the second page, I read the word *ambuk*. An *ambuk* in Dari defines the relationship between a man's multiple wives. He had translated the word into "step-wife."

I couldn't help but laugh. I told the boy, "No, no. We don't have 'step-wives' in English. We absolutely don't say that."

The boy argued with me, defending his translation and his teacher. I told him I didn't care what his teacher had taught him; we don't say "step-wife" in English.

He asked the obvious question: "What word do you use?"

I was stumped. I said we don't allow men to take two wives simultaneously so we don't have that relationship. It's illegal.

He said, "You have to have a word."

I couldn't find one. How can we have a word to describe something that, for us, doesn't exist?

The boy told me the Prophet of Islam directed his followers to take multiple wives and therefore that's what men should do, everywhere. How could we not have a word for it when it's the right way to live?

That struck me as a fair question, even if it didn't map very well to my own language and culture.

The boy asked, "Why don't American men take multiple wives?"

There was reproach in his voice. Clearly, we're doing something wrong.

The boy's mother was a good friend of mine and the only wife of her husband. She married him for love, one of the few women I know who did. At the time, both she and her husband had been living in a small city. Her father had long since died, but her mother and brothers were still alive. She had grown up in the city and attended school until tenth grade, when the Taliban invaded. Her family fled to Kabul, and she finished twelfth grade at a girls' school there. Later, after the violence in her city settled down, her family returned to their home. She took a job as a clerk at one of the first banks to be reestablished after the fall of the Taliban. While working at the bank, she met a young man. They were attracted to each other so the young man approached my friend's brother and asked for his sister in marriage. The arrangements were made, and they married. That's as close to a love story as I've ever heard in Afghanistan.

My friend had lost one pregnancy but gave birth to six healthy children and considered herself blessed. Meanwhile, she lived her entire life behind the walls of her compound. Her older children went out to school and the mosque each day. They played on the streets and in the compounds of neighbors. She stayed within her walls. Her husband wanted her to have more children, but she was tired and felt that six were enough. Sometimes they argued about that, and when they did, he threatened to take a second wife. That threat frightened and angered her. If he wanted to, he could do it and nothing she said would stop him.

Her husband's job was barely able to support all of them, and they didn't even own their property. If he took a second wife, both women and all their children would have to live together. It wasn't that a second marriage for her husband was unthinkable for her; rather it was far too thinkable. She loved it that American men were not permitted to take concurrent wives. Still, she thought it was funny that we didn't have a word for it.

We were sitting in her guest room, a small square room with open screen-less windows on two sides, plush cotton burgundy mats along the walls, and the swirling red carpet so common to Afghan homes stretched across the floor. I sat with my knees folded together and my feet tucked next to my hip. My long coat was draped on another mat, but my scarf was still wrapped around my head. My friend sat cross-legged on the floor in front of me, her hand resting on a tall black thermos of green tea. My friend's son, a boy of thirteen, dressed in Western jeans and a short-sleeved button-down shirt, sat on his shins between us, his book open on the floor.

We were drinking tea, absently waving away flies and cracking almonds against the swirling red carpet with the bottom of a thick glass teacup. From beyond the wall, down on the street, we could hear the music of the ice cream hawker and the occasional bray of a donkey pulling a cart of sand or stone.

The boy asked again, "Why don't American men take second wives when it's what the Prophet teaches?"

I responded with a story. "You remember that God created Father Adam and Mother Eve, don't you?"

The boy was quick to display his knowledge. "Yes, of course. Allah created Father Adam from clay. Then he created Mother Eve to be Father Adam's wife."

"Yes, that's right." Then I added, "We have a little bit more information in the Holy Book, the *Taurat*."

Afghans recognize four books as having come down from God: the *Taurat*, or book of Moses that the Jews call the Torah; the *Zabur*, or Psalms of the Prophet David; the *Injil*, or the book of Jesus, and the Holy Quran, which is considered to have replaced the previous three as the final revelation.

I continued my story. "God created Adam. When God created him, he wasn't a father, but just a man. Then God created Eve. Of course, she wasn't a mother then, either."

Both the boy and his mother nodded. Of course, Adam and Eve weren't parents at first. They hadn't yet met each other.

I went on. "God brought Eve to Adam and introduced them. In this way, God created the first marriage. Do you agree?"

Both the boy and his mother agreed. It's an appropriate story in Afghan culture. It wouldn't be right for Adam to just stumble across Eve and suddenly take her as his wife. Arrangements for marriage must be made by the families of those involved. Since Adam and Eve were the first and had no human family, God Himself would have had to make the marital arrangements.

"In the Holy Book, which includes the *Taurat, Zabur,* and *Injil,* it is written, 'Therefore a man shall leave his father and his mother and hold fast to his wife, and they shall become one flesh.'"

The boy quickly nodded. He had already finished reciting the Holy Quran in Arabic and was learning the meaning of different passages at the local mosque. He was very proud of his developing religious knowledge. His mother didn't nod. Instead she narrowed her eyes, cocked her head sidewise, and looked down at the burgundy cotton mat beside me. She was thinking, and I wondered what had caught her attention.

I continued. "God said that the man should leave his mother and father and become one flesh with his wife. How can the man then become one flesh with another woman? God didn't create four Eves for Adam; He only created one."

The boy looked down at the almonds, smiled shyly, and nodded. It was clear he felt the story had trapped him. It didn't correspond to what the Prophet taught and yet he recognized truth and wisdom in the story. He had no doubt that God created Adam and Eve and brought them together. He also knew there had only been one Eve.

IN THE LAND OF BLUE BURQAS

He leaned his head back and started forming words with the edges of his mouth but didn't speak them right away.

Before the boy could challenge the story, his mother stepped in. "Yes, a man should leave his father and mother when he gets married. Afghanistan would be a better country if that happened!"

The boy stiffened and shot his glance at her.

Often the bane of a young bride's existence is her mother-in-law. The custom is for a man and woman to marry and immediately move in with the man's family. The bride then lives under the authority of both her new husband and her new mother-in-law. Eventually many brides and their mothers-in-law develop healthy, close relationships, but the relationship often doesn't start out so positively. The young bride takes over work that the mother-in-law did before she arrived and often carries the greatest burden of the household chores. It's a great benefit for a mother to find a bride for her son. It eases her load and makes her family complete. Often the son remains more devoted to his mother than to his wife. The scenario creates a great deal of strain for a young bride.

The boy jumped back into the conversation, ignoring his mother and nearly sputtering at me. "But our Prophet teaches that we should take multiple wives. Why don't you obey that teaching?"

I smiled. "I am not a follower of your Prophet. I am a follower of the Honorable Jesus, and He never commanded men to take multiple wives."

The boy's mother nodded and laughed. She said, "That's definitely the better way."

The boy grumbled, "That's not Islam," scooped up his English book with the word "step-wife" still penciled in, and left the room.

My friend shrugged, dumped the old tea from our cups into a waiting metal tray, and poured us fresh, hot tea.

Her son had stumbled on a story he recognized as true, but it conflicted with what he'd learned of the Prophet Mohammed. In that moment, he chose to cling to the example and teachings of his Prophet.

His mother and I continued the conversation. We both agreed that for her son, as a young teen, the example of multiple wives was just an idea. He was too young to marry or understand much of the marriage relationship.

Later I took up the same topic with another young man, Raimulla, who was old enough at least to begin to understand.

One day Raimulla announced, with absolute pride, his engagement to a girl from his home village. His father had won the negotiations for the girl he had wanted. His dream was coming true.

I learned quickly that it would take two to three years for Raimulla to earn enough money to pay for the wedding and the bride price. During that time, he wouldn't be able to see his fiancée at all. He did buy her a phone, though, and called her regularly. That was how they developed their relationship.

On a whim, I decided to convince him of the merits of having only one wife. I didn't get far. Like my friend's son, he was absolutely convinced that four wives is best, two is good, and one isn't the example of the Prophet. Whose example we follow matters.

I teased him. "If you take a second wife, you will have the service of both and the heart of neither."

He made a joke about his desirability and his manhood being enough for two women, then pointed out what seemed completely obvious to him. "Islam says we should take more than one wife. Women know this, and men know this. It's the right thing."

I warned him, "If you do it, you will lose this first wife's heart."

"No, no. You don't understand. Afghan women want their men to take second wives. It's *Sunnah*, the example of the Prophet. They are very happy with it."

At the time I was shocked at his absolute ignorance of the way Afghan women really felt about sharing husbands with other wives.

How could he think that? Then I remembered, as a foreign woman, even with only a few years in Afghanistan, I'd spoken to far more Afghan women than he had in his entire life. After all, men and women live very segregated lives. In the end, we finished our conversation in laughter and complete disagreement.

Some six months later Raimulla came back to me. He had just gotten off the phone with his fiancée and appeared troubled. I asked if everything was all right.

"Yes, yes, it's just that . . . " He paused.

"What's wrong?"

He shrugged, smiled almost apologetically, and explained, "She asked me to promise her I would not take a second wife."

I almost howled but swallowed my delight. I couldn't hide my smile. "So what did you say?"

Raimulla shrugged again, shuffled. "I promised."

I told him he'd made the right decision, and I was proud of him. Then I asked what happened.

He looked down at the floor. "She told me she would stop loving me if I took a second wife. She asked me to promise her I wouldn't. I tried to talk her out of it, but she refused. She said I had to promise, so I did."

I smiled and told him, "The love of one woman is worth more than the service of two."

Raimulla nodded. He wanted his fiancée to become his wife in fullness, heart and body.

I wondered if our conversation had prepared him to listen to his fiancée's voice. I knew she couldn't force him. They were already engaged, and that's a legal contract she would not be able to void. I was glad he did listen to her, glad he had chosen love over the example of his Prophet. Marriage should be a precious gift enjoyed for a lifetime by a husband and his beloved wife. It really is the first relationship.

On a very different occasion, I was visiting with a young male coworker, Naseer, and his family. We were sitting in his family's home, finishing a meal of *mantu* his mother had prepared. *Mantu* is a steamed meat dumpling that takes far too much work to prepare but is wonderful to eat. Naseer's mother and sisters had cooked the feast for us because we had successfully helped a family friend who had a small manufacturing plant. By then, I was firmly established as an adjunct family member. Naseer and I had worked together for several months. At first it had been awkward. Neither of us understood which cultural rules applied to us. Eventually Naseer adopted me as his aunt, with his family's approval, and all was settled.

In those days, Naseer was engaged and working hard to prepare his new house, a set of rooms on his father's compound, for his bride. When the rooms were ready, he would marry her. The project was coming to completion, and he was excited.

That day Naseer and I were left alone, sitting on the floor around the plastic floor-cloth that had served as our lunch table, drinking our tea. His mother and sisters had taken away the dishes and were cleaning up the meal. Naseer asked about marriage in America. I switched the subject to marriage in the Bible and tried to give him an answer. I told him marriage is a good thing, but that in the marriage, a man must love his wife the way the Honorable Jesus loved His students.

For Naseer, that was a very odd statement. He looked at me quizzically and asked, "But a teacher and his students don't do what a man and his wife do."

I smiled. Obviously, the Prophet Jesus would not have had sex with His students. Afghans have a much narrower expectation of marriage than we do.

I told Naseer, "Yes, there are things a man and his wife do that only they should do, but there is more to marriage than that."

He was intrigued.

I went on. "The Honorable Jesus walked with His students. He lived with them and ate with them. He talked to them, and He taught them. He taught them about God and how to live well.

Naseer nodded. He was delighted with his mother's choice of a wife for him and was looking forward to more than sex in his relationship with her. Real companionship clearly sounded inviting.

I wasn't finished, though. "Then, the Honorable Jesus died for His students and for all who would later believe in Him. The Honorable Jesus showed us what real love is. And He tells men they should love their wives the way He loved His students."

Naseer didn't know how to react to that idea, so he just tucked it away. We continued working together for several more months. Often, over that time, he talked to me about his upcoming marriage and asked questions about my faith and the teachings of the Bible. On several occasions, he read whole passages from the New Testament and wondered out loud how such stories and teachings could possibly be true. He was constantly amazed at the love Jesus had for His students while He was on earth and the love the God of the Bible has for humankind.

Naseer told me that Allah is merciful only to those who obey him and specifically only to those who obey him according to the teachings of the Prophet Mohammed. Everyone else, Allah hates. He told me that the Prophet Mohammed was also merciful to those who obeyed and became Muslims. Those who disobeyed, who rejected the Prophet's teachings, were killed.

Naseer had shown me something important. If a husband is like his Prophet, then he should be kind and merciful to his wife when she obeys him. When she does not obey, he should demand submission. That gave me a context to understand the widow who had said that her husband had been a good man because he only beat her when she was young. Eventually, she had learned what he wanted and gave it to him.

Naseer met a different God in my stories and in the pages of the New Testament. He often told me that he found Jesus to be a wise, kind, and loving teacher and my God to be beautiful.

I agreed.

Who we follow really does make a difference. Afghans look to the Prophet Mohammed to tell them who Allah is and what he wants from us. I look to Jesus. The lives of each couldn't be more different.

My Afghan friends often told me stories about their Prophet. They told me how the angel Gabriel came to visit the man Mohammed while he was praying in a cave. It was the angel Gabriel who designated Mohammed as a Prophet and explained his role. According to my neighbors, this Prophet was called to warn people of Allah's judgment. His assignment was to teach pagan Arabs to worship the one true Allah and therefore escape the wrath of Allah that was to come. He was to demand obedience through any means necessary, and this he did.

The Prophet Mohammed is the teacher Afghans follow. Afghan mullahs and imams read, interpret, and declare the teachings and examples of their Prophet as recorded in the Holy Quran and Hadith. They look to the Prophet Mohammed's life for examples and call these examples *Sunnah*. In Afghan society, the religious leaders decide what it means to be Muslim and therefore what it means to be Afghan. Afghans are committed to obeying and emulating their Prophet. Mohammed is their teacher, and they are his students.

I am not a student of the Prophet Mohammed. For my Afghan neighbors, that's obvious. They watched me, listened to me, and recognized that I was not one of them.

My life in their country was transparent. I lived in community with Afghans by my own free will. I had only a scarf, a cell phone, and the goodwill of my Afghan neighbors to protect me. I had left the wealth and ease of my country, my family, and my friends to help a people who called themselves my enemies. I wasn't sent by my government, under orders to carry a rifle. That role is comprehensible. Instead I became vulnerable, both needing and offering help. I came to work and worked hard. I came to love my neighbors and found them beautiful—different, yes, but beautiful. I was astonishingly different and completely incomprehensible to my Afghan neighbors and coworkers.

Often when we sat down to swap stories over tea, we discovered anew how vastly different our perspectives were. In truth, we got to know one another's Teacher through one another's stories, parables, and teachings. They introduced me to their Prophet, Mohammed, and I introduced them to Jesus. It was easy for all of us to recognize our Teachers in one another's lives. After all, a student will become like his or her teacher.

One evening, in the privacy of my own room with my own computer, I developed a rather extensive comparison of the life stories, characteristics, and works of the Prophet Mohammed, the teacher of Islam, and Jesus, the teacher of Christianity. The results were startling on every level. Even a cursory view paints pictures of two radically different men.

While the Prophet of Islam lived as a warrior-king, the founder of Christianity lived as a servant-teacher. The Prophet Mohammed fought battle after battle. Jesus walked from village to village, teaching and healing. The Prophet Mohammed not only took up to thirteen wives including a small girl but also commanded his followers, the Muslims, to claim the widows and girls of conquered cities as their own wives. Jesus didn't take any wives. He killed no one and enslaved no one. Women traveled openly with Him and helped support Him. He spoke with women outside of His family and followers, violating the social customs yet honoring, freeing, and defending the weak and marginalized. On the day of His crucifixion, when Jesus hung on the cross and looked down at His widowed mother standing beside His student, John, He didn't say, "John, behold your wife." Forced marriage was not to be the answer for widows. Instead, He said, "John, behold your mother."

So often my Afghan neighbors challenged me to become a follower of the Prophet Mohammed. Sometimes they did it with a smile and sometimes at the edge of rage. I still shudder at such an idea. There is too much in the life and teachings of the Prophet Mohammed that terrifies me. I imagine living in his land and in his day. How could I have watched the Prophet of Islam and his armies engage in bloody battle? Would I have hidden in horror as his soldiers carried off innocent girls? Would I have said, "Oh, how beautiful. I want to be just like him"? I can't imagine reacting in such a way.

Abraham, Saul, David, and many others from the Bible were warrior kings, but I am not called to emulate them. I may learn from their lives, but I do not follow them.

When I think of Jesus, everything is different. I imagine standing in the crowd gathered around Him while He healed the blind man. I imagine the joy and delight of that man as he suddenly found he could see again. Or the crazy man who lived chained in the tombs—how clean, how joyful he must've felt to finally be free of such awful torment, to stand dressed in appropriate clothes, to be looked upon as a man. How wonderful it would have been to be one of Jesus' followers on the day He lifted the baskets up to heaven and, with nearly nothing, fed five thousand hungry men plus an uncounted multitude of women and children. How amazing it would have been to sit on the hillside and listen to Him teach or watch Him tenderly gather small children around Him, touch them, and bless them.

To me, Jesus is simply astoundingly beautiful. The more I know Him, the more I want to know Him. The more I learn to be like Him, the more I understand that being like Him is good for me and good for the world around me.

Jesus taught us to bless our enemies, to allow those who disagree with us to walk away, those who reject us to live on in peace. He taught us the supremacy of love and invites us to walk in it. He told men to love their wives and reminds us that in Him, there is no segregation between men and women, white and black, Asian and Western. He told us to seek the way of peace, to forgive others, and to ask forgiveness for ourselves. He taught us to live with open hands and to treat others not as they treat us but as He Himself treats us.

I am not a master student of my Teacher by any means, but I am a student of my Teacher. If I've learned anything in Afghanistan, it's how revolutionary, how magnificent Jesus really is.

I spent five years living among Afghans. For the most part, I found them to be precious, hospitable people. I loved drinking tea with them, laughing, and swapping stories. But I also had to face the hard edges of their faith. Sometimes those edges threatened to overwhelm me, to blind me to the beauty of a people created in the image of a beautiful God.

facing Hatred

I often asked my neighbors when they thought there would be peace. It's a reasonable question, considering that there's been war in some part of Afghanistan for years. Sometimes my neighbors answered the question in the context of Afghanistan itself. Often they answered it in the context of the entire world.

One afternoon the older son of a friend entered a room where his mother and I were sitting. Those were the days of the Israeli bombings in Lebanon. We had all seen the horrible images of mangled bodies on TV and grieved the destruction. My friend's brother was working in Dubai, and she was grateful that he was safe. She knew that Dubai and Lebanon are both in the Middle East, but she had no idea how far apart they are. We had been talking about the bombings, the presence of Hezbollah fighters living side by side with innocent women and children, and the sadness of it all.

The boy entered our conversation. He sat on the floor, waved for his mother to serve him a cup of tea, and began to speak. He said, quite simply, "One day everyone in the world will be Muslim. Then there will be peace."

I let his statement pass. I knew, with more experience than the boy's, that when one group bombs another, the other bombs back. It doesn't matter what religion they are. Still, I was intrigued by the expectation that someday everyone would be Muslim. After that, I looked for opportunities to ask different groups of Afghans if they believed that everyone would be Muslim and when they thought it would happen. Their responses often stunned me and sometimes offended me beyond my ability to be gracious.

A family of Sayeds, who claim to descend directly from the Prophet Mohammed, told me with absolute sincerity that the world would come to an end, but that before the end the Honorable Jesus would return. I was surprised to hear they believed Jesus would come back. My first thought was, "Oh, so you see Jesus as more than just one prophet among many?" I had always thought that faith in a returning Christ was strictly a Christian belief. Fortunately for my understanding, the conversation didn't end there.

One of the men explained it to me this way, "Yes, the Honorable Jesus will return. He will return as a Muslim, and He will make all people on earth convert to Islam. He will have a sword, and He will cut the heads off those who don't convert to Islam."

I was shocked and, in truth, offended. This was not the Jesus I knew.

Another man explained that the Muslim armies of Armageddon will march on Israel, utterly destroy it, and kill all the Jews on the face of the earth. He said that would also come at the end of the days.

Again, I was stunned. "Why do the Muslims expect to murder all the Jews?"

"It is the command of Allah." He said, "The Quran says, 'In those days, the rock will cry out, "Oh Muslim, there is a Jew behind me. Kill him." And a tree will cry out, "Oh Muslim, there is a Jew behind me, kill him."' You see, even the natural world is against the Jews."

I once showed a map of the world to a group of women. After I showed them Afghanistan and America and how far away the two countries are, they surprised me by asking me to show them Israel. On a map of the world, Israel is incredibly small. I showed them its tiny outline. Then I showed them the different countries around Israel: Lebanon, Egypt, Jordan, and finally Saudi Arabia, where Mecca lies.

One of the women said, "That's Israel? It's so small! Why is it so important?"

I didn't have an answer for that.

An Afghan man, a graduate of Sharia law school, explained what he called the correct Islamic perspective on Israel. He said that the Jews have disobeyed God and are forever beyond redemption. That means, even if they convert to Islam, they still cannot be saved. He said that God hates the Jews and will never forgive them. He said that God has ordered the nation of Islam, the entire worldwide community of Muslims, to annihilate the Jews.

I listened to his explanation and heard not only his words but his contempt for an entire people group. I tried to tell him God doesn't hate any people group, that no group and no individual is beyond redemption. I tried to tell him God desires that everyone be saved. I reminded him that the Prophet Jesus came into the world as a Jew. None of my words mattered.

It's very difficult to look directly into the face of hatred. A personal hatred is conceivable, comprehensible. A man kills another man, and the son of the victim hates the killer. Somehow that kind of brutal hatred makes sense. But to hate an entire nation of people created by God and in the image of God is incomprehensible. More than that, it's hideous. And yet here was this man politely explaining to me why this hatred is good and right, and not only good and right, but ordered by his god.

I responded with a story that almost caused a small riot in our gathering. I told him that perhaps the Muslims hated the Jews because they were so close to the Jews.

The man's offense grew to nearly uncontainable rage. I should've stopped, but the sight of such pure hatred railed against my heart. I told the man the story of Father Abraham who had married a woman named Sarah. He knew the names and recognized the authority of Father Abraham, whom he calls a prophet. Muslims esteem Abraham as the true father of Muslims.

I continued, trusting that he would contain his rage if only because I was a guest of his family. "God spoke to Father Abraham when he lived in the land of his fathers. That land is now Iraq. God told Father Abraham to take his wife, Sarah, and to travel to the land he would give to him and his descendents. That land was called Canaan. Part of that land is now called Israel, but not all of it. Father Abraham was very old, and so was his wife Sarah. They had no children, so Father Abraham couldn't understand how God could give land to his descendents when he didn't have any."

Afghans normally use a different title for the prophet Abraham. I had chosen "Father" intentionally.

I went on. "During their travels, Father Abraham's wife acquired a servant named Hagar. Later, Father Abraham's wife gave Hagar to Father Abraham to conceive a child. Hagar is the mother of Ishmael, and Ishmael is the son of Father Abraham."

Everyone in the room agreed with this part of the story. They didn't know about the promise of land, but they certainly knew about Hagar and her son, Ishmael.

I continued, "God told Father Abraham that the promise of land would not be received by the children of Ishmael. The land would be received by the descendents of Sarah. Father Abraham was surprised, but he was a righteous man. He believed God. Some time later, his old wife, Sarah, conceived and gave birth to a son. They named him Isaac. Isaac is the father of the Jewish people. You claim that Ishmael is the father of the Muslim people. That makes the Muslim people and the Jewish people related."

At this point, the man nearly exploded in rage. I had pushed him out onto a precipice. He had never heard this story before, even though he had spent years studying the Holy Quran and the Muslim religion. He barely contained his fury. "The Jews are nothing like us. Allah hates the Jews. They have never been anything like us. They have never been related to us."

Unwisely, I pushed on. "The angel Gabriel told the Prophet Mohammed that if he wanted to know the truth, he should read the books that came before—the Torah, the Psalms, and the Gospels. The Torah tells the story of Father Abraham and his sons, Ishmael and Isaac. If you want to know the truth of these stories, follow the angel's advice and read the books that came before." The ledge beneath us narrowed.

Once again, the man hurled his words. "The Jews have changed the Torah. None of it is true. Everything that is true is in the Glorious Quran."

I recognized that I was on far too dangerous ground. I needed to find a way off this narrow ledge, and yet I didn't want to yield. I knew my Muslim neighbors considered themselves to be completely obedient to God's law, including God's law on food. I was also familiar with the Old Testament teachings on food and the conservative kosher practices of some Jews today. I wanted to show this Afghan man and the entire group that there are Jews who follow the dietary laws and do it far better than Muslims. I was being provocative. "If you read the Torah, you'll read the Jewish law, the law God gave through the prophet Moses."

Muslims recognize the prophet Moses, and this man knew that Moses had given God's law to the world. He didn't know that Moses was a Jew. He did know that God gave His final law through the Prophet Mohammed.

I went on. "You will read that God taught the Jews, through the prophet Moses, what kinds of foods the Jews should eat and not eat. Like you, the Jews do not eat pork. They do not eat animals that eat the dead like vultures. Their laws on food are stricter than yours. For example, they do not eat meat dishes with yogurt or other dairy products mixed in. Muslims do these things, but Jews who obey the laws of the prophet Moses do not."

At first this bit of information genuinely intrigued the man. "Jews don't eat pork?"

"No. Not if they follow the teachings of the prophet Moses."

But I had pushed him against a wall. I had made Jews cleaner than Muslims.

The man shifted attention directly to the nation Israel. He began to outline Israel's crimes since its establishment in the modern age, starting with the Israeli bombing of southern Lebanon and working backward. We had all seen the films and pictures of torn bodies and twisted concrete from Israeli bombs that had shattered Lebanese apartment complexes full of women and children. The images and sounds, sorrow and outrage were still fresh in our minds—too fresh for us to be having this kind of conversation. We were standing on a narrow cliff ledge in a rainstorm, intent on passing one another.

The man told me that everything the Jews had done in Israel had been evil and that they and they alone were guilty of the violence between the Jews and Palestinians. He challenged me. "What do you say to that?"

I had to find a way off this precipice. It was too dangerous, too narrow, too slippery. I prayed. Of course I knew that in any war and especially the Israeli-Palestinian conflict, no one was innocent. I also

FACING HATRED

recognized that I had provoked this man. I pushed him and, in pushing him, had set us against one another. I had shown him that Jews and Muslims are related, a thing he hated. Then I had shown him that Jews, at least those who obey the Mosaic dietary laws, kept cleaner than Muslims. That, to him, was equally unthinkable. He was a righteous Muslim. He didn't drink wine or eat pork. He was submitted to God. Jews, in his understanding, had to be filthy and rebellious. Now he had turned the conversation and demanded that I judge between two nations. We were on a cliff's edge.

I couldn't judge the histories of either people. Not only would the storm of our conversation escalate, but for me to judge is to sit in a seat that only belongs to God. I prayed.

Finally I found words. "The problem between the Jews and the Palestinians is very difficult. Both have done evil to one another. Only God can judge in truth, and only God knows the way of peace between them. We must pray that God brings peace to the Israelis and the Palestinians."

Finally I'd said something that wasn't meant to provoke. I called us both to look up, to find a way out of our impasse. "Only God can judge . . . only God knows the way of peace . . . We must pray that God brings peace."

The man did not hesitate. He didn't want a way off the cliff, certainly not if it included peace with Jews. He spoke sharply. "No, we must destroy Israel. And when we are strong enough, we will. Allah hates Jews. He has commanded us to kill them."

I took a deep breath and considered the man who had taken over the conversation. I thought about the others in the room who listened and watched. I knew they had yielded to this man because he had been trained in the law, Sharia law. They considered him an expert who outranked them on such matters. That didn't mean they necessarily agreed with him. It only meant they wouldn't openly disagree. That wouldn't have been permissible. There are rules, and those rules are clear. My other companions would keep their thoughts to themselves, and I would have to honor their silence.

What I was thinking was that Jesus called us to peace, regardless of what the Holy Quran says. I still wanted to find a way off the precipice.

Finally I spoke again. "God has given us two great commandments. The first is to love Him with everything He's given us. The second is to love our neighbors as ourselves. Do you agree?"

"Of course."

"Good. This is what the Prophet Jesus Messiah also taught. Do you also believe that God commanded through the prophet Moses, 'Thou shall not murder'"?

"Yes, of course."

"The Prophet Jesus Messiah said that if a man hates another man in his heart, even if he hasn't killed him, he is guilty of the sin of murder. Do you believe that?"

The man sat straight up. He stated the Holy Quran's teaching again. "Muslims are commanded to destroy the Jews. The Holy Quran is the final word of God. All Muslims must obey its commands."

Like most Westerners, I would prefer to believe this man's opinion was unique in Afghanistan. I want to believe, certainly, that his opinion does not represent Muslims across the world. It's astoundingly difficult to live, to love, and to extend tolerance and freedom to those who would espouse such violence. And yet that's the very challenge Jesus calls us to.

I am also naïve enough to believe that if we, the width and breadth of humanity, choose, we could live in peace and in peace, find prosperity for all peoples. I'm sure that virtually everyone would tell me that such a hope is only naïve. Everyone, that is, except Jesus.

That day, we found a way out of our conversation. We didn't resolve it; we just turned and edged our way off the cliff face onto safer ground. I learned to be more careful and thought and prayed about how I could respond if I stumbled into this subject again. In the meantime, the man's words, his clear hatred, and his resolve continued to haunt me.

Very often Afghans told me stories about their Prophet, Mohammed. They told me how smart and strong he was. They told me he killed all the evil people in Mecca because they wouldn't accept him and become Muslims. He had to kill them, obviously. He was the Prophet of Allah, and they wouldn't submit to Allah. They told me he destroyed Jews because they wouldn't become Muslims. Clearly, the Prophet Mohammed was great.

One day, some men were sharing stories about their Prophet around a *desterkhan*, the floor cloth that we used for eating our meals. It was a lovely spring day, and everyone was in a good mood. We, men and women, were sitting on mats on the floor eating rice and mutton.

The men shared their stories with obvious delight. They were proud of their Prophet, proud of his strength and of his cleverness. They told me the Prophet Mohammed went to the city of Mecca to clean the city of all of its idols. He had a mandate from Allah and went first in peace to teach the people. Mecca, my friends told me, was full of idolatry and all sorts of evil. The Prophet came to set the people on the right path. He preached the one true Allah, a specific form of worship, and a fear of judgment day.

According to the story, the people of Mecca did not agree to put away their idols. They rejected the Prophet and his small band of followers, the Muslims. The Prophet was driven out of the city but that wasn't the end of the story. After all, he had a mandate from Allah. The Prophet raised an army of Muslims, men submitted to God, returned to Mecca, conquered the city, destroyed the idols, and implemented monotheistic worship. It was as if the men around me were saying, "Do you see how great our Prophet is?"

I thought about some of the Jewish leaders, judges, and kings of the Old Testament. Abraham had an army. He put it to good use to retrieve his relative's stolen property. Joshua led the armies of Israel across the Jordan and annihilated those whose land they wanted. All of the judges except Samuel are credited with battlefield victories. Then there was David, the man after God's own heart. He conquered enemies on every side. And yet, I thought, I'm not called to follow Abraham, Joshua, any of the judges, or even the great King David who wrote so many wonderful Psalms. I'm called to follow Jesus. I'm called to learn from His teachings and His examples and apply them in my own life.

Jesus didn't send His students out to destroy those who would not convert. That was never His way.

Over and over in Afghanistan I've listened to these kinds of stories. The Prophet Mohammed, as warrior-king, is kind and generous to his Muslim followers and brutally destructive to those who disobey. The teachings and the examples of the Prophet are well recorded in the Quran and the Hadith. An infidel, an outsider, a person who does not follow the Prophet must be given the opportunity to repent and obey. If he will not, then cut off his toes, then his fingers. If he still won't obey, cut off his head.

I had once heard that during Friday prayers, all Muslim men pray for Allah to convert all the infidels in the world. They pray that if the infidels don't convert, they should be given permission to kill them. Friday prayers are prayed only at the mosque and in Arabic, so my women friends didn't know what was being prayed. They did know that Friday is when the nation of Islam prays for the world and for the community of Muslims across the world.

I listened to the men around the *desterkhan*. I listened to their stories and watched their pride. I recognized myself not in the victorious Muslim armies of the Prophet Mohammed but in the villages and cities conquered by his sword. I thought about Jesus, the Old

Testament warrior-kings, and that rumor I'd heard about Friday prayers. I decided to test the rumor. I asked the men, "Is it true that every Friday when you pray, you ask Allah to convert me, and if I will not convert, you ask him for permission to kill me?" In a single stroke, I had made the conversation deeply personal.

The men around me immediately turned their faces away. They shifted in their places on the floor, toyed with their teacups, and picked at their teeth.

The women just watched, confused, their eyes full of questions. It was as if they were saying, "That can't be true. Is it?"

I asked my question again. Finally, one of the men answered me. He had studied the Holy Quran and knew a great deal of the translation, so his ranking in the gathering was highest. Always there is a man with highest rank. The man said, "Well, we don't actually pray that."

The women were visibly relieved, but I had heard equivocation in the answer. I explored the issue. "What do you mean you don't actually pray that?"

He shuffled around a little and looked down. He started to respond several times and then, each time, stopped.

I watched. The other women watched, also. The men all looked down or away. Clearly different thoughts were swirling in that room, and I didn't know what they were.

Finally the man said, "The mullah prays that. We just say 'Amen.'"

I understood. The rumor was true. This was part of the official prayer of the mosque, the prayer prayed by the religious leader in Arabic.

The other women shook their heads. That wasn't the answer they expected.

I pressed my question. "You just say 'Amen'?"

The man was getting more uncomfortable. "Yes. We have to. The mullah prays it. It's part of Friday prayers. It's always been part of Friday prayers."

"Everywhere in the world?"

"Yes, everywhere in the world, every Friday."

I hope he's mistaken about that prayer's universality. I definitely don't want to believe that Muslims in my community in America, who've been given permission to enter, build mosques, and live and worship among us would pray such a violent prayer against me, my family, and my friends. But I was willing to believe this prayer echoes across Afghanistan each Friday.

I pushed the subject. "And you say 'Amen,' so you are agreeing with this prayer?"

At this, he began shuffling and sidestepping again. The other men looked up at him, expecting his answer. The women just seemed appalled.

At first, he tried to say that he has no choice, that everyone must say "Amen." It doesn't matter what they think; they must say it.

I contained the growing fury in my heart, kept my tone even, relaxed, and hid the deep offense I felt. I had a plan. "Do you want God to convert me?"

"Yes, of course."

I was calm. "I am not going to become a follower of your Prophet, Mohammed."

Some of the more silent men smiled. Perhaps they knew I was laying a trap.

I continued, softly, as though we were talking about whether I would drink black tea or green. "There, I have refused to convert. Do you want to kill me?"

Snap. The trap closed. The silent men in the room chuckled. The women smiled. The educated man had been caught.

"Ah, um, er . . . "

"Do you want Allah to give you permission to kill me?" I was smiling just slightly. I had stood face-to-face with my enemy and gently asked him to declare himself. It was his turn to choose. I still didn't want to believe he really embraced the prayer he agreed to every Friday.

There is often a gulf between what we say we believe and what we actually believe. Sometimes the gulf is broad and full of differing ideas and strong emotions. We genuinely do not believe what we say and will not act on it. At other times, in other situations, the gulf is narrow, changing, in motion. We do believe what we say, but we don't desire to act on it.

Abraham didn't want to sacrifice his beloved son, Isaac, to God. And yet he laid a bundle of wood on the boy, took a knife, and climbed the hill. Fortunately for Abraham and his son, and for all of us, God intervened and gave Abraham a ram to sacrifice in place of his son. Abraham didn't want to kill his son, but he was willing. The gulf for Abraham had been narrow. I hoped the gulf for this man was wider than that. I was disappointed.

The man finally took a deep breath and stood by his faith. "If you do not become a Muslim and God commands, I must kill you."

I remained calm, light-voiced. "And every week you pray for permission to kill me?"

"Yes."

I sighed deeply.

The other men around the *desterkhan* looked away. They didn't want me to ask them the same question. I thought perhaps I might someday, but one-on-one, not in the presence of this man who had already declared what must be the final truth. In gatherings of Muslims, the most educated in Quranic teachings has the final word on all things related to Muslim faith and practice. If I had asked the other men the question, I would have required them to take sides between me and this man who claimed to speak for their faith. They would have had no choice. They would have to offend me and align themselves correctly regardless of what they actually thought, desired, or believed. I didn't press the question. Instead, I told a story.

"You all know that I am a follower of the Honorable Jesus Messiah."

"Yes."

"You know that I have the Holy Bible, the three books that came before, and that I read them every day?" I was establishing myself as a person with the authority to speak, according to their measure, on matters of Christian faith and practice.

"Yes."

I went on. "And you know that even the Holy Quran speaks of the Prophet Jesus?"

Here the most educated man stepped in again, displaying his knowledge. "Yes, the Holy Quran speaks of the Prophet Jesus. The angel Gabriel came to the Virgin Mary and told her that she would become pregnant even though she did not know a man. She would have a son."

I went on. "And the Holy Quran teaches that the Honorable Jesus came from God?"

"Yes."

"And doesn't the Holy Quran also say that the Honorable Jesus knows the way of righteousness?"

The silent men and women stared intently at the educated man. They didn't know the answer to that question. How would he respond?

The educated man said, "Yes, that is what the Glorious Quran says, but your books have been corrupted."

I appreciated the affirmation, passed on the challenge, and continued with my story. "One day, a very wealthy man came to the Prophet Jesus and asked Him, 'What must I do to inherit eternal life?' It was a very good question, wasn't it?"

Everyone nodded.

"The man was extremely wealthy." In Afghanistan, we would call such a man a *sarwatman*. Wealth and power go hand in hand. He could have been a landowner or an extremely wealthy trader. As a man of wealth, he would sit above the law. If he or a family member wanted something, they were able to get it. If they were brought to justice for some crime, they would be able to pay the fine or the bribe and walk away. In Afghanistan, some of these wealthy men raise their own militias, claim the girls they want as wives, and rule their own territories. The poor in Afghanistan, and almost every Afghan considers himself or herself poor, both fear and loathe the extremely wealthy. They fear the *sarwatman* because he has unchecked power and they cannot stand before him. They loathe the *sarwatman* because they believe he should be generous and help the poor. They judge the wealthy as possessing an insatiable hunger of soul that is deeply offensive to Allah and man.

"The man was extremely wealthy, but still he came to the Prophet Jesus and His students. He stood before the Prophet Jesus and then knelt on the ground and asked, 'What must I do to inherit eternal life?' Clearly, this was a very special wealthy man. He knelt before a prophet." So many stories in the New Testament are absolutely stunning in the context of Afghanistan. They require little, if any, interpretation but instead speak directly and plainly to Afghan listeners. This story was no exception.

I went on. "The Teacher Jesus looked at the man. He said to the rich man, 'You know the commandments: Do not commit adultery, Do not murder, Do not steal, Do not bear false witness, Honor your father and mother.'"

Everyone around the *desterkhan* agreed that those are very important commandments. I had said nothing about a specific form of prayer or fasting during a holy month. I had said nothing about taking an oath or making a specific declaration. These are the foundational commandments or pillars that define the faith of my neighbors in Afghanistan.

Jesus didn't teach His students to do any of these. In many cases,

He taught them to do very different things. Yet the context that Jesus entered, first-century Judea with its distant culture and Mosaic laws, is not at all unlike the context of modern-day Afghanistan. Those who sat around the *desterkhan* agreed to the truth of the commandments the Teacher Jesus listed.

The rich man who knelt before Jesus also agreed.

I went on. "The rich man said, 'Since I was young, I have obeyed all of these commandments. What else must I do to inherit eternal life?'"

I paused to allow my listeners the opportunity to see this particular rich man as a man of genuine honor. Then I continued, "The Teacher Jesus said, 'You must do one more thing.'"

Everyone around the *desterkhan* watched me carefully. They were inside the story, following its movements closely.

"The Teacher Jesus said to the rich man, 'You must sell all that you have and give it to the poor. Then you will have wealth in heaven even though you have no wealth on earth.'"

My lunch companions all smiled, the men and the women. What a beautiful answer! Yes, the wealthy must help the poor. Afghanistan would be a better country if all of the wealthy men of Afghanistan stopped taking what didn't belong to them and instead gave to those in need.

I waited as their delight settled. Then I went on. "The Teacher Jesus wasn't finished."

I hesitated until I had their full attention. "He told the rich man, 'After you have sold everything you own and helped the poor, come and follow Me.'"

Each person smiled and nodded. Ah, so the Prophet Jesus is like the Prophet Mohammed. He told people to become His followers. Of course, He was a prophet. That's what He would do.

I had them, but they didn't know it. "Do you know what the rich man did?"

The questions came, "Did he help the poor and follow the Honorable Jesus?"

I smiled. "No." I let the word rest alone for a moment. Then I added, "The rich man stood up and walked away from the Teacher Jesus."

In a flash, everyone around the *desterkhan* judged the wealthy man and found him guilty. I knew they would. They shook their heads, muttered, *"Tobah,"* repent. Each believed that if they themselves were wealthy, they would be different, generous, honorable. They would give to the poor. They would follow a prophet of God.

I waited until they were finished expressing their judgment. My story wasn't finished. "And what did the Honorable Jesus do? The rich man had disobeyed Him. The rich man had refused to become His follower. The rich man had walked away. What did the prophet of God do?"

They all looked at me with expectation.

"Did He call the rich man back? Did He force the man to give all of his wealth to help the poor? Did He punish the rich man?"

According to their own religious stories, that's exactly the kind of thing a prophet should do. Their Prophet required obedience. After all, a prophet represents God and God must be obeyed. I had not forgotten my friend's account of Friday prayers. It's one thing to pray for my conversion. I'll trust God with that. But it's something else entirely to seek permission to kill me if I don't convert.

I smiled. I knew I had them. It was time. I would light the candle and illumine the chasm between us and the Prophets we followed. "No. Jesus did not punish the man. He let him go. He let the rich man walk away from Him with all of his wealth. The Honorable Jesus, the Prophet of God, let the rich man disobey."

Shock. Where was the judgment? Where was the power? Where was the absolute demand, the force that would require all to obey

God? The Teacher Jesus allowed the man to reject Him, to refuse to obey, and to walk away.

The stories of Jesus are astounding in Afghanistan—revolutionary, far different from what Afghans expect. He didn't act like their Prophet at all. He didn't take vengeance. He didn't kill people who refused to follow Him. He simply let the rich man walk away. We, who follow Him, must do the same just as those who follow the Prophet of Islam must do as he did.

I have no idea how my companions found a place in their world-view for this strikingly different Jesus. Perhaps some simply rejected such foolishness. Perhaps others considered the man of peace, who refused to call down fire from heaven, order angels to defend Him, or even send His disciples with swords to conquer their enemies.

I like the Jesus I follow. I like the Teacher who allowed the rich man to walk away. Perhaps sometime later that man returned to Jesus. Perhaps not. The Bible doesn't say. It only tells us the story and invites us to consider the example, to see the sorrow in Jesus' response and the respect, the willingness to be rejected, to allow the one who rejected the freedom to do so. I would rather follow this example. I would certainly rather my Afghan neighbors follow Jesus' example with me.

The truth is, in Afghanistan, I was often challenged with this very clear choice. There are teachings, practices, and closely held beliefs that mark me and most of the people I love as enemies worthy not only of rejection but of death. For me, these are not theories or ideas or even rumors. These are realities embodied by real human beings. The challenge is clear; how will I respond?

5

choosing love

I'll admit, sometimes it was difficult to live among Afghans. Sometimes the darkness overwhelmed me. When my Afghan friends explained Jesus as the prophet who will come and dismember those who would not convert to Islam, I wanted to scream, "No, that's not who Jesus is. You have another Jesus entirely."

When they talked to me about Allah's hatred for Jews and the Muslim community's responsibility to kill all the Jews in the world, I saw in my mind the faces of Jewish friends and family members. I saw their children and grandchildren, some still babies. I recalled the grainy, black-and-white photos of Jewish bodies piled high in concentration camps. I saw the shoes, shaped by the very human feet of Jews who had once worn them, now in a careless heap in the Holocaust Museum in Washington, D.C. My heart raged.

And when they admitted to praying for permission to kill me, well, where does one put that? How does one look into the face of such hatred? How does one choose love? And yet, that's our call.

Jesus is clear: Love God, love your neighbor. Don't love your neighbor because he's good or like you or good to you. Love your neighbor because that's what's good and right. Love your neighbor because God is love. For me, that love should be expressed through the way I live my life.

Every day in Afghanistan, five to six days a week, for five years, I went to work. I worked for the benefit of Afghans. I managed projects, wrote proposals, supervised Afghan and foreign staff, maintained financial records, attended government meetings, submitted reports, applications, and letters, and completed a hundred other similar tasks. I did all this with sketchy electricity, intermittent phone service, slow Internet, oppressive heat in the summer, and brutal cold in the winter. I came to Afghanistan as an experienced project manager but was immediately challenged to pick up a dozen other critical skills—bookkeeping and accounting, negotiating with government officials and village elders, monitoring and assessing security. I developed evacuation and kidnapping contingency plans, supervised staff members who neither spoke my language nor understood my culture, and more.

On most days I rose just after dawn to either a freezing or baking house. I boiled water in a kettle over a flaming burner attached to a gas bottle perched just outside the window. I made my coffee in a neoprene-wrapped French press and enjoyed it with a loaf of hot flatbread brought back fresh from the neighborhood baker. If I had them, I skipped the bread and ate animal crackers mailed by a friend in America. That was my treat.

Each morning, I sat in my room with my coffee and breakfast, my Bible, songbook, and notebook and turned my attention to God. I worshiped. I read Scripture. I settled my heart into the heart of God and leaned into His rest. It was a good place to be.

I explored my raging emotions. The hardness of the culture and the life there pressed in on me like the walls that bound my *aouli*. I often found myself frustrated with staff members—sometimes an Afghan who couldn't quite get the work right, sometimes another foreigner—all beautiful, precious people who were somehow falling short of my sometimes-appropriate expectations. I prayed for each of them. I looked to understand, to remember our Father's love for them, His desires, His always-appropriate expectations for their lives. And again, morning after morning, I found peace. This was the way to start the day, the way not only to live but to flourish in Afghanistan.

After I had resettled my heart into God, I turned my attention to the day before me. My workload in Afghanistan was always beyond extreme, my to-do list always too long. Most of those tasks pushed the edges of my abilities, requiring knowledge and wisdom I did not possess. I could not bear the weight alone. And yet where could I turn for help? What mentor was there who could guide me? All of us, foreigners and locals, engaged in rebuilding a shattered country, were merely stumbling along, picking our way through map-less territory. I turned to God, believing He alone could guide me.

Each morning I took my notebook and wrote down the things I thought I had to do through the course of the day, the decisions I would have to make, and the situations I thought I would have to deal with. I prayed through each one and asked for God's direction. I wrote down the things I thought He was telling me. That became my work list.

I prayed through the conversations I was having with people, the things they were challenging me with and my responses—sometimes appropriate, sometimes not. I listened hard to hear God's voice. What did He have to say about the situations I faced? How would He have me react?

When it was time, I put my Bible, songbook, empty cup, and plate away. I carried my notebook with me.

In the winter I shed my Western-style flannel pajamas and pulled on black *tambons* over expedition-weight long johns. I wore long skirts, normal shirts (sometimes as many as three layers), a sweater and fleece jacket, high-tech sock liners, and smart wool socks. In my house, I wore thick-soled, bright blue snow boots for slippers, gray fleece wristies, a black fleece gator, and a thick black fleece hoodie. In the office, I changed my snow boots for suede-topped, felt-lined winter clogs that protected my feet from the cold radiating through the carpet-covered concrete. Often, my Afghan staff went about in socks or even bare feet. I was not so strong.

Usually I arrived at the office before my staff, prepared their work for the day, and waited. Each day our work was different. There were letters to prepare for the government, applications for visas and work permits, and financial records to be translated and compiled. My staff and I worked hard. We used laptop computers because they can run without consistent electricity and be charged in the evening with city power or in the afternoon with our backup generator system. We used a simple desktop printer and had our copies made at a shop in the bazaar. In the worst of the winter, we moved our desks as close as we could to our little sawdust heater and wore gloves with the fingers cut out.

Some days took us out to the beneficiary communities, groups of people receiving the services we were providing: advanced tailoring training, literacy, business start-up training, or health education. If I was meeting with women, I took these trips alone or in the company of another foreign woman. If I was meeting with men, I usually took one of my male coworkers. We checked on our projects. Were they going as planned? Did they need anything they didn't have? Were the beneficiaries actually benefiting?

I conducted interviews with individual project beneficiaries. That took me into people's homes, where I sat with groups of women and often their male relatives. I asked questions and recorded their responses. They served me tea and treats and watched me—this odd, exotic foreigner who spoke their language. Usually by the end of the interview we had moved from strangers to friends. We answered one another's questions and shared the stories of our lives. We laughed and sometimes cried. If we stayed in a home near lunchtime, the host would invariably invite us to eat. I always declined. As a foreign guest, I knew they would feel compelled to serve me their best, and in many of the areas we visited, the people were too poor to have any extra for me. Instead I would volunteer to return for tea and conversation at another time.

Often people asked who I worked for, where my money came from, why I was there. Those were fair questions, and I always endeavored to answer as honestly as I could. One very cold day, I was sitting with a group of women who had returned from Iran several years earlier. We were in a warm basement room, dim, the bright winter light blocked by thick wool blankets hung over a high row of windows and the single wood-framed, glass door.

We sat in a tight circle on the carpeted floor, wrapped in blankets, drinking bitter green tea out of thick glass cups. Children bounced around the room, fell into our circle, and knocked over our cups and shallow bowls of candy and raisins. Every time a child fell into us, a woman grabbed him and pushed him out of the circle. It was far too cold to send them outside. We were laughing about something, but I can't recall what it was. We had already finished our business and were just enjoying one another's company. I dreaded the long walk in the cold back to the paved road and the line taxi that would take me to my office in town.

One of the women asked, "How can you live here in Afghanistan? I came from Iran, and it was so much better. It was free. Modern. I would go back if I could. How can you live here?"

I knew these women well and had worked with one of them for more than a year. She was a neighborhood trainer in one of our projects, educated and deeply religious. It seemed an honest question, so I tried to give a full answer. "When the Taliban invaded this country, we saw what happened on the news. We saw news reports on TV about how hard it was for women under the Taliban, and it hurt my heart."

These women friends hadn't been in the country during that time, but they had heard stories. They were Hazara, an ethnic minority that had suffered greatly at the hands of the Taliban. They nodded. Yes, it had been a very difficult time for women in the days of the Taliban. But they wondered about the news. "You saw Afghanistan on TV?" America is very far away. So rich. Why should we care about Afghan women?

"Yes, I saw news reports and read things on the Internet. The stories were hard and sad."

They nodded. Yes, the stories were very sad.

I went on. "Those stories hurt my heart. I couldn't see how I could help, so I prayed. I prayed a lot."

"You prayed for Afghanistan?"

I have never met an Afghan who didn't respect prayer. They believe in it. Sunni Afghans pray *namaz* five times a day. Shiites pray three times a day. They pray during Ramadan when they fast. They say prayers for the dead and prayers for rain when the land is too dry or for rain to stop when the land is too wet. These prayers are all spoken in Arabic, but Afghans also pray in Dari. They pray about the things that are important to them.

Usually when I tell Afghans I pray, they're surprised. They ask me if I pray namaz, but I tell them, "No, that's the way the Prophet Mohammed taught people to pray. I'm not a follower of the Prophet Mohammed. I'm a follower of the Honorable Jesus, so I pray the way He taught us to pray." That response doesn't answer all their questions, but it's usually satisfying.

Afghans respect prayer and respect people who pray. But why would I pray for the people of Afghanistan? They're not my family, not from my country, and they're Muslims. They're certainly not my brothers and sisters. At least, that's what my Afghan neighbors commented on.

One of the younger women asked, "Why? Why did you pray for us?"

I doubted if she'd ever prayed for God to bless a non-Muslim, including me, but we don't love people because they love us. We don't help our neighbors so they'll help us. At least, that's not supposed to be the limit of our generosity. I tried to explain, "God is good. He created everyone. We are all children of Father Adam and Mother Eve. In God's presence, we are all one family."

This was a good answer, and my friends nodded. The oldest woman, a kind mountain villager whose toothless Dari often stumped me, said, "Yes, yes. We are one family." The youngest woman, a girl of about seventeen, cocked her head down and looked sideways at her grandmother. Apparently, she didn't quite agree.

I went on. "God loves us. All of us. He gave us two commandments that we must always obey."

It often surprises my Afghan friends that I, as an American, recognize that God has given any commandments. Most seem to have been taught that we Jesus-followers don't believe there's anything we have to obey.

Each face in the circle turned toward me, waiting to see which two commandments I would pick. They knew I wouldn't pick the commandment to perform namaz, because I don't pray that way. They doubted I fasted, so I wouldn't pick that. As a non-Muslim, I certainly couldn't go on Hajj to Mecca. I didn't give *zakat*, the required alms, to the local mosque, obviously. And equally obviously, I didn't follow the Prophet Mohammed and had already steadfastly refused to declare the Muslim creed. They watched me. What would I say?

"God commands us to love Him with all our hearts, all our minds, and all our strength."

They smiled, nodded, and quickly agreed. "Yes, yes. That's right."
They liked my answer.

I went on. "The second great commandment is to love our neighbors as ourselves."

They smiled again. Ah, wisdom. Yes, this is what we must do. Truth resonates in our hearts. It's recognizable. All I had done was answer the question Jesus Himself had been challenged with: "What is the greatest commandment?" My answer had been satisfying, but only for a moment. Then it seemed the reality of the situation settled back into the circle.

The seventeen-year-old asked the follow-up question I knew to expect: "But you're an American. We're Afghans." Implied: You're a *kafir*, an infidel. We are believers. What do you have to do with us?

I answered that question. "We are neighbors."

The women looked at me quizzically, then at one another. There are clear rules in Afghanistan defining neighbor, tribe, family, and Muslim brother. From the Afghan definition, I was none of those.

I waited. The oldest woman who'd spoken earlier spoke again. She laughed. "Of course, of course. We're all neighbors. We're all children of Father Adam and Mother Eve. We're all people." Everyone nodded, even the seventeen-year-old who had clearly not considered such a possibility.

I smiled and was willing to leave the conversation at that. The day was slipping away, and I had to get back to my office before lunch. The women still weren't satisfied. Our neighborhood trainer asked the next question. "But how do you live here? Who pays you? Who pays for our project?"

I told them the story, my story. "When the Taliban were here, I couldn't see how to help, so I prayed. But then, after the big buildings in America were destroyed and America invaded Afghanistan, I thought I could come here to help. I talked to my friends, and they wanted to help too. They collected money and gave it to me so I could come here and live and work. They still collect money and send it. That's where the money for my expenses comes from. I don't make very much money, but it's enough to live on. They send money for the projects, too."

The women were surprised. They asked if it's true that I don't get any money from the US government. "No. The US government doesn't pay me. In fact, I pay the government. I pay taxes in America and in Afghanistan."

They laughed with as much surprise as humor. No one bothers to pay taxes in Afghanistan, just bribes. Everyone knows that. Stupid foreigner. Crazy lady pays taxes here and in America. They mocked my foolishness with money. I let it go. I hated paying taxes to the Afghan government, but they wanted it so I paid it. It was part of the deal. I also paid taxes for my Afghan staff. I knew an Afghan employer wouldn't do that, but I always tried to keep our finances honest and transparent. I knew aid money just poured into private pockets, foreign and Afghan. I didn't want that. I was going to make sure none of our money poured into anyone's pockets. We didn't come to Afghanistan to get rich. Our projects were small, but we made sure they were delivered.

I skipped the tax subject and tried to help them understand why people give. "Your neighbors, people who care about you but live in America, want to help you, so they do. They send money, and they pray for you."

The seventeen-year-old sat straight up. "Americans pray for us?" She was completely incredulous.

"My American friends do. I write them and tell them about the difficulties here, and they pray. They love God, and they know that God loves you, so they pray for you and try to help you."

In Afghanistan, this is a strange thing. When a person gives alms to someone who's poor, the recipient is expected to pray for the giver.

That's the custom. Once, when I was out giving alms in a public place, each woman who received something from my hand put her hands on my face, prayed for me, and kissed my forehead. That's the custom. The giver gives. The recipient prays. Plus the giver receives *sawab*, credit for heaven, just by giving. It's a transaction. To my Afghan friends' way of thinking, they should pray for the Americans who've given money to help them, not the other way around. Of course, they weren't going to pray for the Americans because the Americans are strangers—*not* neighbor, tribe, family, or Muslim brother.

We talked for some time. I watched and listened as the women tried to find a place to put my words in the framework of their understanding. They were surprised to hear of Americans who pray to God. They were confused by the facts that some Americans actually pray for them. They were relieved that I didn't work for the US government and awed by the notion that ordinary Americans would give money to help them.

I told them most of my friends are followers of Jesus and try to love their neighbors, both near and far. I told them my friends are not rich people with lots of extra money, but are just regular people who want to love God and their neighbors. I told them that's why I came to Afghanistan.

In the end, they were happy. I had answered their questions and what I had said made sense. For me, helping Afghans in Afghanistan was just another passage in the journey of my life.

I did not grow up as a Christian. I didn't come to faith until I was well into my twenties. I've shared that with many of my Afghan friends, to their complete amazement.

Most tell me that all people on the face of the earth are born Muslim. The first time I heard that, I was both shocked and offended. I told the one who told me not to tell my mother. She would not have appreciated it. Once when a foreign friend was visiting me, one of my Afghan coworkers told her that her children had been born Muslim. She was a woman of deep faith, had raised her children in her faith, and viewed Islam as fundamentally false. The accusation that her own children had actually been born Muslim infuriated her. I don't think I'd ever seen her quite so angry.

I definitely don't consider myself to have been born a Muslim. I didn't even know there were such things as Muslims until I was much older, perhaps a teenager. I don't remember when I first heard of Muslims, but I didn't know any in school. As a young adult, I met a great many Muslims, mostly from Iran. I came of age during the Iranian revolution and met Iranian students at university who seemed both angry with the revolution and angry with America. I tried to stay away from them. Their anger frightened me. I didn't learn about Islam from them. That would take a few more years and some intentional research.

Religion was not part of my life growing up. My mother had faith, but I don't think she even owned a Bible when I was a child. We certainly didn't go to church. I did go to Vacation Bible School one summer while I was staying with my grandparents. I got to wear one of my grandfather's white shirts with his tie wrapped around my waist. We children shouted down the walls of Jericho, and that's all I remember from Vacation Bible School.

Sometimes I went to church with my grandparents for Christmas or Easter. Easter used to fall on a school holiday, and since my mother was a working single parent, I was often shipped off to my grandparents. The only thing I really remember from that is that the pastor gave each child a tulip bulb. It was meant to represent the death and resurrection of Christ. My grandmother buried the bulbs at a spot in the backyard, and each year they bloomed. I was always amazed at that.

When I was eight, my mother married a nonpracticing Jewish

man from New York City. We didn't keep a kosher household, nor did any of us go to synagogue. I did hear the stories of what it was like for him to grow up as a Jew in Brooklyn. He didn't have a good attitude toward Judaism, and I inherited his cynicism.

As a teenager, I developed a fascination with the study of philosophy. I was too young to read direct texts, but I read about many of the great philosophers and the ideas they proposed. I was taken with the existentialists. I'm sure that was more a reflection of the times in which I lived than anything else.

In college, I continued my study of philosophy, although my focus was history. I was fascinated with the great ideas that shaped Western thought. I also read about other religions. I found Hinduism and Buddhism particularly interesting. By then, I was reading direct texts and read the Bhagavad Gita and parts of the I Ching. However, I still leaned toward the existentialists. That seemed to fit my way of thinking.

If I had any real, deep Christian influence, it came in the form of a much older black woman, Miss Lillian, who worked for one of my great-aunts. I adored Miss Lillian. For several months, I lived at my great-aunt's house and fell under Miss Lillian's care. I was about five years old at the time. I have fond memories of sitting on the stool in the kitchen, shelling peas or shucking corn, and listening to Miss Lillian's stories, stories about her life and stories about Jesus. I remember she took me to church, but all I really recall is playing in the churchyard with a dozen black kids who eventually accepted me, despite my bright yellow braids.

Years later, when Miss Lillian lay on her deathbed, she called me to her. I remember driving to her house along back roads in Chester County, Pennsylvania, sliding through a fresh snowfall. It took everything I had just to stay on the road. Seeing Miss Lillian was a shock. She had once been a robust, dark-skinned woman with a wide smile and glowing eyes. But when I saw her that last time, racked with cancer and lying on her bed, she seemed more the color of ash. All of her fatness was gone. Her skin stretched around her joints, and her eyes were just muddy. I was seventeen, and I was terrified.

We arrived late, but Miss Lillian obviously wanted to talk to me. She had something to say. She had skipped her morphine and was in deep pain. I was completely unprepared. I absolutely could not accept her sickness nor her impending death. I told her she would still be around when I graduated from high school. I don't know why I expected her to get well. It was unreasonable. She was completely riddled with cancer and had been sent home from the hospital to die. She did die, just two days later.

As I stood by her bedside, she wrapped my hands in hers and drew me close enough so I could hear her low, rasping voice. She had a message, and she was going to deliver it. Miss Lillian told me she was going to heaven. She said she was going to dance with Jesus, and I needed to rejoice. I had no place to put that in my understanding of reality. She was old. She was sick. She certainly wasn't going to dance!

I had heard the message she had to give me, but I couldn't receive it. Still, for years, it haunted me.

When I was twenty-five, I heard the gospel for the first time. Of course, many people had tried to tell me about Jesus before then. Those were the days of the Jesus movement in America, and I had met long-haired, bearded, or granny-skirted followers of Jesus everywhere. Still I didn't hear, really hear, until I was twenty-five.

I had flown to my grandparents' city and gone to church with them. It was Christmas Eve. The pastor explained who Jesus is, why He came, and what it meant to become one of His followers. At the time, I felt enchanted. The story was beautiful. Then the congregants celebrated communion. I had absolutely no understanding of what communion meant, but the bread and the cup were given to me. I ate the bread and prayed, "God, if You're out there, and this is real, make it stick." It was an honest prayer.

A few days after Christmas, my grandfather took me to a shelter for lost girls in his town. He was on the board of directors and had a meeting. The shelter was run by a group of nuns, and one of them took me by the hand and showed me around while the others were discussing business. She talked to me about the girls with such love that I simply assumed she was naïve. How could she possibly know what those girls had been into? I considered myself worldly and had been exposed to a great deal, so I thought I had a better understanding than the old, naïve nun who led me. Eventually, though, as we continued our walk around the grounds, I realized that this precious old nun understood exactly who her girls were and loved them anyway. I thought her love was pure and beautiful and wondered if I could ever experience anything like it.

Several days later I flew back to southern California and went back to work. I shared the story of the nun and her love with a coworker. He responded with the gospel. I was furious and wouldn't have any of it. Exasperated, he challenged me to read the Bible and figure it out for myself.

I took up that challenge.

I'm very particular about books and always assumed that one must read them from one end to the other. In those days, I didn't understand that the Bible is really a collection of books written over several thousand years by different authors. I thought of it as one book, so I started in Genesis.

It took several months for me to read the book, but the results were cataclysmic in my life. In the pages of the Old Testament, I met the God of the universe and found Him beautiful. I was astonished, first, by how honest the Old Testament is about the nature of people. We're always running off in wrong directions. I suppose I expected the Bible to make all those Jewish heroes look perfect, but it didn't. Every one of them seemed to put his foot down his own throat, and that was a thing I recognized. What really captivated my attention was God's unremitting love, His patience and willingness to continually forgive and restore.

Somewhere during my reading of the Old Testament, I prayed my second real prayer: "God, if You're out there, if You're real, I want to know You."

Eventually I got lost in the minor prophets. I had managed to finish the book of Hosea, but only barely. I struggled. I still thought I needed to read the Bible from one end to the other to understand it, but Hosea had completely baffled me and the next prophetic account wasn't any easier.

Someone, I can't remember who, told me to jump ahead to the New Testament. They told me that was where I'd find the story of Jesus and I needed to read it. Since Hosea was so baffling, I thought I might as well take the advice. I read through Matthew and then started on Mark. By Luke, I was pretty sure I was losing my place because I seemed to be reading the same stories over and over. I think that's when I realized that each book in the Bible was written independently.

At that time, I absolutely did not believe that Jesus was God. I understood from reading the Gospels that the disciples did believe that, but I couldn't. I'm sure it was a reflection of the Jewish influence I'd had. I was absolutely convinced that Jesus was just another prophet. Somewhere in the middle of Luke, I prayed my third seeking prayer: "God, if this Jesus is You, You have to prove it to me because I don't believe it."

I suppose by then I was convinced that God is real. I'm not sure when that happened, but it had. I would love to say I had some sort of revelatory experience when I just knew that Jesus was real and that He was God come in the flesh to save me. If there was such a moment, it must've happened in the middle of the night because I just woke up one day and knew that I knew that I knew. Much later, I read that faith is a gift of God. By then, I had received it.

I still didn't know what to do in response to what I was learning and experiencing. It never occurred to me to go to church. I really didn't associate church with faith. I continued reading. The book of John was mesmerizing, the book of Acts, stunning. I skipped Paul completely. Somewhere along the line, I had learned that Paul was a misogynist, a man who hates women, and since I'm a woman, I figured it was best to skip him. I jumped ahead to Hebrews. I had no idea that some people think Paul wrote Hebrews. I just read it.

Hebrews put the pieces of the Old Testament in order and explained how Jesus fulfilled what was written before. I was astounded. I had read so many passages in the Old Testament about sin, repentance, and confession that the explanation in Hebrews clarified how Jesus fit into all of that. By then, I believed completely that Jesus was the Lamb of God, the perfect sacrifice who took away the sins of the world.

I still didn't know what to do about it. After all, Jesus wasn't in my apartment for me to lay hands on.

Finally, I reached the first letter of John. There's an amazing verse there that says, "If we confess our sins, He is faithful and just to forgive us and to cleanse us of all unrighteousness." The pieces clicked into place. I knew exactly what I had to do.

Now I should probably point out that none of this was easy. At first I had been quite offended that God had the audacity to tell me how much in my life was sin. Who did He think He was? My life was my own. Eventually, my desire to know God and my amazement at how beautiful He was overcame my attachment to my lifestyle, but that was a slow process. I came to understand that I had to give my entire life to God, not just part of it. It took me several months to agree to that, and it was definitely an agreement.

Finally, by the time I reached 1 John, I was ready. I read the words about confessing my sins and remembered the Old Testament model of laying hands on the sheep and confessing the sins of the people. I was sure I had to confess all of my sins, so that's what I tried to do. It wasn't easy, and of course I couldn't even recognize all my sins, let alone confess them, but I did what I could. I got down on my knees and began. I confessed everything I could think of, and as I did, I felt as if layer after layer of chain mail was being pulled off my body. I wept through the experience. When I stood up, I knew that I knew that I was a new person. I was totally forgiven and completely cleansed. I absolutely understood that. I also recognized, with deep gratefulness, that God had loved me before I committed my life to him just as much as He loved me afterward.

Later I found my way to church and, more than a few years after that, to Afghanistan. When I boarded the plane in America, I carried with me the many lessons I'd learned about God, His love, and His invitation to love others as He has always loved me.

Over the years in Afghanistan, I struggled to explain myself, my faith, and my journey. My beliefs are so strikingly different from my Afghan neighbors'.

Then there are the words themselves.

I would sit down with Afghans over cups of tea and face questions that startled me: "What do you believe happens when you die?" "Why don't you pray namaz?" "Why won't you become a Muslim?"

At first I didn't even have the vocabulary to respond. I would listen to their questions and stumble through my answers. In the early days, Afghans would just give up and move on to another topic. I would return to my house, search through my small Dari-English and larger Farsi-English dictionaries to find the words that would clarify my meanings. I wrote out a brief account of my conversion story and practiced it until I could say what I really meant. I took their questions and prepared responses that seemed truer, more accurate than my stumbling first attempts. Then I returned or visited another group and tried again.

Over time I acquired the unique vocabulary of faith. I adopted the habit of calling Jesus the Honorable Jesus Messiah, Teacher and Master. I learned to explain the Trinity and found words for helping my friends understand Jesus as both the Son of God and the Son of Man. I started referring to the Bible as the Holy Bible. I found words for prayer and how to address the great God of creation. I learned to explain myself.

I also learned metaphors and analogies that made sense to my listeners. I found in the annual *Qorbon* sacrifice an image that helped my friends understand the sacrifice of Jesus. I learned words for *cross, atonement, forgiveness,* and *resurrection.* I found ways to explain what it means to follow Jesus. I collected simple illustrations—teacups and bowls of treats, broken bread, a child sleeping peacefully in her father's arms. In time I learned how to answer my neighbors' and coworkers' questions.

Still, I knew that no matter how hard I tried to explain myself and my faith, I could never talk anyone into becoming a follower of Jesus, any more than Miss Lillian could talk faith into me. People become followers of Jesus when they both hear the gospel and receive, from God, the faith to believe. Without one and the other, it's impossible. Over the years, many Afghans have tried to convince me to convert to Islam. I've never done it. I've never received faith in the Prophet Mohammed nor the teachings of the Holy Quran.

I listened to my neighbors' stories. I answered their questions and listened to their explanations. Often I asked my own questions. I learned to understand their perspectives and to explain myself in terms they could relate to. They planted their ideas and understanding in my heart, and I planted mine in theirs. I can see how I've interpreted the things they've taught me, but I can't see what they've done with the things I've taught them.

In Afghanistan, faith is foundational. It motivates and defines virtually every aspect of Afghan life, so we talk about it, often. We share our stories and our understanding. We ask one another our questions and seek to understand one another's perspectives. We puzzle through what we hear. Perhaps we've come to know one another better through these conversations. Perhaps we've learned to recognize one another's journey of faith and quest for God. Certainly we've learned to see one another as strikingly different, yet also as deeply human.

Often, through our conversations, I've come to more clearly understand my own faith and the reasoning behind my own practices. I've been challenged to clarify my beliefs and have seen them contrasted to those of my neighbors. Understanding their stories has helped me get to know them, and it's helped me as I've tried to answer their questions and explain what is, really, a work of God in people's hearts. More than anything, though, our conversations helped me see Jesus anew. I saw Him reflected in the glass of a strikingly different culture, and I realized, more deeply than I had before, how powerful and beautiful His love is.

who is god?

Once, while I was in America, one of my American friends asked, "What do Afghan women do for fun?"

I immediately thought about all the things that Afghan women in my community didn't do. They didn't go to the movies. They didn't talk above a whisper in the bazaar. They didn't read books simply for the pleasure of it. They didn't go to plays, concerts, or even the library. Most families didn't have the money to redecorate their houses simply because they'd found something new. In my town, there were no gyms for women, no summer softball leagues, no restaurants women could easily visit. There were no mosques they could attend, no women's groups or Quran study groups. The reality is, there are few diversions for Afghan women in most of the their country.

What do Afghan women do for fun? It struck me as a good question, a question borne out of a society that values leisure and experience, where people take classes, participate in civic groups, and go on vacation. But what about Afghan women?

I thought about the Afghan women I knew and the lives they lived. I thought about the things I could do in Afghanistan.

Afghan women, like women everywhere, value relationships. They value social interaction. Their biggest fun events are social. Afghan women visit one another's houses, sit in one another's rooms and talk. They go to engagement parties and weddings, women-only affairs where they can wear their finest clothes, makeup, and shoes, events where women can dance with elegant and sensual abandon. They go to funeral gatherings, where they eat sumptuous meals and share conversation with one another.

I've been to more than my fair share of Afghan weddings. I've learned to stuff cotton in my ears to protect them from the blaring Indian music blasted through oversized, rented speakers. I've even learned to dance like an Afghan, to the great delight of my women friends. I've adapted to visiting homes, drinking tea, sharing lunches, and attending weddings and funerals.

When I lived in their country, my foreign coworkers and I were always looking for things we could do to build relationships with our Afghan neighbors. One year a foreign woman friend and I decided to throw a party for our neighbors in celebration of International Women's Day. Women's Day is not a true holiday in Afghanistan. Men go to work and the shops are open, but it is a day to recognize women. Across the country, there are official gatherings where speeches are made and sometimes photographs are taken for the TV news. I've attended some of these gatherings, too. For the most part, they're stiff and boring affairs. Important women attend but not the average Afghan tucked away in her little compound.

We wanted to do something fun for those average Afghans in our neighborhood, so we hosted a special party. We spent the two weeks before the party visiting neighbor after neighbor, inviting our friends and their families. If it was a wedding, we could have written out invitations in Dari and delivered them by the hands of neighborhood boys. Instead, we made the invitations personally.

It's nearly impossible just to walk into a compound, deliver a message, and walk out. That's not the way things are done. Every invitation was met with hot cups of tea, treats, and at least twenty minutes of conversation. I cannot even begin to quantify how much tea I've drunk in Afghanistan.

The women we talked to were delighted with the invitation. They all wanted to know if we were going to give them gifts in honor of Women's Day. We told them the party was the gift. They chided us, but they still came.

We prepared presentations for the party. One friend wrote a sweet and very honest poem about what it means to be a woman in Afghanistan. Others prepared short stories about aunts, mothers, or grandmothers who had influenced their lives.

I prepared a talk. I wanted to encourage the women, to help them understand that they are absolutely precious to God, to one another, and to the society at large. I wanted them to hear that God made them unique and beautiful. I wanted to tell them God loves them.

In Islam, there are ninety-nine names for God, but none is "love." In Afghanistan, no one tells people that God loves them. They tell each other God is kind, all-powerful, and omniscient. God created everything including people. God commands, and people must obey. God will reward or punish depending on how people obey. It's not that Afghans tell one another that God doesn't love them. It's just that they don't tell one another that God does love them. I wanted to do that. I wanted to give our women guests a glimpse into the truth that they are absolutely precious. That's what my talk was about.

The week before the party, I wrote my speech and carefully translated it into Dari. My Dari is good but not perfect. I wanted my speech to be perfect, so two days before the gathering, I visited my local language tutor and asked her to check my translation. We went through the first part of the speech without a hitch. My translation was good, and the speech was affirming and beautiful. My language helper loved it until I got to the last part. I said, "God loves you. God loves you because God is love. Each one of you is precious in the presence of God. God loves us all."

My language helper immediately stopped and corrected me. "God is not love; God is kind."

Those are very different words. My language helper had assumed I'd picked the wrong word. I hadn't. I knew exactly how to say, "God is kind." It's one of the most common expressions in Afghanistan. There's a bombing in Kabul and at the end of the conversation, some-one says, "God is kind." A child dies, and after the tragedy has been discussed, someone says, "God is kind." A man finds a job and is delighted, and someone says, "God is kind." The only appropriate response is agreement. "Yes, God is kind."

But "God is love"? No. That's not a thing Afghans say. Later I read that Muslims can't say that Allah loves because love implies need and Allah is so great that he has no needs. I agree that God has no needs, but He still loves.

My language helper and I debated the translation. She didn't want me to say it, but of course I was the one giving the speech. I would say what I wanted.

I didn't expect that our guests would listen to my words and in-stantly, wholly, and completely believe what I said. Sometimes truth is like a flash of lightning on a dark night. For just a second, a split second really, everything becomes visible. And then, just as quickly, the flash disappears and the darkness returns. Still, one doesn't for-get what one has seen when the lightning flashes.

The day of the party, my friends and I, both Afghan and foreign, sent men out to buy cakes, fruit, cookies, raisins, tea, nuts, and sweets. We borrowed thermoses from our neighbors and collected all the cups and serving trays we could find. We boiled kettles and kettles of water over a row of propane tanks with gas burners mounted on top. We filled our thermoses with green and black tea and all our little plates and bowls with treats. We even made popcorn, one of the most popular American treats I've ever prepared for my friends in Afghanistan.

The Afghan style of serving is to set clusters of full plates before each guest or at the very least, within arm's reach of each guest. Every guest must be able to eat every kind of treat without asking someone to pass her a plate. We spread the brown plastic tablecloth on the floor from one end of the room to the other and arranged our plates, bowls, and plastic-flower filled vases from one end of the tablecloth to the other.

We hung sparkly plastic garland across the ceiling and draped the twisting strands over curtain rods. We bought toys for the small children to play with and put them in baskets in the wide hallway outside the sitting room. We borrowed coatracks so we could hang our guests' burqas and banished all men except the guard who opened the gate and ushered our neighbors to the house door. We were ready.

The women arrived. Of course they did. A party is a wonderful thing. Some brought their small children, several brought new babies, tightly swaddled, others brought relatives we'd never seen before. Several of those relatives were visitors from distant towns and provinces. They came in their best, wildly colored clothes, discreetly hidden beneath blue burqas. They came in their fancy-heeled shoes and gold jewelry. And they came with excitement, curious to see what the inside of a foreigner's house looked like, delighted for the diversion.

We greeted each woman with three kisses on alternating cheeks and the standard questions: "*Salaam*, welcome, how are you? How's your family? How are your children? How is your health?" They lifted off their burqas, stepped out of their shoes at the door, and entered the large living room. They scrutinized the display of treats and were mostly satisfied. They fingered the heavy paisley cloth on the floor cushions and matching drapes. They admired the flowers and decorations. They commented on everything but only to one another. They both admired and found fault, and they waited for us to serve the tea. We didn't disappoint.

Finally, when the women had gathered and taken their places on the cushions around the room, and the children had overturned the baskets of toys in the hall and made themselves busy if not quiet, we began.

My foreign friend stood and welcomed everyone into her home. She opened the celebration "In the name of God." That's the custom when making any kind of speech. She offered a simple prayer, asking God's blessing on our gathering. The recitation of a prayer at the beginning of a gathering is common practice, but of course we did it a little differently. Instead of reciting a verse from the Holy Quran in Arabic, my friend prayed her blessing in clear Dari. While she prayed, most of the women lifted their hands palms upward and closed the prayer by passing their palms over their faces.

My friend made a speech about Women's Day and how important women are. Our guests clapped. Then a local woman stood and recited her poem. Again our guests clapped. Finally, it was my turn. I spoke in the most careful and clear Dari I could: "In the beginning, the great and all-powerful God of the universe created the first man and the first woman, Father Adam and Mother Eve. He created them beautiful and called them 'good.' They were precious in His presence. He also prepared a very special garden, the garden of God, and brought Father Adam and Mother Eve to live in His garden and to take care of it. Father Adam and Mother Eve were very happy. They loved one another, and they loved God. This was the will of God and God said it was good."

Our guests quieted and listened carefully. I watched them as I spoke. Questions passed over their faces, doubts, and in the end a sweet and gentle joy.

"God created each one of you, each of us. We are unique, like flowers in a garden. Some of us are big, bright flowers. Some of us are small, sweet-scented flowers. Some of us are blue flowers, and some are red. Some are pink, and some are white. We are all beautiful like the flowers in a garden, precious. God made us this way.

"God knows each one of us. Before we were formed in our mother's womb, He knew our names. He saw us, even before we were born. He sees us now. His spirit is with us, everywhere, all the time. If we go up to the highest mountain, He is with us. If we go down to the deepest sea, He is still with us. He is with us here in this room. He is with each of you in your houses every day and every night. And He calls us 'precious.' We are each uniquely and wonderfully made.

"God loves us. God loves each one of you. God loves us because God is love. He loves us when we are good, and He loves us when we are not good. He will always love us. He has loved us from the very beginning of the world. God loves you—each of you. God loves you."

When I finished, the room was silent. Each woman looked intently at me. Their faces were relaxed, and there was a gentleness, a sweetness in the room. It was as if their eyes were saying, "Really? Thank you."

After a moment they clapped, and the celebration went on. Another Afghan woman stood and shared brief biographies of amazing women—some who'd worked for peace, some to improve the lives of women, others who had created art. Then several of our guests stood and shared stories about aunts, mothers, or grandmothers who had protected them, sacrificed for them, and loved them. After the stories, we poured more tea and spent the rest of the afternoon eating treats, talking, and laughing. It was a good day.

Here's the thing: God does love us, and our souls ache to know it. We are meant to live in the light of His love like a child is meant to grow in the love of her mother and father. His love is what we're made for, and it really is a beautiful thing.

I can't remember the first time someone told me that God loves me. My family was not in the least bit religious, yet I grew up knowing that if there was a God, He loves. I was taught from earlier than I can recall that I'm to love my neighbor, forgive and seek forgiveness, give to those in need, and in general treat others as I would like them to treat me, not as they actually do treat me. When I grew up and read for the first time that God is love, that His kingdom is a kingdom of love, I wasn't surprised. The words in Scripture clarified and confirmed what I had already been taught.

The Afghan experience is completely different. Afghans don't grow up in a society that's been deeply influenced by the teachings of Jesus. Most have never heard His teachings in any form, just as most have never heard the words, "God loves you." For Afghans, there is only the kingdom of this world, with all of its violence, war, and oppression. This life is a test, a challenge Allah has set before each person. If a person passes the test, he or she may reach paradise. Everything that happens along the way is considered to be the will of Allah.

Once an old woman shared her story with me and one of my foreign visitors. She and her family had lived in a neighborhood in Kabul during the days of the brother war. That was the civil war that shattered the country after the Russians left. One of the Afghan warlords stationed his men on the mountains around Kabul and launched thousands of rockets down on the city. The old woman's neighborhood was destroyed. She told me that in one day, fifty-three members of her family were killed. The remnants of her family had fled the rockets on foot, their children without sandals. "What else could we do?" Then the old woman said that somewhere in the mountains, on the road northward, she stopped.

She stood in the middle of the half-destroyed road, her white hair hidden beneath her headscarf, raised her hands, palms open toward heaven, and cried from the depths of her loss, "My God, what have we done to you that you should hate us?"

When she told me this story, her old brown eyes washed with tears. The memory of the whole experience still grieved her heart. "What have we done to you that you should hate us?"

I listened carefully, translating the story line by line for my foreign guest. I could see the old woman in the middle of the refugee-clogged road, surrounded by the high mountains of central Afghanistan, crying out in her grief and horror to the God she had always believed in and yet didn't know, "What have we done to you that you should hate us?"

When the old woman finished her story, my guest asked permission to speak.

The tears were still in the old woman's eyes. About a dozen other women, all refugees from the same bombing, sat quietly around us, waiting.

My foreign friend was careful. She spoke slowly, and I translated sentence by sentence: "God loves you. He has always loved you, and He always will love you. His desire is to bless you. He does not curse you. He does not hate you. He loves you."

The room was quiet, very still, absorbing my friend's beautiful, life-affirming words. She had responded to the first part, "Why do You hate us?" If we believe that everything people do is somehow the will of God, then we ascribe to God the destructive works of people. My friend responded to that lie: "When people do what is evil, they are not doing what God wants. God wants us to love each other in the same way that He loves us."

The women listened deeply. This was perhaps the greatest gift we could give them, the message they most needed to hear: "God loves you. God wants us to love each other in the same way that He loves us."

When we left that day, the women were different; their hearts were encouraged. They had heard, perhaps for the very first time, that God loves them, that the great, all-powerful God of the universe genuinely loves them.

God's will and desire for us is not war, violence, or destruction. God is love, and His kingdom, His will and desires for us, are birthed from that love. We are meant to love God who loved us first. We are meant to love our neighbors, even those we don't know, as God loves them, wholly and completely.

The men who launched their rockets from the mountains above Kabul, rockets that slaughtered innocents in their homes, were not doing the will of God. I have told many Afghans, "If we do what is evil, we are not submitted to God. It doesn't matter if we pray five times a day or go to church every week. If we do what is evil, we are not following God."

Often my friends ask me if I pray namaz, the formulaic Muslim prayers. Sometimes I explain that I do pray, just as Jesus taught us to pray, "Your kingdom come, Your will be done, here in Afghanistan as it is in heaven." I tell them that living in God's kingdom is about living in love. It's about doing the will of God—what is good and right—and doing it from a motivation of love.

This is a revolutionary concept. It changes everything. Usually when Afghans hear it, they either reject it completely because in their minds and by their theology, living according to God's will is a matter of saying the creed, praying the formulaic Arabic prayers, and fasting during Ramadan. It's obeying the Holy Quran, the Hadith, and the *Sunnah*. It's following the teachings of the mullahs, wearing headscarves, and calling themselves Muslims, submitted to God.

Others hear this message and recognize the truth. Their hearts fill with hope, and indeed their lives are changed.

Often I found myself sitting around teacups discussing some new horror in Afghanistan. An aircraft shattered into a mountain rock, killing everyone on board. Avalanches buried hundreds alive in deep, unmarked frozen graves. Bombs landed on wedding halls, and brothers and cousins were shot dead in attacks on police outposts. Most days we heard the helicopters coming into our town. My neighbors said they were carrying the dead, bringing bodies home from Kandahar or Helmand. This was the shadow under which we lived. It's hard to see a God who loves when loss and destruction are so close.

One day I listened to yet another death story. There had been a car bombing in Kabul near the old presidential palace. The bomber had targeted an American military convoy but had detonated his load right next to a packed civilian bus. At first no one knew how many Afghans were killed, but the slaughter had been extreme. One victim's death was particularly horrific. A sheet of shattered glass ripped through the body of a young mother while she cradled her infant child. The glass cut her in half but left the child unharmed and wailing in her dead mother's arms.

I was sitting in a very small, dark house when I heard this story. There were six women with me, lounging on cotton mats, leaning against the cool, mud-brick walls. As always, there were cups of tea in front of us and trays of treats. One of the women related the story, her voice trembling as she spoke. Of all the horrors in Afghanistan, this one was especially troubling.

Each woman, including me, whispered, *"Tobah, tobah,"* repent, as we looked down at the swirling red carpet beneath our knees. *"Tobah."* I think each of us wept. I certainly did. I also prayed. After a long silence, I found some words. "This is not the will of God."

The women looked up at me. Afghans almost universally believe in the concept of kismet, fate. What happens happens because Allah wills it, no matter whose hand has accomplished the thing.

I repeated, "This is not the will of God."

I know I have no power to change an individual's worldview. I can't compel people to accept my words. The interpretation and reaction belongs to my listeners. If I speak truth, that truth will resonate within them. If they can receive it, they will. If they can't, they won't. My responsibility is to follow Jesus and share the faith I have. In my understanding, God is good and certainly not the author of death and destruction.

The women in the small room with the swirling red carpet were still looking at me, so I went on. "This is not the will of God. God came to give us rich, deep, and full lives."

The women nodded.

"Satan came to destroy, to kill, to lie, and to steal. That's the work of Satan, not God."

I told them that when people kill, lie, and steal, they are doing the will of Satan. They are serving Satan. When people love, forgive, and bless, they are doing the will of God and serving God.

Afghans have a concept of Satan. They recognize him as evil, as the destroyer. I reminded this group of women of what they already knew to be true. Satan is evil, and they agreed. But I said something else, too. I said that the man who bombed the bus and cut the young mother in half while her child wailed in her arms did the work of Satan. The Taliban had claimed responsibility for the bombing. I took them at their word.

"The Taliban say they are the fist of Allah. They say they do the work of Allah, and they do it in the name of Allah. But God is love. God loves all of the children of Father Adam and Mother Eve, including the Taliban, the people on the bus, and the foreign soldiers in their trucks."

The women nodded. One woman said, "Yes, we are all the children of Father Adam and Mother Eve."

Affirmed, I continued. "God told us not to kill. We cannot disobey God in the name of God. That's a lie. God told us to love Him with all our hearts, all our minds, and all our strength. Then He told us to love our neighbors. If a man kills his neighbor, he is disobeying God. This man who blew up the bus and killed that mother did not do the will of God. He did the work of Satan. God will judge him."

One woman in the room responded by sharing another story. "Our town was at peace. We didn't know war. We were very happy. One day my cousins and aunts were gathered in the house preparing trays of *mantu* for a wedding party. A bomb fell. We found pieces of dough, bundles of meat, hair-ties, scarves, and scraps of bloody fabric. Even the part of the ceiling that didn't fall was covered with blood and pieces of bodies."

Sometimes stories in Afghanistan are most brutal in their brevity. They are rarely related with great drama, though occasionally with tears. These are simply facts, experiences, reality, the shadow under which so many have lived their lives.

Once again, we all looked at the swirling red carpet. Each woman muttered, *"Tobah,"* repent.

After a long pause I restated what I absolutely believe to be the truth: "That was not the will of God, either."

"No," the women agreed. "That was not the will of God."

Conversation about God, faith, and what it means to live submitted to Him is more common in Afghanistan than any place else I've ever been. For Afghans, God is important and religion is central. Perhaps it's the influence of Islam, although there are many Muslim countries where talk of faith is not so common. More likely, it's the reaction of a people of deep faith to the darkness that's settled over their lives. My Afghan neighbors pray five times a day, fast during Ramadan, and do whatever they can to obey the teachings of the Holy Quran and Hadith, and yet their lives are marked by trauma—violence, oppression, and poverty. Perhaps many of my Afghan neighbors are secretly like that old, white-haired woman who stood in the middle of the mountains and cried out to Allah, "What have we done?"

For many Westerners, the question of who God is and what He wants for and from us is simply not relevant. We are, after all, wealthy and busy. For Afghans, it may be the most important question of all.

One afternoon, after a long day of work with more to do in the evening, I was sitting in a neighbor's house drinking tea. I had known the family for some time and felt quite relaxed with them. Suddenly the husband asked, "What do you believe will happen to you when you die?" We had not been talking about religion or faith or even death, so the question surprised me.

In the New Testament, it's written that we should always be ready to give an answer for the faith that's within us. I wasn't ready. I did give an answer, but it wasn't much. I said, very simply, "I'll wake up in heaven." Then I asked my own question. "What do you believe?"

The entire family was in the room, both men and women, boys and girls, all sitting together. One of the men explained his faith to me. He told me that when a Muslim dies, he must first cross the *pul-e salat*, the bridge spanning the chasm of chaos, separating heaven from earth. He told me the bridge is as thin as a human hair and as sharp as razor. If a person is righteous and has enough *sawab*, credit from the good works he's done, he can go across the bridge. If a person is unrighteous, he will be cut to shreds and fall into hell. Then each person will be judged by Allah. Allah will weigh his good deeds against his bad deeds. Allah knows everything and has written our actions in a book. His measure will be just. If a person has enough good deeds, Allah will welcome him into paradise.

I wanted to make sure I understood the message. I drew a line on the swirling red carpet with my thumbnail. That was the bridge. I put the thermos on one end of the line. That was heaven. I put my teacup on the other. That was me. Then I took two cut glass bowls of treats from the floor between us, one full of wrapped candy and the other of almonds. I weighed the bowls in my hands and asked,

"So this bowl, the candy, is like my good deeds, and this other bowl, the almonds, is like my bad deeds, right?"

"Right."

"And God weighs them? Right?"

"Right."

I understood. My neighbors recognized God as judge and we mere mortals as working to be accepted by Him. This life is a test—enough points, and we pass. I wondered if the judge cares who passes and who fails. I asked another question, still weighing the bowls in my hands. "How do you know if you've done enough good deeds, if you have enough candy, to outweigh your bad deeds, the almonds?"

Almost everyone in the room smiled and shrugged. "You don't know until you get there."

I realized how I could explain what I believe. I said, "Yes, I believe what you said. I believe God will judge us, but I also believe God knows that we will not be good enough. We will not have enough *sawab*, good works to earn our way into heaven. The *Injil*, the book of Jesus, says that God loves us and wants us all to go to heaven."

I took another small bowl, a nearly empty one, and turned it upside down on top of the bowl of almonds. The two bowls—one covered, one open—sat on the floor, side by side. I said, "God loves us, so He sent Jesus to cover my sins, my bad deeds, so that when I stand before God, He doesn't look at them."

The entire family watched me carefully.

I picked up an empty cup and set it down on the floor next to the thermos. I said, "You're right. It's difficult to have enough of our own righteousness to get across the bridge. I don't believe I have enough. I am not that good."

My friends immediately disagreed, but I waved them away. "I may do good things, but God sees every corner of my heart. He knows me completely, and believe me, I'm not that good."

They couldn't argue with that. No one can see into another person's heart, and only we know what lies hidden in our own.

I went on. "Here's the thing: I don't have to be good enough to get across the bridge on my own righteousness." I put my hand on the cup that I had set next to the thermos and said, "The Holy Quran teaches that the Honorable Jesus came from heaven to earth."

My companions nodded. They knew that part.

"God knew I wouldn't be good enough, but He still loves me, all of us, and wants us to come to heaven, so He sent Jesus to help us." With that, I slid the cup across the line I had marked in the swirling carpet with my thumbnail. My cup and the Jesus-cup sat side by side on the carpet just in front of me, the two bowls beside them.

I went on. "He gave me faith to believe in Him. When that happened, it's like He picked me up." I stacked my cup on top of the Jesus-cup. "When it's time, He will carry me across the bridge on His righteousness, His *sawab*. He hasn't done any bad deeds, only good. You know that. He will carry me to heaven on His *sawab*."

I slid the two cups back along the line and set them down next to the thermos. Then I pointed to the two bowls, one still covered, and I said, "When God judges me, He will not look at my bad deeds because Jesus took care of them. He will welcome me into heaven. This is the will of God." I smiled. "That's what I believe."

My friends looked at the bowls, the thermos, and the cups. They looked at me and at one another. They were thinking about what I had just said. Finally, the gray-bearded father said to me, "You have a beautiful God."

I smiled, put the cups and bowls back where they belonged, poured myself another cup of tea from the thermos, and said, "Yes, I think I do."

Often when I talked with Afghans, I looked for analogies they could relate to. Jesus did that, too. He talked about farming and fishing and herding because that's the work His neighbors did. He talked to the woman at the well about water, because she had come there to draw water. He talked about broken bread and cups of wine because broken bread and cups of wine lay on the table before Him. The analogies He chose made sense to His neighbors.

I looked for analogies that made sense to my Afghan friends. Often I sat in rooms with children crawling around, knocking over cups of tea and scattering plates of raisins. I watched mothers, fathers, and grandmothers pull their babies away from thermoses of scalding tea. I found analogies.

I wanted my friends to know God loves them, to know that recognizing God's love changes everything. Sometimes I told my friends, "God's love is like your love for your child, only greater, because He's God. If I understand that God loves you and even loves the stranger down the street, how could I throw a stone? How would you feel if I took your small child and threw him against the wall? You would think, 'This is a horrible woman. I thought she was my friend. I welcomed her into my home, and she's hurt my child. How could she do that? She's not my friend.'"

It's a clear analogy. "If I hurt someone God loves, how could I say I love God?"

Sometimes my Afghan friends understood. The very nature of God is love. It's the foundation of all things. God loves us, each of us, wholly and completely. His love is pure and without the kind of need we mortals mix in with our love. God's love defines us, heals us, and brings us into joy and peace. God wants us to love Him and one another. That's the foundation. It's what Jesus showed us when He called love the greatest commandment. Love God, and love your neighbor.

God doesn't want us to throw rockets at one another or blow up buses and slaughter innocent people. That's not the will of God. This world we live in is crowded and confused, full of both good and evil. Our challenge is to find the light through shadows of violence and oppression, pain, and loss. That's not easy for us, but Jesus showed us the way.

HOW DO WE RESPOND
TO EVIL DONE TO US?

In Afghanistan, the lives of many women have been extraordinarily difficult. For some, war started in the middle '70s when government troops and rivaling warlords attacked their villages in the countryside. In those days, the government of Afghanistan was communist and trying to modernize the country. They wanted to do away with the practice of selling young girls into marriage. They tried to establish schools, hospitals, and clinics throughout the countryside. They even attempted to change debt structures and to redistribute land. The major cities, Kabul, Herat, and Mazar-i-Sharif were, compared to today, stunningly modern and free. Outside these major cities, the country was completely the opposite—remote, traditional, and overwhelmingly illiterate.

The ideology and efforts of the communists and other Kabuli modernists slammed hard against the power of the very conservative religious leaders on both the Shiite and Sunni sides of the Afghan religious house. They also threatened the moneyed landowners who controlled large swaths of countryside. Throughout the 1970s, violence exploded erratically and devastatingly in pockets of the Afghan countryside and even in Kabul itself.

Like most Americans, I had always thought Afghanistan's problems really began with the Russian invasion in 1979. I was just out of high school when our city newspaper carried grainy black-and-white images of Russian tanks pouring into the country. Throughout the '80s, I heard heroic stories of brave and presumably good mujahedin warriors who defended their poor and vulnerable nation against one of the strongest military powers on earth. Later, when the Russians finally left and the country descended into a brutal brother-war of competing mujahedin warlords, I, like most Americans, looked away. I couldn't make sense of the chaos. What happened to victory? What happened to peace? I had naïvely assumed that the departure of the "evil" Russians foretold the restoration of all that was good in Afghanistan.

Throughout my five-year journey in their country, I interviewed several hundred Afghan women and pieced together their stories. I learned that war in Afghanistan is and has always been regional. Different Afghan communities experienced war at different times depending on where they lived. I met women whose families were driven from their villages several years before the Russian invasion. I met others who didn't see war until Taliban planes raked their villages with bombs and Taliban soldiers burned everything standing.

I listened to the stories, mostly of women, but also of men. I found their villages on maps and placed their experiences in timelines. Afghanistan uses a different calendar from the one we use in the West. The year is counted from the time of the Prophet Mohammed, not the time of Christ. Their calendar recognizes twelve months, but the dates of the major holidays change from year to year. To most of my Afghan friends, calendar years and months just weren't significant. Instead, they counted time by events, people, and harvests. I heard dates like "In the days of Daud" and understand that the subject we were discussing took place between 1973 and 1978. Another woman marked the time of her flight to Iran as a refugee from "the days Russian tanks rolled through the streets of Kabul," and I recognized the Saur Revolution in 1978. Once I asked a woman when the Taliban bombed her village. She thought for several moments and replied, "At the time of the grape harvest, yes, we were drying grapes." Another woman told me, "We fled our village when the first wheat was in the field." I listened to their stories and translated to understand their experiences.

When I started interviewing women, I expected to hear horror stories involving the Russians. I had read books and came with very Western assumptions. Perhaps if I had been working in the south of the country or along the Pakistan border, I would have encountered an Afghanistan with decidedly different collections of stories and experiences. The stories I did encounter were strikingly different from my assumptions. The stories revealed an Afghanistan riddled with tribal violence, dominated by local competing warlords who took what they wanted and killed and maimed with abandon. I had expected to hear brutal stories involving the Taliban, and I did, but I was surprised to hear equally brutal stories from across most of the country —stories involving mujahedin militias, disparate groups of fighters, usually under the leadership of a local, non-government warlord.

One woman told me that a mujahedin militia came to her father's house in the middle of the night. They dragged him out of his *aouli* to the street and beat him mercilessly. His crime? Sending his daughters to school. They told him that if he continued to do this, he would be killed and his daughters taken. That was the end of that woman's education.

Another woman told me of a different mujahedin gang. They came to a neighbor's house, deep in the night, took the entire family out to a field, and raped the girls in front of their father and brothers. Again, the crime was sending the girls in the family to school. The father and the brother killed the girls for the shame of the rape.

One woman told me that a local warlord came to her father's house and demanded her as a wife. That's not the way marriages are meant to be arranged, but what could the girl's father do? The warlord and his men told the father that if they didn't hand over the girl, the entire family would be killed and their household burned. The girl was given to the warlord as his third wife. She was twelve years old. Later the warlord himself was killed, and the young woman became a widow with one small child and another in her womb. She wasn't yet eighteen years old.

There were other stories—stories with terrible outcomes. One woman was eleven when her father was dragged from their home. Later the man was found dead in the street. The mother took the children, including her eldest, the eleven-year-old daughter, and fled to the mountains. There they threw themselves on the hospitality of strangers. They were impoverished and hungry. The mother sold the eleven-year-old to a gray-bearded man. He was not only old; he was brutal and beat her regularly.

Jesus tells us to forgive those who have sinned against us. He tells us to bless our enemies and to pray for those who abuse us. In the West, we find this teaching difficult. Those of us who've embraced it understand the freedom forgiveness brings. In Afghanistan, neither the teaching nor the freedom it brings exists, and yet the need is exponentially greater.

Another Afghan woman told me of her police officer husband who comes home each evening from his work in the city. When her children cry, the man, enraged, beats the entire family with cables. She showed me the bruises on her son's back and told me that hers was covered as well. While she told me this story, her mother, who lived with her, wept. She was powerless.

How does one forgive such brutality? How does one forgive these events when they are in the past—completed traumas that, one hopes, will not be repeated? How does one forgive them when they continue, when each night, they are repeated? And yet we know that forgiveness is a foundation stone in the kingdom of God. It's absolutely critical. *Forgive us our trespasses as we forgive those who trespass against us.* We also know that the kingdom of God is good news—that somehow even this forgiveness, the grace to do it, is good for us. We know the kingdom of God was meant for us and we were meant for the kingdom.

One day, while I was setting up a training class in a very poor neighborhood, I met with the woman who would host the class. Nazira was a sad woman, perhaps in her late thirties, living in deep poverty, but she was also educated. She had completed the tenth grade.

We went through the process of negotiating the training class. Nazira had the approval of the community elder, his signature and stamp, and a list of students. We walked through the contract and clarified each requirement. She was in agreement. She would be paid for the job, and although the money wasn't much, she still very much wanted to do it. We signed and stamped the contract and then enjoyed a cup of tea.

Nazira's sitting room was unusually small, no more than six by seven feet. The doorway was low and narrow, blanket-covered against the cold. It led onto a narrow alley that, in turn, led into another *aouli*. Her small house had been carved from someone else's property. She had no swirling red, machine-woven carpet, so common in other homes. Her floor was covered first with empty flour bags cut open and patched together and then with a cheap woven mat of faded colored yarn. We sat directly on the floor. Nazira poured two cups of thin, bitter tea from a plastic thermos. She had no treats to offer.

In Afghanistan, it's rude to just conduct your business and go, so we sat and talked for a little while. I asked where she was from and how she had managed to get an education. Nazira told me her story. Her father had been killed by a mujahedin militia when she was very young. She didn't know whose militia it was. Her father wasn't a soldier, but just a working man caught up in the violence.

Her mother remarried and, amazingly, had been able to keep the three children she bore with her first husband. Normally, upon the death or abandonment of a father, the children become the possessions of the father's family. During the time of war and displacement, such rules were often broken. For Nazira's mother, that meant she was able to keep her children.

The mother's second husband was cruel. He regularly beat the children and his wife. When Nazira was about thirteen years old—she's not sure of her exact age—her mother made arrangements to marry her off. The girl was ready to go. She couldn't imagine that any life could be worse than the one she endured with her stepfather. She was wrong.

Nazira was sold to a man as his second wife, but his first wife had already died. Initially, Nazira was unable to conceive children, a failure that provoked her husband's wrath but also allowed her to continue her education.

In Nazira's tenth year of school, she became pregnant and brought forth her first child. She thought her success in birthing children would assuage her husband's violence. It didn't. The beatings continued. Two more children followed. It was when she was pregnant with her third child that her husband was killed by yet another mujahedin militia. The story surrounding his death remains a complete mystery. Neighbors came and told her he had been killed, and that's all she ever learned. In her mid-twenties, she became a widow. She did not grieve her husband, but she did grieve her immediate and desperate poverty.

Even though I've listened to so many such stories, each one steals my breath and presses my heart painfully against my ribs. The extent of human devastation is staggering. So many stories—and how could I respond? What could I say? How could I encourage or comfort this precious lady?

Nazira related these details dry-eyed and steady-voiced. I don't know how Afghan women do that, how they control their emotions so well. Their stories, so often, fall flatly from their lips like a lunchtime tablecloth spread before a guest. Here it is: my story, my experience, my life. And they pour another cup of tea.

I listened to Nazira and prayed silently as she spoke. I eyed the flat "tablecloth" of her life story and thought, no, this is not what any of us should eat from. This is not the will of God, not the will of a God who is good, not the will of a God who tells husbands to love their wives as Christ loves the church, not the will of the God who says don't kill. We were not created to be abused, to be beaten, or to be hated. No, we were created for love, for joy, and for peace. But what could I say? What response could I give? What words of hope could I offer? I so desperately wanted to give Nazira a gift she could use, a gift for her heart.

As I listened and prayed, I felt I should share a sketch of my own story. I had never experienced anything as devastating as this dear lady had known, but I had experienced hardship. I had experienced abuse. I had tasted the bitterness of anger and rage and carried wounds and offenses in my heart. Perhaps most importantly, I had learned the sweet freedom and peace of genuine, heart-breathed forgiveness.

I took a deep breath and began. I told her that I, too, had once had a stepfather who had beaten me.

Nazira looked up into my face with unspoken questions washing over hers. *Really? Do such things happen in other places? It isn't just us?* So many Afghan women believe that every place else in the world is safe and only in Afghanistan does brutality happen. But of course, this isn't true.

I told her I hadn't grown up with faith in God. That, too, surprised her. From her perspective, God is a reality everyone recognizes and religion is a faith one is born with. I didn't grow up with that kind of faith.

I told her that I received faith in God when I was in my twenties, that I met the Honorable Jesus and realized God loved me. I explained to her that when I met Jesus, I confessed all of my sins and He forgave me.

Again Nazira looked at me attentively, questioningly. Most Afghans don't admit to having sin, and here I was, a foreigner, admitting such a thing. And I was speaking about being forgiven, that precious gift we receive through Christ Jesus. When we know Christ, we know the sweet freedom of being forgiven.

I went on. I told Nazira that after I received faith, many months afterward, I learned that I needed to forgive my stepfather.

Nazira nodded as though she understood, but I doubted if she did. Afghans do believe that both Allah and people can forgive, but forgiveness itself is understood differently. It's almost as though the person who forgives simply chooses to ignore the sin. Allah agrees not to count it; he doesn't wash it away.

I told Nazira, "When God forgives us, He looks directly at our sin. He sees it. We confess it, agreeing that we see it, too. Then God takes our sin away from us and puts it on Christ."

In Afghanistan, that concept of forgiveness is a revolutionary one, and Nazira didn't understand it. It was too foreign for her, and came across to her as just pure theory—a nice idea but too far away for application. I sought an analogy to help her understand what it means to forgive someone who has hurt us. I told her this: "Our hearts are created like deep wells. The water is sweet, and we need it to live. But as we live, things happen. Sometimes other people do very bad things to us. Each time they do something bad to us, it's like they are throwing a rock into our well. Every day we drop our bucket into the well and draw water to drink. Eventually we drop the bucket into the well, but it can't reach the water because there are too many rocks. We have to clean the well."

Afghans understand wells in a way we don't in America. Most wells in Afghanistan are deep, open pits dug straight down into the earth. A stone ring is built around the opening or a concrete well ring is buried into the lip. This keeps the dirty runoff water out of the well. Sometimes a frame with a winch is mounted over the top. The bucket, often made from the rubber of a used tire, is tied to a rope wrapped around the winch. When a woman wants water, she lowers the bucket into the well and then cranks it up to the surface. It's hard work, but necessary. If a woman has a well in her yard, she may do this work several times a day.

Sometimes wells become full of rock, gravel, or dirt, or the water level falls beneath the rock bed. The well must then be cleaned. A man descends deep into the well and fills the bucket with rocks and other debris. Another man on the surface pulls up the heavy bucket, tosses the rocks and debris away, and lowers the bucket again. The process continues until all the rocks and dirt are gone and the bottom of the well is full of sweet water once again.

I chose an accessible analogy to help this lovely lady understand what it means to forgive. "Each time someone does something bad to us, it's as if they are throwing a rock into our well. If we leave the rocks, we won't be able to draw water. We must go down into the well. We must pick up each rock, one at a time, and put it into the bucket. Then we must lift the rocks out of the well and throw them aside. It's hard work, and it takes time. Our wells might have many rocks or just a few. When we have taken them out, we can draw sweet water from the well again."

Nazira understood the story. She grasped the wisdom of it. For Afghans, a story speaks far more powerfully than some reasoned explanation. A story is accessible, applicable, and somewhat detached. We could discuss a well and rocks, understanding completely the implications. Nazira knew the rocks that had been thrown into her own heart.

I watched her consider the analogy, watched her face move from comprehension and acceptance to confusion. Finally I saw a question. She turned her attention back to me and waited. She had entered the story.

I didn't know what specific question had brought her attention back to me, so I simply went on. I applied the story to myself. "One time my stepfather beat me with a leather belt. I was very afraid. I was angry, too. I hated him. I prayed and asked God to punish him. Instead God asked me to forgive him. This is what I said: 'Dear God, I forgive my stepfather for beating me. When he beat me, it hurt and I was afraid. It was wrong, but I forgive him. I ask You to forgive him too.'"

Tears slid silently over Nazira's cheeks. Her shoulders trembled. She looked away, searched the walls, and then looked back at me. Finally she asked, "You did that?"

I breathed. The story was working. Nazira was learning to forgive. "Yes. And each time I thought of something else that he had done to me, I prayed again and forgave him."

We fell silent, each of us fidgeting with the heavy glass teacup in front of us.

Finally I spoke again. "When I forgave him, my heart became lighter. The anger and the pain left. The water in the well of my heart became sweet."

At this Nazira wept openly, without gasps or sobs. She simply wept, the tears sliding down her cheeks, collecting unchased in the corners of her mouth, staining the wrapped edge of her scarf and the collar of her long shirt.

I didn't say anything more.

In time Nazira took a deep breath, sighed, and wiped her face dry with her scarf. She poured our last cup of tea, and we drank in silence.

I put the signed and stamped contract, the attendance list, and the letter from the village elder in my bag and reminded her of the next steps for the work. I spoke a blessing over her life, unfolded my crossed legs, and pushed myself up from the floor.

As I leaned forward to walk through the low door of her tiny room, she reached around me, wrapped my hands in hers, and pulled me back into the room. Once again her eyes were full of tears. She laid one rough, calloused hand gently around the side of my face and breathed, "Thank you, thank you," then kissed my cheek and bid me good-bye.

I only saw that lovely lady two more times. She had not been able to accomplish the work she agreed to undertake. The others in the community decided not to participate in the training. They thought they would receive more than the class, like bags of rice and flour. They were disappointed when they didn't and went away.

I would love to know what that precious woman did with my words, with the story I shared, but I never found out. I prayed my story would give her courage and hope. I prayed that in the privacy of her own room, away from the prying eyes of neighbors or the presence of an odd foreigner, she would find the strength to descend into her well, pull up the bitter rocks, throw them over the wall, and laugh, really laugh.

The kingdom of God is like a farmer who plants seeds. He sleeps and wakes, and the seeds grow. He doesn't know how they grow; he only knows they do. My confidence is in this: If the seed I planted was a good seed and the soil that received it was ready, the seed grew and that gentle lady found peace.

Sometimes we imagine that all that is good in God as revealed in Christ only belongs to those who've adopted a complete framework of theological beliefs. We imagine that until a person understands and confesses belief that Jesus is God, that He died on the cross for our sins and rose the third day, the teachings and blessings of God remain inaccessible. We sometimes make the mistake of viewing ourselves and others as either in or out, as either wearing our team's jersey or not wearing it.

How much better to remember that we are all on a journey. Each time we see or hear or in some way grasp a teaching or revelation of Christ, we are drawn out of an area of darkness within our lives into His light and truth, into His beautiful kingdom. He invites us to walk with Him, to learn from Him, and to find in Him the healing, love, joy, and peace that our souls desperately need. The good news is that we can walk with Jesus. We can receive His healing long before we understand who He is and why He came in the first place.

In Afghanistan, I feel as if I've met the Canaanite woman who came to Jesus begging healing for her daughter. I've met the daughter of Abraham, an old woman whose back was bent. I've met the shamed woman with the issue of blood who simply reached out and touched the hem of Jesus' robe. All of them found the answers to their prayers in Jesus, and yet when they did, none of them understood, really, who He was.

One afternoon I was sitting with a group of Afghan women, friends of mine, drinking tea and sharing stories. I can't remember how we got on the subject, what story brought it forward, but a special story came. Afghans tell me their stories. Each in turn, men and women—so many tell me their stories.

Sometimes one will start to tell a story, and the others will object:

"Don't talk. Everyone has suffered. Be quiet." Perhaps this is a collective response to trauma: Put it away, be silent, your story isn't unique, it doesn't matter.

Sometimes I think they're right. After a while, the stories begin to sound the same. The trauma, always shudderingly intense, enters the room we're sitting in. It chases away the laughter and unlocks the trunks where other traumas lie hidden in each person's heart. Trauma is never really shared. The entire community may experience the same event, but each person's story of it is unique and deeply personal.

The tragedy of September 11th happened to all Americans, but it didn't bring us together inside of our trauma. It brought us together because we were side by side, each experiencing our own stories at the same time.

When 9/11 happened I was in Paris, conducting a business workshop. The first calls came in via cell phone. For us, it was around three o'clock in the afternoon. I remember the events with clarity: the cell calls from North Jersey, German coworkers fighting the Internet for news, misinformation and inconceivable reports that proved true. We were together in a conference room—Germans, French, Americans, Canadians, Japanese, and British—yet each of us experienced our collective trauma uniquely. The bits and pieces of my experience are packed into a locked trunk in my heart. They belong to me.

Since 9/11, I've often found myself, somewhere early on in a relationship with a Westerner, swapping our stories of that day. "I was in Florida at a conference. I rented a car and drove home." "We landed in Pakistan that very day. Never left the airport. Turned around and went to Thailand." "We were in Italy. It was our honeymoon." "I watched on TV." "My father never came home."

There's something in the human spirit that longs to tell the story, to make sense out of our unique experience. We open that trunk and unpack its scraps of memories. We invite others to look at them and tell us what they see. Somehow, in the unpacking and repacking, we define and contain all those scraps. We shine a little light into the corners of that trunk and feel better about its presence in our heart.

The storyteller says, "This is my wound. This is what happened to me, and it's important. It's not important because I'm the only one who suffered. No. It's important because I suffered and I'm important."

When I was new in the Afghan country, I told a very experienced foreign worker that real freedom would come to Afghans not through democracy or economic development, but through forgiveness. That's where real healing and true freedom would begin. By then, I had only heard some stories. I only spoke the local language well enough to get the things I needed from the bazaar, and if I understood anything of importance, it was through a translator. That foreign worker listened to me, then rebuked me sharply. She told me I was expecting far too much. I was too naïve. Afghan pain was far too deep.

Over time I learned the language. I listened to stories and recorded them and then took them back to my room and listened again. My language improved, and the stories I heard transformed themselves from black-and-white sketches to high-definition movies.

That foreign worker who told me I was expecting too much was mistaken. Yes, the stories are far too hard. No, I haven't walked the journeys of my Afghan friends or experienced their trauma or their losses. But Jesus never said, "Forgive if the offense is small. If it's great, just carry it. You can't get rid of it. You'll carry it until you die." That wasn't His message at all. I figured He knew best.

So one afternoon I was sitting with a group of Afghan women friends, drinking tea and sharing stories. It was hot, the season of yellow mangoes imported from Pakistan. We had already sliced ours open, scooped the soft, bright fruit into our mouths and returned the long nut and empty skins to the bowls before us. We had been talking about mangoes. None of the women ate them when they were growing up. They hadn't been available in those days. Somehow, that became the bridge—mangoes.

The women tripped through one story after another, as they so often did with me. The foreigner is safe. The foreigner doesn't judge or silence. The foreigner listens.

They were Hazara women, born into a Shiite tribe hated by the Taliban. That day they were tripping through stories of their exodus from their home villages, their refugee journeys, and then the Taliban invasion. That invasion had been a deeply fearful time. They saw horror. They heard horror as they crouched behind their walls and war raged in the streets. They lost fathers and brothers, uncles and sons. So often these were the kinds of stories women, especially Hazara women, told me.

We were drinking tea in the safety of a small room. The curtains were drawn against the hot summer sun, and the room was cool. The Taliban were gone, and people walked the streets of our town in safety. The rockets and machine guns had been silenced. Shiite men sat in their shops not worrying if a gang would come arrest them for not having long beards or drag them into a Sunni mosque for prayers at a time they didn't pray. So much had changed, and we were all grateful.

I listened to the stories until each woman fell silent. I inhaled the old horror and deep sadness, and I considered how to respond. I prayed, "Father, is there something for me to share? Something for me to say?"

These women were my friends, good, generous women who, even in the face of deep loss, had found the strength to keep living. They were old and had raised their children through years of trial. They hoped for more for their grandchildren. They were women who had welcomed me, the stranger, into their lives, and I appreciated them deeply.

I recognized the enemy in most of their stories: black-turbaned, bearded men with Kalashnikovs, men who rode the streets in Toyota pickup trucks and Range Rovers, shooting, beating, or just taking

Hazara husbands and sons. Those were men who sat in the city and fired rockets into the wide, arid fields that bridged the city and the mountains. Those rockets fell on fleeing Hazara women and their babies.

I thought about forgiveness—sweet, true forgiveness, the only answer, the only solution for the remnants of horror in the hearts of my friends. A grudge is a heavy thing, rocks in the heart. Hatred turns to bitterness or fear. Fear becomes immobilizing, paralyzing. Bitterness becomes acid that burns us and everyone around us. A wound festers until it cripples. That's not what we were made for— no, not at all. We were made for peace, love, and joy. We're made to breathe, to laugh, and to dance, but it's hard to dance when our hearts are full of rocks.

I was sitting, knees folded together and bare heels against my hip, leaning against a cool inside wall. My scarf was as loose as I could allow it in the late afternoon heat. I shared the words I knew, the only response to such horrible stories that made sense to me.

Forgiveness isn't just ignoring what happened. It isn't pretending it was okay or justifying it. It's looking an evil act square in the face and saying, "I forgive that evil act." It's asking God to forgive, as well. It's letting go of the desire to punish, kill, and destroy. And then it's going one step further. It's blessing the person who perpetrated such horrific evil. It's praying for the one who was once an enemy and may still be an enemy. It's giving the evildoer—the murderer, the rapist, the thief—love. Forgiveness is freedom. In so many ways, it's the only true path to freedom, and it's a hard path to walk.

That afternoon I shared stories about forgiveness, and my women friends nodded as though they agreed and understood, but I knew they didn't. For so many Afghans, forgiveness is a matter of looking the other way, of ignoring the offense. Only the powerful can really do that and get any credit for it. God and the rich man and the warlord can choose to look the other way, to refrain from exacting revenge. For the weak, the options are different. They can't exact revenge. They can only accept the offense, and in their acceptance they are more shamed than ever.

Finally I shared stories from my own life. My stories are nowhere near as horrific, but they're real. My friends listened. Once again I told a story from my experiences with my stepfather. Then I showed them how I forgave. I lifted my hands palms upward, turned my eyes toward heaven, and began to pray. I had chosen an event in my life, a trauma I'd experienced. I recognized the trauma and then prayed forgiveness for the man. Finally I prayed a blessing on his life. I was offering a model. I repeated something I had actually prayed many years before to give my friends a tangible example to help them understand what I was really trying to say.

Somewhere in the middle of my prayer, one of the women in the room gasped. I didn't look around to see who it was. I just kept praying, but I wondered.

When I finished praying there was silence. The women were looking down at their tea, picking threads out of the hems of their clothes. I waited. When the silence seemed long enough, I asked, "Is there someone you want to forgive?" I had intended to ask each woman in turn, but the first woman I looked at responded.

Immediately, without explanation, she lifted her eyes toward heaven, raised her hands palms upward, and began to pray. I thought she would pray about one of the stories she had shared—those days of violence and destruction when the enemy had been clearly identifiable. But that wasn't what was on her heart. Instead, she prayed to forgive a man who had violated her and shamed her some thirty years before, before the mujahedin came to her village, before the desperate run for safety under exploding rockets, before the Taliban arrived. The offense that weighed heaviest on her heart was a deeply personal one, an old one, a shaming one.

When she finished praying, she breathed. It was like a sigh that rose up from the arc between the crests of her hips. She shook her arms and rolled her shoulders. She smiled. "This is good. This is good." She breathed again. "Ah, this is good." Then she looked at each of us. "This is very good."

I wanted to ask a hundred questions—what she was thinking, how she felt, what all this meant to her—but I didn't. I allowed her journey to remain a private one, her own story experienced in the company of others.

After a while, I looked at one of my other friends who seemed to be hiding beneath her bowed head. I called her by name. "Masuma, is there someone you want to forgive?"

She wouldn't look at me. Instead, she just shook her head and continued to pluck errant threads from the hems of her clothes.

I'll admit I didn't know what to do. We had entered into a very precious, holy space, and I wanted to honor it. I wasn't going to push. I sat quietly until the air in the room returned to normal and the sense of the sacred faded. Then, gently, I filled bowls of pistachios and candy, poured old tea from our cups into a glass bowl, and refilled our glass cups with fresh green tea. I found another conversation subject, and we moved on.

For days after that, I wondered about my silent friend and what had been troubling her under her bowed head. I thought I would never know, but I was wrong. Perhaps she was counting the cost. Perhaps she was wondering if she was strong enough, if she could really do it even if she wanted to. I don't know. She never told me what was going on in her heart or her mind, but a week later when we sat together once again she shared her story.

This time it was just the two of us and the plate of rice we were sharing. She ate with her hands and I with a spoon. I had not yet learned how to eat with my fingertips without dropping rice everywhere. Sometime during the meal she began to tell a story, and I tried to listen.

Masuma was a precious friend—in some ways, like a mother to me. She had taught me so much about right and wrong in Afghanistan. She had laughed with me, and I love to laugh.

She was also remarkably difficult to understand. Her family came from some very distant mountains and she had never been educated, so her village accent was thick and hard to decipher. Also her mother tongue was Hazaragi, not Dari. Hazaragi and Dari are closely related, but they're different. I had been studying both languages but in those days wasn't very good at either. Listening was exhausting and understanding difficult. I found that if I understood the context, I could piece the story together quite easily. But if someone changed subjects in mid-conversation, it might take me awhile to catch up. Masuma was telling me a story in an odd mixture of Dari, Hazaragi, and village speak.

Through the beginning of her tale I only pretended to understand. I thought it was just another story of her family and it would be okay if I didn't get it completely, but in the middle I realized it was much more. Masuma had always been incredibly patient with me, and I counted on her goodwill. I stopped her story and asked her to repeat it. Without the slightest hint of irritation, she began again. In the end, she had to repeat her story three times before I understood it. It was another hard story.

By the time the Taliban invaded her city, Masuma's husband had already died. He had been a very old man when she married him and she was his second wife, much younger than his first—she was a girl for his old age. She gave birth to two sons. One lost his leg in a mine when he was just a small boy. When that firstborn son was a young teenager, the Taliban arrived. At the time, her second son wasn't much more than a toddler. He was at that age when children only want to run and play.

When the Taliban invaded, many of the Hazaras took to the mountains. They had to run across wide-open rangeland to get away, but Masuma couldn't do that. She would have had to carry the toddler on her back while her one-legged son shared his weight between her arm and his ill-fitted prosthetic leg. She would never make it across the rangeland up into the mountains. Instead, she fled her Hazara neighborhood and made her way through the walled neighborhoods of different ethnic groups in the city.

Somewhere on that journey, a Pashtun family took her in. The Taliban are Pashtuns, and tradition says the Pashtuns hate Hazaras. Masuma couldn't understand the Pashtun family's generosity. She was terrified but desperate, so she accepted their help.

The family hid her in a small, dark room with her two sons. They hid for hours, but it wasn't safe. In time, a black-turbaned, black-bearded Talib, a single warrior, came and searched the house. He found the small woman, her crippled son, and her toddler. He leveled his Kalashnikov at her boys. Horror. Terror. Desperation.

Masuma begged, negotiated, gave him everything she had—the coins in her pocket, the bundle of rice she had dragged with her, and more. She felt the blade of his knife against her body as her boys watched in helpless horror. And then it was over. She had saved her boys—her sons, the only thing in the world she had.

Masuma related her story between bites of rice. She told me the whole thing, three times over, dry-eyed and even-voiced.

I had already been in Afghanistan long enough to be able to picture the room, hear the cries, and smell the desperation. The trauma of it crashed against my heart. This was my friend, one of my closest friends in Afghanistan. I knew her sons, both of them, now grown. Sometimes, even when we know the right things to do, it's hard. There are moments when all I wanted was a sledgehammer to smash down the walls, moments when everything within me raged against the brutality, the injustice. Masuma's story brought me into that bitter place.

Once I met a man who admitted to being a mujahedin warrior. At first, he denied it. I don't know why. Everyone else would have known. When I met him, he was about forty years old with a gray-edged beard down to the middle of his chest, a small turban, and a checked man-scarf. He was working as a taxi driver, and I was sitting in the backseat of his old Russian taxi. I imagined that if I searched his house, I would find not one Kalashnikov but a dozen, buried in a shallow well beneath a carpet in his house or out in a covered pit in the yard.

"You were mujahedin, weren't you?"

"No, no," he protested and then sighed. "No."

I don't know why I challenged him, why it mattered, but I pressed the question. I knew too many stories. The Taliban don't have a corner on the market of cruelty.

In the end, he admitted it: "Yes. Yes, I was mujahedin." He sighed again. He told me which group he fought with, and I saw a deep sadness in his eyes through the rearview mirror. I wondered what stories haunted his mind, but my ride had already come to an end. I walked away thinking, the victims and the victors in this land both suffer.

Masuma finished her story, and we finished the rice on our plate. She prayed the Arabic end-of-meal blessing, and we collected the plate and bowls and stacked them on the tray. We tossed the bread scraps into the middle of the tablecloth we had spread out on the floor and folded it up. I poured two glasses of tea, and we began again.

"Can you forgive him, Masuma?"

She thought for a long time, and I wondered if she would be able to do it. In the end, she turned her head downward and said very simply, "Nakhair." No.

I waited and prayed silently. I didn't know what to say. Forgiveness is hard. Jesus must've known that when He told us that it's something we must do. He showed us how hard it is when He did it Himself, from the humility and violence of the cross. After a long pause, I asked, "Can you bless the Pashtun family who helped you?"

Masuma looked at me as though she were seeing something for the first time.

I told the story of Jesus, the Honorable Jesus who God sent to earth through the Virgin Mary to show us who God is and what it means for us to live His way, the way He made us to live. "Jesus said, 'You have been told to love your neighbor and hate your enemies. But I say to you, love your enemies.'" The family who had helped Masuma were not neighbors but enemies, enemies who had chosen to do her good. I asked again, "Can you bless the Pashtun family who helped you?"

Afghans understand the power of speaking blessings just as they understand the power of prayer. My friend thought for a long time and then nodded. She lifted her hands palms up toward heaven, raised her head, and spoke a wonderful blessing over that Pashtun family. Then she looked at me and smiled. "This is good. This is good. They helped me. They helped my sons."

We continued drinking our tea, and I continued sharing stories. I paraphrased the prayer we call the Lord's Prayer, including the petition to forgive us our sins as we forgive those who sin against us.

I retold the story Jesus told about the man who forgave another man who owed him a great deal of money. At first, the man wanted all the money back, but the debtor couldn't pay it and begged for forgiveness. The man forgave him and erased the debt completely. That's the part we always like—the generous part that offers restoration and life. It's the second part we don't enjoy. The debtor went out, found a man who owed him a fairly small amount of money, and demanded repayment. Perhaps he didn't understand that his own debt had been completely forgiven. Perhaps he thought he would collect as much money as he could and buy off his financial debt so that he wouldn't owe the rich man even a debt for his generosity. I don't know, but that recently released debtor harshly demanded repayment from a third man who owed him a small amount of money. When the third man couldn't pay him, he had his family thrown in prison.

If the story ended there, we might walk away simply not liking the man who threw the debtor into prison. But the story doesn't end there. Word got around to the first, forgiving man about what the second man had done. The man who had forgiven so much became angry and called the second man to accountability: "I forgave you such huge debt. Why couldn't you forgive this other man?" He had the unforgiving man thrown into prison. Jesus tells us to forgive even as we have been forgiven.

I told Masuma that story in my timid, tripping Dari. I had learned the words for debt and jail and pay, but I had never practiced telling that particular story in Dari, so I stumbled through it. Masuma corrected my sentence structure and pronunciation as I went along.

When I finished, I turned the focus back to Masuma's story again. "Can you forgive that Talib, the man who showed you pain?"

Masuma thought for a long time. She knew me well enough to say no. I waited. Finally, she looked into my eyes. "Yes, I can forgive him."

Masuma lifted her eyes and hands to heaven and prayed. I watched and listened. I bore witness. It was a beautiful prayer, honest and pure. She told God exactly how she felt about that Talib. Then she forgave the man. She asked God to forgive him as well. She sealed her prayer by passing her palms over her face before letting her hands fall, still, into her lap. She smiled, not at me. She just smiled. Then all she could say was, "This is good. This is very good." And she smiled more.

We drank another cup of tea. Eventually I asked her if she could bless that Talib.

She thought and then said, "No."

I told another story, but it didn't matter. She couldn't do it. I understood. I told her she had done well, but she already knew that was true. We cleaned up the lunch dishes and went our separate ways, I back to writing project plans, reviewing financial books, and crafting emails, and Masuma back to her housework. Yet neither one of us walked away the same.

For me, forgiveness has been a difficult and fruitful journey. So often I've watched Afghans walk this journey in spaces of deep personal pain. When I've been privileged to share the journey, I've been astounded anew at the beauty of Jesus' ways. I've watched precious friends and near strangers breathe and smile and taste the sweetness of a freedom that's more inner mystery than outward show.

Afghanistan is not only a society deeply traumatized by war, violence, and personal damage; it's also a culture that easily and quickly takes offense and expects to exact revenge for personal and even cultural insult. Many times over the years I've entered into conversations about insult and the best response. And, like so many in the world who follow the news, I've seen the tragic outcomes of our neighbors' practices.

HOW DO WE RESPOND TO INSULT?

In Afghanistan, honoring and defending the Holy Quran, the Prophet Mohammed, and the name of Allah from any insult is quite simply a foundational requirement. I learned that lesson early in my journey and over the years endeavored to be respectful of my neighbors' sensitivities. I tried not to do or say anything that could offend them or insult some aspect of their religion. Part of my caution was blatant fear: I didn't want to be killed for some offense I might see as minor. Most of my caution, though, grew from trying to love my neighbors in ways that made sense to them. I didn't always succeed.

Once while I was sitting at lunch with a group of women in our office I stumbled directly into offense. There was a mosque with its loudspeaker right next door to the office. Every day, in the middle of lunch, the loudspeaker crackled and the mullah sang his long call to midday prayers. I've heard this call to prayer five times a day, seven days a week, and have grown so accustomed to it that I usually barely notice it.

Every mosque has its own mullah, so we get to know his voice. Some are quite melodic and beautiful. Some, well, less so. The mullah in the mosque next to our office had a beautiful voice, and we were accustomed to his call to prayer. One day there was a startlingly different sound.

I was sitting with a group of Afghan women coworkers at lunch, when we heard that very unusual sound. I'm almost afraid to describe it because I know that if I write what I said at lunch, I will offend—and I don't want to do that again. Let me just say, there was a slaughterhouse in the city in which I lived as a small girl. Occasionally, we drove past the stockyard and heard the squeals of animals coming to their end. For me, what came out of the neighbor's loudspeaker recalled that stockyard, and I said so. I should not have.

There were twelve Afghan women sitting on the floor around me. I counted them as friends and knew each one well. We had helped one another, prayed for one another, and always laughed together, but not that day. That day my comment about the mullah's voice fell on our group like a rotting blanket. Each woman reacted in stunned silence, their eyes wildly searching me and one another. I absolutely could not be allowed to say what I had said. It was dishonoring, insulting.

I knew my fault immediately. As quickly as I could, I apologized, but my apology fell unreceived onto the floor. My coworkers didn't know how to react. They held their breaths and watched one another.

Finally one woman spoke. She said simply, "The mullah's sick. That's his nephew."

Someone else quickly changed the subject; gratefully, we went on with our meal.

My friends chose to look away from my offense. They didn't accept my apology. They didn't forgive me. They simply chose to ignore what I had said. At the time, I didn't realize how generous they had been. I had, however, learned a valuable lesson on the importance of showing honor to that which my Afghan neighbors honor.

In Afghanistan, the Holy Quran must be honored above all other material things. Any defilement of their holy book must be punished. I knew I would never rise to such a defense of a printed copy of the Bible, but still I tried to learn what it means to my neighbors to show respect for a holy book. I paid attention to their rules for how the Holy Quran should be handled and treated. I knew they would assume that I would treat my book in the same way. I watched their examples, asked questions, and learned what was expected of me.

For a little while I lived on a lovely, shaded street with a mosque on each opposing corner. Each day I watched clusters of children stream past my house to the mosques. The girls usually wore long, black jackets and matching black slacks. They covered their heads with small white scarves pinned under their chins. The boys usually wore the traditional *Shalwar kameez,* long cotton shirts with matching cotton trousers. They covered their heads with small white caps. Each child carried a Holy Quran, wrapped in colorful cloth, and held respectfully above their waist.

Every household owned a Holy Quran. Often when I entered homes I could see their book, wrapped in its cloth, tucked intentionally on a shelf above everything else in the room. The Holy Quran is honored above all other things. It must be treated with care and respect and shown the greatest honor because it's deemed the exact, verbatim words of Allah.

The text is printed in Arabic, the chosen language of Allah. Children learn to recite it in the mosque, but most don't learn to understand it. The reading has value. The recitation of verses is, in and of itself, a spiritual act. Honoring the book is an absolute requirement.

My Afghan staff watched how I handled my Bible. I knew they judged me by my treatment of it. I adapted to some of their expectations. I made a colorful cloth bag for storing my Bible. That actually proved to be convenient, and I still use it, even in America. The wind can't blow the pages into a mess, and I can always find it easily. In Afghanistan I kept a Bible I never wrote in. Writing in a holy book is defiling. One of my Afghan friends brought me a folded wooden reading stand, and I used that when I sat on the floor and read my book. Since my house didn't have chairs, I sat on the floor a lot. My Bible never touched the carpet.

When I considered my Afghan neighbors' expectations, I differentiated between those that were simply not cultural for me and those I understood to be wrong. I figured that adapting to a culture by doing things like wearing a scarf or wrapping my Bible in a special cloth were fine actions that reduced friction between us. I drew the line at actions contrary to the teachings of Jesus.

Often Afghans asked if I accepted the Holy Quran as the final revelation from Allah to humanity. I tried to sidestep the question to avoid offense. Usually I would only say, "I'm a follower of the Prophet Jesus. I read the book that shows what He did and taught. I also read the books He recognized as holy." By that, I included three books—the Torah, which are the first five books of the Bible, the Psalms, and the New Testament.

Afghans were quick to point out that they accepted those same books, as well as the fourth, the Holy Quran. They also pointed out that they accepted Jesus as a prophet of Allah.

Once I entered into what proved to be a very humorous conversation about this. I stumbled across an effective metaphor from Afghan culture to illustrate our different understandings of the concept of acceptance.

Afghans have an important social concept called *raft-amad*. *Raft-amad* just means going and coming, but it's used to describe the nature of a person's relationship with another person. Two people have *raft-amad* if they visit each other's houses and share meals. If they don't have that kind of relationship, they don't have *raft-amad*. They may be acquainted and speak in the public sphere or at social gatherings, but they don't have a personal relationship. *Raft-amad* is a meaningful social distinction.

I borrowed the metaphor.

One day a young Afghan male friend of mine taught me carefully about the Afghan attitude toward the three books that came before: the Torah, the Psalms, and the gospel. He told me that Afghans and in fact all Muslims accept these three books as having come from Allah. He said, "We accept all four books. Why don't you accept the Holy Quran?"

It seemed a fair question, but I figured a full explanation about the misalignment of the Holy Quran to the previous three books wouldn't be helpful. Instead I responded with a challenge. "You say you accept the first three books as from God. You also know that in the Holy Quran, the angel told your Prophet to read the first three books. Yet you've never read those books. How can you say you accept them when you've never read them? You don't know what they say."

The young man smiled. It really was a gentle conversation, and we were both enjoying it. He went on to explain his concept of acceptance. Basically, he said he believed that the three books came from Allah. That meant he accepted them, even though he'd never read them. Then he challenged me again. "We accept the Honorable Jesus as a prophet of Allah. Why don't you accept the Prophet Mohammed?"

I thought that was another fair question but recognized that we used the word *accept* in very different ways. That's when I stumbled on *raft-amad* as a metaphor. I smiled, cocked my head, and said, "You say you accept the Honorable Jesus, but you don't welcome Him into your home, and you don't invite Him to eat with you. You don't have *raft-amad* with the Prophet Jesus."

My young friend howled with delight. I'd caught him with his own cultural metaphor and he knew it.

I pressed on. "You will not read His book. You will not listen to what He says. You say to the Honorable Jesus, 'I accept You. Please enter my gate, but sit down on the porch. You cannot come into my home.' You don't honor Him. You leave Him outside where you can't hear Him."

By then both the young man and I were laughing.

He protested, "No, no, that's not the way it is. We respect the Honorable Jesus. He is a prophet of Allah."

"Then let Him in. Sit down at a meal with Him. Pour Him a cup of tea. Listen to what He has to say to you."

In the end we parted, still laughing. I don't know if he carried anything away from our conversation, but I did. I learned that not only do we have different views on what it means to accept a book as coming from God, we have very different views on what it means to honor. For my Afghan neighbors, honoring their holy book above all other things is absolutely required, and yet most don't know what their book actually says. They would defend any insult against the book with extreme retribution but cannot draw its teachings directly into their heart.

For me, honoring the Bible really isn't a matter of cloth covers, wooden stands, or high storage places. It's a matter of getting to know God the Father, God the Son, and God the Holy Spirit through its pages. It's a matter of listening, learning, and applying what I've heard to my life. For me, that's what it means to honor the book I count as holy.

A few months after that incident, a Danish newspaper published a series of cartoons depicting the Prophet Mohammed. The series became perhaps the most famous cartoon series in the world. One image depicted the Prophet Mohammed with a bomb in his turban. When the cartoon was published, riots swept the Muslim world, including Afghanistan.

Through the winter and spring of 2008, the cartoons were re-published. Some men had tried to kill the cartoonist in Denmark and were credited as heroes in Afghanistan for even trying. Everyone I knew in Afghanistan said the cartoonist should be killed because he had insulted the Prophet.

We discussed this event one day around the *desterkhan* at lunch. Our gathering that day included both men and women, although the conversation was dominated by the men.

I had been in the country for some time and definitely understood the need to defend any insult to Islam, the Prophet of Islam, or the Book of Islam. Still I couldn't comprehend the intensity of my neighbors' and coworkers' reactions to the cartoon.

I had looked at the images of the cartoons on the Internet, although I didn't confess to that. The cartoons seemed more political than anything else. And of course, as a Westerner, I believe in free speech. I couldn't fathom why such images were worthy of death— not only the death of the cartoonist, but also the deaths of Muslims swept up in the protests and riots. It didn't make sense to me, and I genuinely wanted to understand why the offense was considered so extreme. I did what I always did when I wanted to understand some aspect of Afghan culture: I asked questions.

One of my coworkers explained. He was sure that I would not only understand but I would also agree with the rightness of his re-action. He told me that no one can be allowed to dishonor either the Prophet Mohammed or the Holy Quran. Because the cartoons insulted the Prophet, all Muslims everywhere are required by Islamic law to rise up and defend the Prophet by killing the offender.

I did understand his meaning. All Muslims are compelled to defend the Prophet because the Prophet has been insulted. The insult diminished the Prophet's honor, and that simply cannot be allowed.

It was the next part of the conversation that actually became difficult. My coworker, Ghulam Sadiq, turned the situation around and put it to me. "Of course, you would do the same if anyone insulted the Honorable Jesus or your Holy Book."

In fact, when I saw the cartoon images on the Internet, I had immediately compared those images with others I'd seen over the years that insulted, mocked, or degraded Jesus, the cross, or the Bible. I thought of art, movies, plays, and books that had sparked protests in the West or statements of offense by Christians. I could not remember any Christian I respected calling for the artist's death. Sometimes, the images were removed. Usually, the play continued, the movie found its way into theaters or onto DVDs, or the book appeared and was purchased from bookstore shelves.

Ghulam Sadiq's challenge revealed an unbridgeable gulf between us: "Of course, you would do the same if anyone insulted the Honorable Jesus or your Holy Book."

Did he really think I would kill or call for the death of someone who insulted Jesus or the Bible? In all the things I'd seen and read, images much more insulting than the Danish cartoons, I had never considered the murder of the artist. Yes, I'd been shocked and sometimes revolted, but to call for death? No way. To burn down movie houses and bookstores? Not a chance.

I shook my head. "No, I would not. It's not possible."

My Afghan coworkers, both the women and the men, found my response incredible. "You would allow someone to insult your Prophet Jesus?"

These coworkers knew I was a follower of Jesus. They knew I regarded the three books that they say came before the Holy Quran as from God and that I read those books regularly. They knew I was a woman of prayer who endeavored to live a holy and generous life. Surely such a person would never allow her own Prophet to be insulted. Surely.

I tried to explain. "I would not like it, have not liked it when my Prophet has been insulted. That's true. There have been many books and many films that insulted the Honorable Jesus. However, even the Prophet Jesus says that I cannot respond to insult with violence." I pronounced those words with finality. I wasn't considering alternatives. To respond to an insult with violence is completely contrary to the teachings of Jesus.

My coworkers were unconvinced. How could that possibly be true? My words made no sense.

We look at one another across nations, religions, and even tablecloths and assume that beneath our clothes and customs we are somehow all the same. We believe that if we just communicate, we'll understand one another and find our ground common. We don't realize that we look at one another through our own eyes, from our own frameworks and worldviews. My Afghan coworkers knew that any insult should be defended against and any insult against their religion should be met with overwhelming punishment so that it never occurs again. That's good and right, the solid framework of their thinking. So when they looked across the *desterkhan* at me, they assumed I lived within the very same framework.

As Westerners, we do the same. We assume our neighbors really agree with us about the things that are most important to us. Surely, our neighbors must just want to live and let live. To us, that perspective, that framework, is simply good and right. The reality is, we see the world very differently.

My Afghan coworkers questioned me again and again. They were incredulous and simply could not accept the notion that insult must be tolerated.

From my perspective, how I respond to insults against myself, my family, my country, and even my religion is another aspect of my life that's defined by who I understand Jesus to be and how I understand my responsibilities as His follower. His teachings and example are my guide. My coworkers followed the Prophet Mohammed, so his teachings and examples are their guide.

I tried to show my coworkers why I couldn't respond to insult with violence. Once again, I chose a story. "One day, when the Honorable Jesus was on earth, He taught a group of people what it means to live in the kingdom of God rather than the kingdom of man."

Ghulam Sadiq interrupted me to ask me what "kingdom of God" meant.

I told them, "The kingdom of God is the will of God. It's the rule of God. When we live in the kingdom of God we live in the will of God, under the direction, teaching, and leadership of God. We submit to God. God created His kingdom for us to live in and created us for His kingdom."

For Afghans, submission to Allah is defined as obeying the laws of the Holy Quran and Hadith. Submission starts with declaring the Muslim creed and then is expressed through praying namaz five times a day. For Afghans, the will of God is whatever happens. A woman is raped, and they say it's the will of God. A man dies in a suicide bomb, and they say it's the will of God. Ghulam Sadiq interrupted me with this correction.

I listened then responded, "God says you must not kill, do you agree?"

"Of course."

"Then killing is not the will of God, is it?"

The entire group watched me.

"If a man kills another man, then he has broken the law of God. His work is against the will of God. We cannot say that the act of murder is God's will."

Ghulam Sadiq remained quiet. I didn't think he agreed, but at least he passed on the challenge.

I went on. "God is always good."

I had thrown out another new thought but didn't wait for a comment. "God made it clear through the Prophet Jesus that He has made us to live in peace, love, and joy. Then He showed us the way to do it."

I had gone to the heart of the question. Beneath the question of what we think is the proper response to insult is really how we view the character of God and what He desires for us. If God is good and does not want us to kill other people, then we ought not kill people. If God wants us to live in peace, love, and joy, then we ought to pursue peace, love, and joy in all our relationships.

My coworkers around the *desterkhan* thought about this, but again I didn't wait for them to respond. I went on with the story. "Once, while the Honorable Jesus was on earth, He was teaching a large group of people. He told them, 'You have heard that it is said, An eye for an eye and a tooth for a tooth.'"

Ghulam Sadiq interrupted again. He was a man who knew Sharia law. "That's right. If you knock out a man's tooth, you must pay a certain number of camels. If you knock out a man's eye, you must pay with your own eye. This is what the Glorious Quran teaches." He went on to explain how many camels one must pay for different teeth.

I was amused at the thought of getting a camel in exchange for a lost tooth. I told Ghulam Sadiq that in America we can't use camels and that if someone put a camel in my yard I would think that they definitely didn't like me. I explained that my house was in town, and the government doesn't allow me to keep a camel in town. That bit of information was simply nonsensical to him.

Finally I got back to my story. "The Honorable Jesus said, 'If anyone slaps you on the right cheek, turn to him the other also.' This is the will of God."

The room erupted. Words flew and clashed. "Crazy." "Impossible."

"That makes no sense." "He couldn't have said that." "He couldn't have meant that."

I waited. When they were finished I responded, "Yes, He said that and He meant it. Not only did He mean it, He did it."

A stream of questions followed.

I responded with another story. "When the Honorable Jesus, the prophet sent by God to earth through the Virgin Mary, was arrested . . . "

Ghulam Sadiq interrupted to correct me again. "The Honorable Jesus was not arrested. That was another man. The Holy Quran is clear. Jesus was not killed."

I was patient and respectful in my response, but I did respond, "I understand that's what you believe, but the *Injil*, the New Testament is clear: Jesus was arrested." I waited to see what would happen.

Ghulam Sadiq challenged, "The *Injil* has been changed."

I let that objection fall and continued with my story. "The *Injil* says that when the Honorable Jesus was arrested, the men who arrested Him insulted and beat Him. They whipped Him and put a crown of thorns on His head. Then they took His clothes off and nailed Him to a cross. He was insulted. He was also killed."

Ghulam Sadiq let me continue, and so I did.

"When Jesus stood before the judge, the judge said, 'Don't You know I have the power to condemn or free You?' The Honorable Jesus said, 'I could call down thousands of God's angels to save Me.' Yet, Jesus didn't. He was insulted, shamed, and beaten. Then He was killed. He did not respond with violence. Instead, while dying, He prayed, 'Father, forgive them.' The Honorable Jesus prayed for His enemies. He didn't kill them."

Everything I had said went against my coworkers' understanding of what's good and right. Everything.

Still I went on. I closed my explanation. "The Honorable Jesus taught us that when we're insulted, when we're slapped on one side of our face, we must respond by allowing our enemy to slap the other side as well. We must pray for our enemies and bless those who hurt us. Jesus taught us this, and then He did it. He prayed for God to forgive those people who killed Him. So, no, even if the Honorable Jesus or the Bible are insulted, I cannot respond with violence."

Ghulam Sadiq listened to my story and obviously rejected it. He responded only by summing up Sharia law on the subject of insult. "In Islam, if someone insults you or hurts you, you must respond with ten times the amount of force. Then they will never insult you again."

Initially my male coworkers agreed. Each told story after story of insults and responses, some from the Prophet Mohammed, some from other heroes of their faith. The women in the room remained silent but watched us carefully. They would listen and decide in the privacy of their own minds what they would accept.

I listened and prayed. I felt the men's anger and justification. I heard clearly why these men accepted vengeance as the good and right thing. They were telling me their stories, showing me the examples of their Prophet, and justifying their fellow Muslims' reaction to the offensive Danish cartoons.

Eventually they were satisfied that their point had been well made and fell into silence. They looked at me as if to ask, "Now, what do you say?"

I hesitated. What could I say? Had Jesus said anything that would challenge these men, that could encourage them to forsake violence and embrace peace, to even consider a different way? I prayed.

Finally I spoke softly but definitely, with neither accusation nor apology. "Satan came to rob, kill, and destroy. Jesus came to bring us life—deep, rich, full life. God is good."

At first the room fell into silence. Every Afghan knows that Satan is evil, that he destroys. Effectively I had said that the way of tolerance, forgiveness, and peace is the way of God. Violent retribution is not, no matter what justification it carries. I hoped that to some of my coworkers, their hero stories of cunning retribution might have lost a bit of their brutal glory. I hoped that at least some, in the privacy of their own thoughts, would consider another way. I knew that all wouldn't.

Ghulam Sadiq broke the silence. He reiterated Sharia law: "An eye for an eye, a tooth for a tooth. That is the way it must be. We Muslims follow Allah's law." His words carried a rebuke. They implied, "You Christians don't."

I picked up the challenge but responded in a tone as gentle as I could find. "Perhaps that's why you're constantly at war."

Ghulam Sadiq's cheeks burned. He clenched his jaw and looked away, but the others listened. It was an interesting thought, a new thought. I wondered what memories they were each considering. Were they remembering the brother-war in the days of the mujahedin, when one group of Muslims rose up against another, killed, robbed, and maimed? Were they thinking about the retribution of Muslim families, when the life of one was demanded in payment for the life of another? Were they thinking about the Muslims who died in the riots over the cartoon? They didn't say.

One man, not Ghulam Sadiq, broke the silence. "Perhaps."

I let the conversation fall like a seed. We had traded our stories, and now our stories lived within each of us. All of us would consider, in the quiet of our hearts, what we really thought and believed.

We gathered the plates and serving dishes, tossed the leftover bread into the middle of the *desterkhan*, rolled it up, and put it away. We went back to work.

I thought about Ghulam Sadiq's perspective, his commitment to retribution. The heroic stories of retribution my coworkers had shared provided me with a framework to understand some of the other stories that I heard from neighbors and the accounts of violence

I heard on the news. I learned to see from my coworkers' perspective, and I learned to fear.

Once again I recognized how revolutionary Jesus' actions and teachings were. Surely He lived and died in a cultural context much more like Afghanistan than like my America. He had often been insulted and yet had not responded with violence. His followers, James and John, the ones who were called the "sons of thunder," wanted to rain down fire on the village that refused to offer hospitality to Jesus and His companions when they were traveling through that territory. Surely such refusal had been an insult. It would have been in Afghanistan. Hospitality is so important, so basic. To refuse to host the Prophet Jesus and His students was a deep insult. Perhaps James and John and their request hadn't been so absurd after all. Perhaps they were responding as their culture said they should. The village insulted their teacher, a prophet of God. Surely retribution was called for, but Jesus would have nothing to do with it.

I'd always read that story with some amazement. My Western eyes, my sensibility could never grasp why those two students, so long with Jesus, would request such a thing. Even if they hadn't known Jesus, how could they even consider such an option? But I've internalized the notion of bearing with insult.

I focused on Jesus' actions and teachings in contrast to the stories my coworkers had shared—stories of villages burned to the ground because they'd refused to convert, to embrace the Prophet of Islam and his religion. I considered my own beliefs of what is good and right. Once again my faith in Jesus was strengthened, not because I saw Him as a powerful, not-to-be-rejected leader, but because I saw Him as patient and good. I thought, "I would rather be like Jesus." I admired Him all over again.

A couple of years later I read in the news about a Floridian pastor who intended to burn a copy of the Holy Quran. I feared the outcome. I'd already heard stories of foreign soldiers who'd reportedly desecrated the Holy Quran. In one report, some European soldiers were accused of using the Holy Quran for target practice. My Afghan staff members were furious. The men in my neighborhood argued about how to respond, and I knew I could become a target. When that report came out, I told my staff that neither I nor anyone in our office supported the destruction or shaming of any book that any religious group counts as holy, including the Holy Quran. Fortunately, there had been no films or still pictures of those reported desecrations, so the storms blew over. But in the fall of 2010 when the Floridian pastor threatened to burn the Holy Quran, there were pictures, and even films and interviews. The threat was public and deeply provocative. I prayed that the man would restrain himself. I even wrote him a letter explaining why he shouldn't do it. I begged him, and I prayed more.

I assigned our office the task of preparing letters of condemnation. If the Floridian went ahead with his plan, our staff would distribute those letters to the local government and to the mullahs of our local mosques. I kept praying. When the Floridian pastor withdrew his threat, I breathed again.

Some months later, in the spring of 2011, that pastor did destroy a Holy Quran. He made a spectacle of judging the book of Islam, condemning it, and burning it. By then I was safely back in America. I had missed the initial news reports on the man's actions. In Afghanistan, all was quiet until the story hit the Afghan press. Not only had the man burned a Holy Quran, he had recorded doing it. That film made it to the Internet.

Ghulam Sadiq had said, "No one can be allowed to dishonor either the Prophet Mohammed or the Holy Quran" and "In Islam, if someone insults you or hurts you, you must respond with ten times the amount of force. Then, they will never insult you again."

I recalled his words as I watched the news from Afghanistan. Riots swept through cities, and protests threatened small towns. In Mazar-i-Sharif an angry mob attacked the UN establishment and brutally killed seven foreigners including several Nepalese Ghurkas. Those victims had not participated in any way with the Quran burning. Still, they were foreigners and served as proxy victims of retribution.

My coworker had spoken for at least some in Afghanistan when he said, "If someone insults you or hurts you, you must respond with ten times the amount of force. Then they will never insult you again."

I wondered how he and the rest of those Afghans who had listened to me share the teachings of Jesus on insults interpreted the violence and murders in Mazar-i-Sharif. Had they all thought, "We have done what is good and right," or had some considered an alternative? Ghulam Sadiq and the other Afghans in the room that day when we discussed the Danish cartoon had heard a very different approach. Had they ever considered it? Did they remember that conversation when their neighbors and friends charged into brutal violence? Had the ideas I'd shared taken root in any of their hearts? Perhaps someday I'll know.

For me, the teachings of Jesus took on new life in Afghanistan. In contrast to my neighbors' stories and teachings, I saw Jesus' ways reflected in magnificent beauty. I also learned much about the context of the world in which Jesus walked and taught. Even His warnings spoke with stronger, clearer voice. My Afghan neighbors taught me their approach to responding to insult just as they showed me their approach to judgment and condemnation. They challenged me to understand and explain what Jesus said about these things.

who can judge?

One lovely spring day, while I was walking down the tree-lined street in front of my house, a group of six small girls, somewhere around eight to ten years old, saw me from a distance and ran toward me, shouting and calling out. I heard them, turned, and waited. They were precious, delightful children. Their sparkling scarves billowed like pennants behind them. Their plastic sandals flapped against the soles of their feet. Just before they reached me, a white-bearded, gray-turbaned man stepped directly in front of the shouting girls. He chided them fiercely. They snapped to attention, hung their heads in shame, turned, and walked silently, shoulders bent, back down the street. He had spoken so sharply I didn't have a chance to catch his words. I only saw the consequences.

The girls had violated some rule, some understood expectation for appropriate behavior. The gray-bearded man had enforced the rule, and the girls had recognized his right to correct them.

I wondered what the girls had done wrong. Was running and

IN THE LAND OF BLUE BURQAS

shouting on the street a crime? Were they too old for such behavior? Had they become young women, who must act accordingly? Other girls shouted and ran toward me on the street. What was different about this group? Why had they provoked such strong chastisement? Later that day I sat with an Afghan woman friend and sipped cups of tea. I told her the little story and asked if she could interpret it for me. She did.

The girls were too big to run and shout on the street. Their behavior was inappropriate for Muslim girls. The gray-bearded man had been correct. Children must learn, and it's the community's responsibility to teach them. In Afghanistan, virtually every aspect of the culture finds its support in some Islamic teaching. Religion and culture are intertwined; the first justifies and defends the second.

For a long time, I focused on learning the rules. What clothes should I wear on the street, in people's homes, at government offices? Where should I sit in taxis and rickshaws? How should I address the governor, a community elder, police at a checkpoint? Early on I recognized the role of peer pressure and looked to my neighbors and coworkers to help me construct the strange, hybrid rules that applied to me, as a foreign woman.

I understood that my neighbors would decide, based on dozens of small social cues, if I was a good woman or not. If they judged me as good, they would welcome me into their lives. If they judged me as bad, the doors and gates would lock before me.

I chose a fairly conservative path and was careful to test, question, and observe the outcome of each decision I made. It was exhausting but necessary. Most of my neighbors did accept me as a good and honorable, if strange, woman. In a sense, I accepted my neighbors' right to judge me. It was, after all, their country, and I was the visitor.

I knew that violating the rules in Afghanistan could expose me to serious retribution or punishment. Once when a driver asked why

I wore a scarf in Afghanistan, I had smiled and said, "Because if I don't, people will stone me." He laughed and agreed. There was the possibility of rocks, broken windows, or worse. It wasn't just a matter of my being an awkward and foolish foreigner. There could be serious consequences.

One spring a European woman, another aid worker in the city, caused a stir. The local Afghan security forces picked up a specific kidnapping threat and substantiated it easily. I was informed because the specific target hadn't been identified. The police didn't know if I was in immediate danger or if some other foreign woman was intended.

After a couple of days, the Afghan police decided that the European worker was the actual target. She was known to attend government meetings without the long, somber-colored coat that would hide both her colorful clothes and female form. That was a violation of the rules. I, on the other hand, "dressed respectfully." That was the way the police explained it to me when they told me I was off the hook. The police turned out to be right, but the woman's offense extended beyond her clothes. Still, the incident underscored the importance of all the small decisions I made in their country.

I accepted reality. I didn't question the underlying motivation or worldview that compelled my neighbors to judge me or one another's behavior and to punish deviations. I simply focused on adapting.

Then one day while I was praying, I stumbled onto an understanding of this Afghan need to control and judge. The revelation was like a flash of light in a dark room; the contrast became clear, the implications, astonishing. In that flash the conversation in my mind shifted from how to accommodate cultural rules to how to deal with judgment.

Afghans are part of the Ummah, or community of Islam. They understand their responsibilities to other Muslims. It's the role of the

Ummah to demand the obedience of all others, and especially their neighbors, to the rules or laws of Islam. That means that the Ummah, the Afghan community, is teacher, guide, judge, prosecutor, and punisher. That's a powerful self-identity, an authority that I understand only belongs to the Holy Spirit.

The realization that the community had usurped the authority of the Holy Spirit recast my attitude toward my neighbors' judgment. Who can be God but God?

As a follower of Jesus, I too have a concept of the believer's community. The New Testament speaks of those who have embraced the same faith, hope, baptism, and heavenly Father as belonging to the body of Christ, the church in *mysterium*. We have responsibilities to one another, and they're similar to the role of the Ummah, yet the differences are subtle and profound. For one, judgment is forbidden us as members of Christ's body.

In the West, we often assume that the judgment Jesus prohibited is an opinion on right and wrong. If a person believes some behavior is contrary to biblical teaching, then they are accused of judging. But judging in Afghan society is not a matter of an opinion held in private or even spoken openly. It's both a judgment on the inner condition of another and the enforcement of the rules defined as true Islam. Judging, in Afghanistan, always comes with condemnation or the threat of condemnation. Afghans understand this more intense practice of judgment. They participate in it.

Once while I was in the States, I saw a television program that included two Muslim women as part of the discussion group. One of the women was Azar Nafisi, the writer of the book, *Reading Lolita in Tehran*. I had read her book and been absorbed by her account of living in Iran during the days of the Islamic revolution. She saw firsthand the violence and oppression of the hard-line followers of the Ayatollah Khomeini, and she had suffered as a result. The other woman on the stage was Daisy Khan, the wife of the man who wanted to build a mosque by Ground Zero in New York City. Both women were articulate and clearly Muslim. Neither was wearing a headscarf.

During the program, a Muslim leader living in London participated via video conference. In the middle of his overtly conservative discourse, he chastised the Muslim women on stage for not wearing headscarves. Those women were breaking the rules, and that distant Muslim leader rebuked them for it. I knew that most of my Afghan neighbors, if they saw those women on TV, would agree with the leader. My neighbors would judge those women and declare them disobedient Muslims who must learn to submit to Islam.

I remembered a conversation I once had with a young Afghan girl. Aziza was about fifteen years old and still attended school. Often, in our town, older girls went to school with black scarves wrapped carefully around their heads and faces so that only their eyes showed. When I first met Aziza, she was wearing this kind of scarf with her black coat and matching slacks.

One day while I was drinking tea in the home of one of her relatives, Aziza came chattering into the room, flinging her steel-blue burqa off on the way. She dumped her schoolbooks in the same motion. I was surprised to see her wear the burqa and asked about it.

She said, "Oh, I hate this thing!"

The other women in the room laughed in agreement.

One of the women scooped up the tangled burqa, shook out the creases, and carefully laid it across a cotton mat on the floor. She left the book bag where it was.

"Then why are you wearing it?" I was fairly certain she didn't have to since I had seen so many other girls her age and older wearing their headscarves double wrapped. I assumed she had chosen the burqa for herself, yet she had declared contempt for it.

Aziza responded to my question. "The Holy Quran says I must wear this. That's what the mullah says and what my brother says. If I don't, I'm not a Muslim."

I recognized the finality of the threat. Her brother had not said, "You should . . . " He had said, "You must . . ." If she didn't obey, she would be judged, condemned, and punished. Afghans fear their community's judgment with very good cause.

Several years ago, a woman friend told me she could no longer drink tea with me. She was a neighbor and a widow with a house full of sons and daughters. I enjoyed her company, and we often laughed when we sat together. Then one day she told me she could no longer welcome me into her home nor could she come to mine. Breaking relationship is significant in a land where hospitality is everything, so of course, I asked why.

"People are talking. They're saying I'm becoming a Christian."

She wasn't becoming a Christian. She was not in the least bit interested in discussing the things of God—or even of Allah. Still her neighbors had judged her and found her guilty. I thought, "So what? It's just gossip. What could that matter?"

She explained it this way: "I still have four daughters to marry off."

Ah, I understood. Her innocence was not relevant. The neighbors had judged, and their judgment carried consequences. She had to end her friendship with me, or she would pay for it when it came time to sell her daughters into marriage.

Another woman told me that if her neighbors knew she was a follower of Jesus, they would, at the very least, throw rocks over her wall. I thought about the size of rocks in Afghanistan; baseball- and softball-sized stones littered the land. I imagined my friend squatting in her yard, washing clothes in a shallow basin while her small children played around her. I imagined the rocks silently fired over the wall from unseen hands. Without warning, a child would scream in pain. No, hers was no trivial fear.

Judgment in Afghanistan is a serious matter. It comes with the threat of punishment. That punishment might include gossip, public shaming, or shunning. It might include stoning, beating, rape, or even murder. These are the strongest tools the community uses to enforce the rules of their religion on its members.

There have been Afghans who have genuinely left Islam. Their stories provide the entire society with terrifying examples of what can happen if an Afghan is judged to be a non-Muslim.

In one such case, the community discovered that a Kabuli man named Abdul Rahman had converted to Christianity. Through a disturbing course of events he was arrested in Kabul and thrown into jail. His crime was, of course, conversion. I didn't know the man personally, but like everyone else I had heard about him on the news. His story broke across our office like a dust storm. Some of our Afghan staff argued that the man must be killed. Others said, "What's the difference if one man becomes a Christian? Leave him to it." Once the argument erupted into violence between two of our staff members.

I was shocked and deeply disturbed at both the office violence and the protests that had swept across the country. I asked one of my Afghan friends why he thought this apostate should be executed. His response was intriguing.

He said, "If one man is permitted to become a Christian, then all Afghans will become Christians, and we will no longer be a Muslim nation."

I recognized his thinking: The convert was a threat to Islam; to punish him was to protect the Islamic community of Afghanistan. Afghans must teach their neighbors what it means to be a Muslim. If a neighbor or family member drifts outside the boundaries they've established, the community must bring them back, using any means necessary. Such correction protects the community and ensures that others don't drift away from Islam as well. If one man were allowed to convert, then others would convert. Secret Afghan Christians would come out of hiding, and even more Afghans would leave

Islam. Those who called for the man's execution saw themselves as protectors of their community.

My Afghan neighbors have appropriated the authority to judge and condemn. They recognized lists of specific enforceable rules—verbal declarations of faith, defined prayer times and methods, fasting during Ramadan, even women's clothes. They focused on appearance. Does the man show up in the mosque for Friday prayers? How often does the girl go out to the street? Does the woman keep her face hidden in public?

I understood. What else can we see but these outward signs of devotion or compliance? Only the Spirit of God knows if the man praying namaz actually believes in Allah. Only the Spirit knows if the girl who hides from the street secretly lusts for a boy she's seen or imagined. Afghans enforce observable rules because observable rules are all that can be enforced, and they applied those rules to me.

I enjoyed learning about the Afghan culture and adapting to it. I loved my neighbors and wanted them to be comfortable with me, the stranger in their midst. I would have endeavored to acculturate out of respect, without the threat of punishment. Instead I lived daily under the pressure of my neighbors' expectations and judgment. For me, punishment would not come in the form of a gray-bearded man chastising me on a public street. It would come with locked gates, rocks, bullets, or rockets.

Each time I stood inside my gate and prepared to walk out onto the street, I put on a cloak of outward conformity. I tried to balance my desire to respect my neighbors with my need for self-protection and my inclination to be honest, open, and transparent. But when I realized the implications of my neighbors' judgment, that they were usurping the role of the Holy Spirit, a role that only belongs to God, I knew I needed to reframe the conversation. I would not intentionally break the rules and infuriate my neighbors, but I would challenge the judgment, shrouded in careful definitions of what it means to be obedient to God, that my neighbors hurled at me. Sometimes that led to uncomfortable conversations. Sometimes it led my neighbors to reconsider their position.

When an Afghan friend provoked me to confess that I would judge and condemn my family member if they left Christianity, I knew what I wanted to say. This man believed I would respond the same way as he would to a family member's apostasy. He challenged me: "What would you do if your sister converted to Islam?"

I replied, "I believe God is just and good. I also believe, as you do, that on Judgment Day each person will stand before God and give an answer for his or her life. God will judge, not me. God sees and knows everything. I don't. Judgment belongs to God."

That Afghan thought I had missed the point. I had not. Instead I had shifted the conversation from a question of the right judgment to a question of who has the right to judge.

Reframing this conversation usually wasn't easy. I often found myself responding to the specifics of a story or accusation and missed entirely the foundational beliefs the conversation expressed. Plus, there are two sides to judgment. One is the usurpation of the authority to guide people, and the other is an assumption that we can see what lies hidden to all but God.

One morning an Afghan friend launched into a deep and bitter complaint about a foreign office manager. She accused the foreigner of tricking her and lying to her for spite. She accused the man of intentional deceit.

At the time I looked for a way to assuage my friend's anger. I tried to help her understand that perhaps the foreigner hadn't intended to lie at all but had changed his mind. Things just hadn't worked out. In effect I had stepped to the defense of the foreigner as though I could simply convince my friend she had judged incorrectly.

On the way to my office, I mulled over our conversation and

wondered at my frustration. I replayed the story, without names, over lunch to see how my coworkers, both Afghan and foreign, would judge the situation. In the middle of that discussion I recognized the point we were all missing.

"Wait," I said and took my little backpack, with all the zippers closed, and tossed it into the middle of our lunchtime group. "What's in my backpack?"

Each one stepped right into the trap. "A computer, a notebook, keys." They took their guesses. Some were right, some weren't.

I mocked them gently. "You have no idea what's in my backpack. You can't see inside. All you can do is guess."

My companions laughed at the ease with which I'd trapped them.

I said, "This is what it's like to judge. We guess what's in a person's heart, but we can't see it. Only God can see inside my backpack. Only He knows what it contains."

One of the young Afghan women at the table went into a fairly long discourse on when it's right to judge and when one should abstain. Her argument was reasonable and described a clear portrait of the Afghan approach to judgment and condemnation.

We listened patiently.

At the end of her explanation, she asked, "When do you think it's right to judge?"

I said, "Never." Then I added another metaphor. I took my water bottle out of my backpack and put it in the middle of the table. "Now you see a water bottle. That is my action, my words. You can see that. You can say, 'There is a water bottle.' You can respond to my actions but not to the contents of my backpack. My friend can say, 'The foreigner changed his mind, and I'm angry.' She can say, 'I don't like that water bottle,' but she can't say, 'The foreigner tricked me and lied to me for spite.' Whether he wanted to lie or not is still inside the backpack."

My friends, both Afghan and foreign, embraced the metaphor. Each agreed that we can only respond to the action or words presented before us. Only God can see inside the human heart. We spent the rest of our lunchtime teasing out the boundaries between the heart we can't see and actions and words we can.

That day the judgment had not been against me. I had no real stake in the original situation, and no one at lunch knew the participants. In a way it was an abstract example. That wasn't always the case.

One day I was sitting in a friend's home eating lunch when a sister-in-law of my host joined us. The newcomer had never met a foreigner before and was intrigued. Like always, we started our conversation by discussing familial status. She was married to a difficult man and had too many children. I told her I'd never married. Immediately she chided me and told me I certainly must marry. There was reproach in her voice. I was disobedient and must submit.

I was ready. I shot back, "Are you God that you know how I should live?"

The woman looked straight at me, eyes wide and mouth open. She stammered but found no coherent words.

I had meant to shock, to seize her attention. I invited her into my paradigm. "My friend, really, don't you agree that God is the all-powerful, all-knowing God of the universe?"

Immediately she nodded.

"And do you not agree that God has a path for each person?"

"Yes, yes." She definitely agreed with the premise.

"If God is all-powerful and if God has a path for each person, then only God can judge a person's life. God called you to marry, and you must be obedient to God as a wife and mother. God has not called me to marry. I must be obedient to God in my work and with my friends. Each of us must live submitted to God where we are."

173

My new friend was puzzled. She knew the rules: A woman must marry. She knew her responsibility: to tell me how I must live. Finally and foundationally, she knew that only God is God. Her beliefs clashed. Slowly, she chose God as the greatest truth.

I completed the structure of my thoughts. "God has given you and me different paths. You are an Afghan woman, a wife and mother. I am an American woman. God chose where we were born. We did not. Now we are here. You are married, and I am not. Each of us must accept the paths God has given us. Let us leave God to judge us."

The woman had stopped eating and listened hard to my words. My logic made sense to her, but my worldview didn't. Later, when our lunch was finished and the plate of fruit cleaned, I returned to the subject but challenged more gently. I talked about us, a group of women trying to live good lives that honor God. In the end, I think this new friend did understand but perhaps just barely.

I was satisfied with the conversation. I had stood firmly on the ground Jesus gave us. Judgment belongs to God. In the process, I hope I invited my neighbors to consider what they really believe about who God is and about who they are.

That day the challenge thrown at me came from the hand of a relative stranger. In truth, that woman's judgment didn't matter to me. My friend Zarmina's judgment did. I found that more difficult to confront.

One of my closest Afghan friends, Zarmina, and I had fallen into a conversation about my lifestyle. She knew I always looked for humor in situations. That day I related what had been, to me, a comical exchange I'd had with some women in another home. At that house, the women had called me a *duktar-e-khana*, meaning, a daughter of the house, and I had mocked the definition. I told that group that if I was a daughter of the house, then my house was the whole world and God my Father was with me in it, everywhere. The women in that house had laughed at the obvious incongruity. After all, my own house, my mother's and father's house, was on the other side of the world!

Zarmina, though, was not amused. She didn't like it that I called myself a girl of the world. She saw deep shame in my lifestyle. She didn't like the idea that others in the community might see me as an immoral woman. That would be bad for me and for her, my closest friend.

Zarmina formed her questions cautiously. She was a very dear friend.

She asked me, "Do you travel alone, alone across the world?"

It must have been the first time she had considered how I traveled. She knew I came from America, that the trip included four airplanes and nights in several different cities. We had talked about the distance and the difficulty of the trip. She had just assumed that someone else traveled with me.

I told her that my friends in America drive me to the airport. They drop me off at the terminal, and I go through security. From there I travel alone until I arrive in our town. Then, when I arrive, my male coworker hires a local taxi and drives out to the small dirt runway to meet me and take me to my Afghan home.

She asked again, "Do you travel alone, alone across the world?"

I understood that my actions violated Zarmina's careful definitions of what it means to be obedient to God. If I continued, I would incur my dear friend's judgment. I thought about somehow softening or hiding the truth and yet I also recognized that her judgment itself was inappropriate.

I took a deep breath, laid aside my cloak of conformity, and chose transparency. I told Zarmina that I did travel alone. I told her I had spent much of my adult life traveling and working in Europe and Asia. I had stayed in hotel rooms by myself, bought meals at local restaurants, and had eaten them in the presence of the other patrons. I knew, even as I spoke, that my dear friend was regretfully judging my life. I knew she wanted to perceive me as a good woman, but that my account prohibited her.

I waited, wondering how she would frame her condemnation. Finally my very dear friend gently told me, "You are an unclean woman because you travel alone."

I sighed. Certainly I had brought this onto myself. I had taken off my cloak and asked, "Will you throw a rock?" Now I had to respond to the rock my friend had thrown.

She had said, "unclean." She could have easily said, "sinful, infidel, condemned to hell." They mean the same thing, but "unclean" was perhaps the softest word she could find. She had judged me. Yet even in her judgment, there was deep sadness.

I could have bristled. I could have said, "How dare you!" I could have been offended. I could have walked away from this beautiful, uncomprehending friend and counted her as lost to me. But we were friends, and I did want to reframe the conversation. I wanted to step out from under her judgment, not because I hid the truth or because she ignored it, but because judging is wrong. We are not meant to judge one another. Jesus was clear on that account. Judging another is a usurpation of God's role. Only God sees into the human heart. Only God sees the actions of people when no one else is watching. Only God is truly qualified to judge.

Zarmina had not judged me for some immoral act I had confessed or that someone else had witnessed and testified to. She had judged me as her society, the community, judges, based on an expectation that anyone would, if left alone, sin against God. I traveled alone. Therefore, I must have done sinful things. She counted her judgment as completely true and appropriate. She counted herself as not only qualified but required to judge.

I gently reframed the conversation. I did not protest my innocence. I challenged Zarmina to see the arrogance in a model that requires mere mortals, limited human beings, to step into the role of God in someone else's life.

I responded evenly, almost innocently, "Why? Why do you say I'm unclean?"

My friend instructed me. "You must have a *mahram*, or chaperone, wherever you go, otherwise, you are obviously unclean." Zarmina went on to explain that the nature of woman is crooked always and that if we don't have someone to look out for us, we will invariably do things that are evil, sinful. "A *mahram* is necessary. He will protect you from yourself. He will make sure you don't do anything wrong. If there is no *mahram*, then people must assume that you've done wrong things."

My friend had been patient, advising a dear but lost friend. She did not want to condemn me, but she had.

I responded with a story, one I had told her before and knew she agreed with. I picked up my teacup, half filled with tea, and began to speak. "When you washed this cup, did you wash just the outside or the inside also?"

Zarmina was fastidiously clean. I knew she would never serve me tea in a dirty cup. "Both, of course."

"One day when the Honorable Jesus was teaching, He warned the people to beware of the religious leaders. They knew the law of Moses and were very diligent to obey it. They worked hard to make sure everyone else obeyed the law too. But the Teacher Jesus told people that the religious leaders only obey the law to be seen as righteous by other people. He told them that their insides—their hearts and their thoughts—were not the hearts and thoughts of God. The religious leaders became angry. The Teacher Jesus told them they were like people who washed only the outside of the cup and leave the inside dirty. He told them that, inside, they were full of hypocrisy and rebellion. He told them God cares about who we are on the inside.

God judges our hearts. He sees who we are and why we do what we do. The inside is important."

My friend became uncomfortable. It was obvious she was seeing herself and her culture in the story. She knew the hypocrisy in her own society. She recognized that she and her neighbors could only judge the outside—whether it's a scarf that doesn't cover a woman's face, a group of girls shouting in the street, or a man who doesn't go to the mosque on Fridays. These things the community can judge. We mere mortals are not God. God judges our hearts. He sees who we are and why we do what we do.

I hoped she was following my desire to move the context of judgment from our actions to our hearts, and from human eyes to God's Spirit.

I went on. "God is with me always. The last night He was with His students, my Teacher Jesus told them that even though He was going to die, come back from death, and go away to heaven, He would not leave them alone. Instead, He would send them the Holy Spirit, the Spirit of God who is living. God is spirit and truth. The Teacher Jesus said He would send the Spirit of God to His followers. The Spirit of God would guide them, teach them, and help them not to sin. The Teacher Jesus told them that the Spirit of God would be with them always."

My friend was accustomed to hearing me talk about Jesus, but my description of the Holy Spirit was a difficult concept to grasp.

Afghans recognize that Allah is spirit and that he is nearer to us than the vein in our neck. They believe he is watching our every move, recording our deeds in his book, waiting for the day he will judge us. Allah sent the Prophet Mohammed, the Holy Quran, and the Hadith. Those are the instructions. Allah is everywhere, but he is not guiding us into understanding and empowering us to live good lives. That's the responsibility and authority of the community of Islam. My friend Zarmina had accepted her part in that role.

I challenged that authority. "The Teacher Jesus said that if we love Him, we will obey Him. Everywhere I travel, God is with me. It is as though Jesus is walking beside me. The Holy Spirit, the Spirit of God, is with me, helping me obey God. If I travel with another person, they may see my outside actions, what I do and what I say, but they cannot see my heart. God sees my heart, and I know that. I am a follower of Jesus. I want to live my life in a way that pleases God. I know He sees me always—and not only what I do and say, but what my heart is feeling and thinking. The Holy Spirit is my *mahram*, my chaperone. I try to do what is good because I love God, not because people are watching, but because God is watching. It's God who judges, not people."

I was finished. I had neither declared my innocence nor confessed my guilt. Instead, I had shifted the conversation from outward holiness judged by people to inward and outward holiness judged by God. I could have just said, "Judge not, and you will not be judged," but such a simple statement would not have answered the question, "Why not judge?"

My friend thought about my words for a long time before she responded. There was so much in what I had said that she already believed. Yes, God is spirit and He is always near. Yes, He does see both our actions and our hearts. Yes, if we really want to serve God, we will obey even when others aren't watching, and we will obey from our hearts, not just our hands. I knew she already agreed with these ideas. We had talked about them before. They had been revolutionary at first, but eventually she had recognized them as truth.

Finally, she responded, "I believe you. I believe you are a clean woman and you do not sin when you travel."

My friend had repented. When we started our conversation, she had judged me. Her judgment was not only wrong, but she had also been wrong to judge. She had listened to the things I shared with her and changed her way of thinking.

I'll admit I was relieved. I didn't want my friend to think that I was wandering around the world doing things we both know are wrong, but I was also aware that her thinking and acting had just changed—and that was the greater gift. She had heard a truth, recognized it, and realigned herself to it. She had learned from the teachings of Jesus, considered His words, and decided to follow them.

Then Zarmina added something that surprised me. "But you mustn't tell anyone you travel alone. No one else here will believe you. They will all think you are unclean."

As I walked back down the rocky dirt road to my house, I thought of the people around me. They were, of course, judging me, each and every one. They had assumed that responsibility, that authority. I escape the punishment of their judgment because I'm a foreigner and, obviously, an infidel. I am already judged. If I were an Afghan woman, I would undoubtedly have been killed. If they could see me in America, in my jeans and T-shirt, with my naked face and head, talking to men who are not related to me, they would know without a doubt that I am a sinner. If I were a Muslim, like those scarf-less women on TV, they would condemn me. Yet I know exactly who I am and who is able to judge me in truth. I walked down my dusty Afghan street aware that I walked with God, and I thanked Him for being with me always, for guiding me, for protecting me, and for teaching me.

Afghans have not only usurped the role of judge; they've also taken the responsibility to protect. They define the walls that outline proper faith and practice. Often, in their country, I stumbled into conversations about those walls. I learned that the society is meant to protect its members from temptation. Once again, my neighbors and I faced the same subjects across the chasm of very different worldviews.

who protects us
from temptation?

Occasionally, in the Afghan country, I gathered with other foreigners to talk about the things we were learning from our neighbors. Once an American man shared about how much Afghans love music and delight in singing.

I said, "Really? I don't see that as true." I reflected on my experience with Afghan women. I had collected local songs—bawdy wedding-eve songs, sweet sleep-time lullabies, and sad dirges for lost mothers. I'd found very few women who could sing, and when they did, their range approximated a chant. Many of my friends, especially the more religious, had told me that the music videos on Afghan TV were sinful. Most of my Afghan friends, both men and women, were appalled when I told them that in America, women and men sing together in church. I wondered at the young American man's perspective.

He elaborated for some time on his experiences with Afghan men. He talked about the musical instruments they played and the songs they wrote. He reminded us that we could hear men singing, even as they walked down the street.

I recognized those things as true, but I reminded my companions that women walk the streets silently, hiding their faces and their voices. That conversation sparked my desire to go out and learn what Afghan women really thought of singing.

One afternoon I sat down with my audio recorder and a tribally mixed group of Afghan women. They had agreed to answer my questions about music and allowed me to record their responses if I promised not to let any men hear the recording. I was good to my word.

We started the interview in the basement room of a home out in a new area of our community. The women were Tajik, Hazara, Sayed, and Uzbek. Some were Shiites, and others Sunni. I had a list of questions and stepped through the first several easily.

The women disagreed on whether music videos were evil and on whether singing, in and of itself, was a sin. They did, though, agree on two things, and those two things became the focus of our conversation.

I had started the interview to learn about Afghan women's participation in music, but I really learned about the source of sin—who is responsible for temptation and how we protect ourselves and one another from it.

One woman explained the group's perspective best. "If a woman sings and a man hears her, he will think her voice is beautiful and will lust after her. Maybe he will be on the street separated by the wall or in a neighbor's *aouli*. Maybe he will never see the woman who sings, but he hears her voice. If that happens, he will want her. It's her fault. She has sinned. She made him want her. The sin is hers. She will be punished. That's why a woman should never sing, even in her own *aouli*."

The women in that gathering agreed unanimously: It's a great sin for a woman to allow a man to hear her sing. A woman's voice is seductive. She must hide it. She must protect the man from temptation. They also agreed that no woman should sing to Allah. That stunned me. I love to sing to God. The women agreed that men could sing to Allah although there was no reason for that. However, women should never sing to Allah, even if men aren't present. Men and women can chant and recite, but singing, like traditional Afghan folk songs or the music on TV, is completely unacceptable.

They never did give me a reason for that last part.

The interview was long, but I transcribed it for the young man who had told us that Afghans loved music and loved to sing. He read my notes with surprise. We both learned, in a fresh and deeper way, how different the lives of men and women in Afghan society are.

I learned another important lesson as well, one I explored repeatedly. I learned that in Afghanistan, the influences that cause or encourage a person to do what the society defines as wrong are the real sin, not the person who actually does the wrong. People are weak and must be protected. The society provides that protection. Any influence that tempts a member of the community must be eradicated, silenced, or walled out. Over time, I learned there are no boundaries limiting the community's responsibility to protect. The differences are found in the disparate opinions of which influences constitute a threat to the community.

One day I went to a home to celebrate an infant's fortieth day. I'm not sure why forty days are significant, but for newborns they are. By that time, the woman has healed, is ceremonially clean, and can entertain guests. Often we sent over small gifts, like a bag of fruit or an infant outfit, as soon as a child was born. Sometimes we sent a tray with bowls of soup or plates of *palao*, a common, rice-based meal, but we didn't go ourselves. We'd wait until forty days had passed.

On the fortieth day of one of our neighbor's children, an Afghan friend and I packed up a bundle of infant clothes, a small blanket, a tube of foreign diaper ointment, and a bag of bright kinos (a type of sweet orange). We put on our best clothes—sparkly shirts, matching skirts, white baggy pants, and silky black headscarves trimmed with dazzling silver-colored plastic bits. I slipped into my long, blue coat and draped a heavy burgundy scarf over my head and around my shoulders. My Afghan friend threw a steel-blue burqa over her head and pulled the embroidered, sewn-in cap tight around her crown.

We trooped off to our neighbor's house through a chilling early spring rain. We slid along the mud-and-rock streets, careful not to fall into the Afghan mud. It was only a two-block trip, but slow and cold. The neighbor's gate was open, but a soaking wet, mud-splattered, tan canvas curtain separated the *aouli* from the street. I pushed it aside, careful to keep my clothes clean, and we stepped into a small, mud courtyard surrounded by several low, mud-brick buildings.

We called out our presence, and a young girl appeared in one of the doorways. Her presence showed us which room the mother had chosen for her forty-day visitors. We knew the men and older boys were hiding in the other rooms. We walked slowly along the mud-slicked path, holding on to each other for balance. At the doorway, we handed the girl our bag of fruit with a simple statement, "This is nothing." We kissed her, stepped out of our shoes, shed our wet over-clothes, and entered a long, narrow sitting room.

The room was beautifully appointed for the occasion, much nicer than on normal days. Narrow, swirling, red, machine-woven carpets had been laid over the raw cotton *toshak* floor mats. Large, thick pillows in swirling burgundy and brown leaned against the wall behind each space. Heavy, satin-like, cream-colored drapes with red diamonds, lines, and trim framed the single window. White sheers covered the glass. A plastic floral tablecloth covered most of the open floor. On that were bowls of candy, cakes, and other treats displayed in clusters before each sitting place. Six women with their small children and young daughters sat on the *toshaks*, leaning against the oversized pillows.

The room was cold and damp, heater-less against the early spring rain. A thick lung-antagonizing mold tore at my throat and threatened my breath. I inhaled slowly, swallowing coughs. We took our places, far from the door, in the seats of honor. A young woman brought hot green tea, and I was glad for it.

Whenever I entered an Afghan room, I was always the center of attention. I was the foreigner, and most Afghans in my area had never seen a foreigner up close. Strangers never expected me to speak the language and were always delighted when they found I could. Usually they started by asking one another questions about me. "Who is that? Where is she from? Why is she here?" The mood was typically more curious than hostile. I waited and allowed others to answer until someone pointed out that I could speak for myself. Then the attention turned directly to me.

That particular room included relatives of the mother from deep in the mountains. It also included two mostly grown daughters from the *aouli*.

I drank my tea and answered questions, beginning with the usual: "Where are you from? Do you have a mother and father? Where are they? How many children do you have? You've never married? Why not? You can marry an Afghan man."

That day I told my companions I would only marry an Afghan man if he would wash the dishes, a line I'd borrowed from another foreigner. The women laughed, and we went on to other discussions.

Abruptly one of the older girls took over the conversation. She was wearing the black, nearly knee-length jacket, matching black Western-style slacks, and black scarf common to older schoolgirls. She looked to be about seventeen. She announced, in clear Dari, that she was studying English in the high school and taking courses after her classes.

In our town, that's not uncommon. Many families send their children to private education centers. They pay up to ten dollars for each course. Students study math, literature, or Holy Quran, but the most expensive and popular courses are in computer or English.

There was a tone of bragging in her voice and accomplishment in her body. She had sat straight up when she made her declaration, speaking loudly and distinctly. I knew my friend, the mother of the forty-day-old child, was completely illiterate, and I guessed that the rest of the women were as well. This girl, who sat in the place of least honor near the open door, declared her status. She was literate and could speak some English. She had rank.

I was careful to indulge her status and then asked why she was studying English.

Her response was the same as every other Afghan student's: "It's the language of the world. We must learn it to advance."

I'd heard that answer over and over and am convinced it's one of the stock phrases memorized in school. Usually the answer to the next question was more unique to the individual. "What will you do with the English you learn?"

The girl answered, still sitting straight up, "I will be a teacher."

I started to affirm her choice and her efforts, but she cut me off. She segued into a brusque dissertation on Iran and the evils of satellite television. I had to scratch my head at that conversation bridge and the antagonism in her manner, but I followed along. I thought perhaps she'd stepped into her own bully pulpit and was making a point specifically articulated to tell me or someone else in the room something significant. I watched the other young student who sat beside her and wondered if she were the real audience.

That second girl sat on her shins in the doorway. She was leaning slightly, her weight resting on one hand, palm against the carpet. With her other hand, she picked bits of dust and crumbs out of the red carpet and made a small pile of her findings. She wore the same student clothing, but she didn't speak or even look up while her companion was speaking. Obviously, the first student was in control.

The older women also remained silent. The girl had already established her greater status and spoke with the authority that came with being literate.

The girl had a rehearsed speech, and I listened to it. "Iran allows satellite television. It's illegal for Iranians to watch satellite television, but they do it anyway. Satellite television brings anti-Islamic teaching to people. These people cannot be Muslims. If they were Muslims, they would not watch anti-Islamic teaching. This is against Islam." She finished, obviously satisfied with her denunciation.

Confused, I looked at each face in the room. This was a discussion I had never entered before. I didn't know how to respond or even if I should respond. Satellite television is against Islam and therefore must be banned? People who watch it, even if they are Muslims, are anti-Islam?

I recalled that the Council of Mullahs, the official body of the highest Islamic leaders in Afghanistan, had in the past gone to Afghanistan's President Karzai and demanded that he ban Indian soap operas from Afghan television. I had watched a few of those broadly popular serials in the homes of my Afghan friends. They're not like the American fare, but they do depict a world quite different from Afghanistan. The Indian women don't wear headscarves but drape their long, silky scarves over their shoulders. Women wear short sleeves and low-cut saris, revealing both their elbows and the soft flesh of their stomachs. Afghan broadcasters paint blurry clouds around any inappropriately exposed flesh.

The thing that really impressed me about the Indian soap operas was the depiction of their homes and the fascinating commercials that went along with the shows. The homes contained couches, tables, and lamps elegantly arranged on wall-to-wall carpet. Men and women drove automobiles. Once in a while, a scene would take place in a clean, modern, indoor kitchen, where the women stood to prepare meals. Unrelated men and women talked to one another. There was nothing Afghan about the world displayed.

Then there were the commercials. The ones my Afghan friends and I always talked about were the bathroom and kitchen cleanser commercials. It wasn't the cleansers that were so exciting, since they're mostly useless in our part of Afghanistan. But the bathrooms and kitchens depicted were amazing—sparkling white tile, flush toilets, bathtubs. I say these things with a smile because they're so unusual in the Afghanistan I know—and what Afghan woman wouldn't rather have a modern, Eastern bathroom than a little shed with a hole in a concrete floor ten meters from the front door? I could see the mullah's point. I'm told that TV is revolutionizing Afghanistan. Even Afghans up in the mountains are seeing images of worlds outside their own, and they're wondering, "How did we fall so far behind?" But was that what the girl saw as anti-Islamic?

The student's diatribe had amazed me, and I wanted to understand. I wondered if she'd even seen satellite TV. Perhaps someone important had told her it was evil and must be banned. Afghans must be protected from non-Islamic influence, and the Afghan society must protect them. Or perhaps the offenders were specific presenters like Iranian Bible teachers who broadcast from Canada or the Middle East. No one else in the room picked up the conversation, so I braved it. "Why is satellite television anti-Islamic?"

The girl offered another short speech. "Satellite television shows cultures that are against Islam. A real Muslim would never watch satellite television."

I had my own ideas of what aspects of Western culture threatened the strong framework of Islamic control but didn't want to assume. I asked, "Do you think that if a Muslim watches satellite television, she will stop being a Muslim?"

The girl wouldn't respond to that question. She simply repeated her position. "Satellite television is anti-Islam."

"Are Indian serials against Islam?"

"Yes. If an Afghan watches an Indian serial, he is not a Muslim."

I was sure most of the women in the room watched those Indian soap operas. I noticed that none entered the conversation, and each looked away when the girl spoke. I also knew that everyone in the room considered themselves a Muslim. I knew better than to expose them to direct condemnation for the vice of TV watching, so I kept my attention on the girl. I simply asked, "Why?"

"Muslims should not see things that are anti-Islam. Muslims should not think about things that are anti-Islam." She delivered her words forcefully, head up, jaw forward.

I tried to explain that television can sometimes show us people and cultures different from us and ours. I told her that learning about different people helps us develop a respect for the lives of people in different places.

She found that idea objectionable.

I asked if she knew that I was a follower of Jesus, and she said, "Yes." I asked her if she knew anything about what it meant for me to be a follower of Jesus. She said that to know such things was anti-Islamic. I asked if she thought followers of Jesus were evil. She did. I asked how she could know that if she didn't know anything about followers of Jesus. She said that followers of Jesus must be evil because they're not Muslims.

I gave up. In the end I put on my wet coat, slipped into my muddy shoes, handed my last gift to the mother of the forty-day-old child, kissed everyone good-bye, and simply walked away.

Ideas can threaten the status quo. I'd often watched my Afghan friends consider my ideas, my stories, and the way I understand right and wrong, good and evil. Some changed their opinions. The ideas I brought—both those that reflected my American culture and those that reflected Jesus' teachings—were radical in Afghanistan. Yet those ideas often made a great deal of sense to Afghans.

This young student sought to erect walls around her society, to protect herself and her neighbors from what she saw as temptation. For her, that was the way to defend the Islamic culture of Afghanistan. Others may not have shared her indictment of satellite television, but they did often agree on her overall approach.

For several months when the snows inundated our small town and I couldn't go out to the villages for our projects, I took two young women as English students. Both were studying at the local university. They were hardworking, highly intelligent, and deeply committed students. Sometimes English students are accused by other Afghans of giving up their faith and embracing Western ways. These girls were absolutely committed Muslims who prayed namaz five times a day and fasted during Ramadan. They had no intention of leaving Islam. The only aspect of the West that they particularly liked was the practice of choosing one's own spouse. They both agreed and dreamed that such would someday be the case in Afghanistan. One of the young women also liked the idea of a husband and his wife leaving the households of both parents and living separately. The other didn't agree. They were also interested in the economic opportunity that development money brought to the country. These were the only benefits they wanted from the West.

Both of these young women looked forward to teaching careers. One dreamed of teaching at the university, any Afghan university, and the other dreamed of teaching in a girls' school. A university teacher is afforded great respect and honor. A schoolteacher also gains honor as well as pay. Teaching is one of the few jobs that genuinely welcomes Afghan women.

Both girls, according to their professor, were excellent students, but neither could speak English well. They were silent in their university English classes. I'm told it's different in the capital where girls take their places beside boys and engage fully, even in the presence of men. But that wasn't the way in our small town. Female students clustered in the back of their male-dominated classes. Sometimes there were as few as four girls in a classroom with more than twenty boys. The girls answered questions when absolutely required but used as few words as possible. As a consequence, even though their reading comprehension was fairly good and their ability to understand spoken English reasonable, their ability to speak and write was lacking. I agreed to tutor them a few hours a week until spring to help them develop those skills.

Each week they came to my office, sat on mats behind a closed door, and practiced their English. They always brought a small boy with them, sometimes a brother, sometimes a cousin. I had a beautifully printed Dari children's encyclopedia with pictures of oceans and animals, stars and machines. Each week I gave that to the small boy while my students and I talked.

Our goal was to practice conversational English, so I would come prepared with a list of topics. I asked the girls to bring topics, and once in a while they did. One day one of the girls, Shafiqa, asked, "Why do Americans believe Islam is a religion of war?"

This put us on socially dangerous ground. With that subject, it would be easy for me to offend. For Afghans, Western culture is full of myths and misinformation. One young man once asked if it was true that all Americans discard every one of their possessions, even their cars, on New Year's Eve, then buy everything new on New Year's Day. I'm afraid I laughed. Graciously, he chided me. "Don't laugh. We don't know about your world. I'm trying to understand." I apologized and offered an explanation. In the end, we both laughed, but it was a together-laugh that felt much better. The truth is, most Afghans know virtually nothing about American society.

We Westerners spend a great deal more time and effort trying to understand a religion whose customs baffle us and whose leaders have declared war on us. Despite our efforts, the culture, and therefore religion, of Afghanistan remains inscrutable.

We approach one another from two entirely different perspectives. Our understanding of right and wrong, good and evil, and what it means to live honorable lives is simply poles apart. Our experiences of life in our respective societies bear no resemblance. We in the West live in a multicultural world with Jews, Muslims, Christians, and the flat-out nonreligious living side by side in our workplaces and schools. Our tribes—black, white, Hispanic, and more—have taken their places in our government, our police forces, our judicial system, and our classrooms. Men and women sit at the same conference tables. Boys and girls participate in the same classrooms and study groups. We have not, as a society, reached a state of complete social peace and mutual respect, but our level of social integration is completely beyond anything my Afghan neighbors could imagine.

I wasn't sure how to respond to Shafiqa's question or even if I should, but then I thought, "These are English students. They're reading our literature and learning about our culture. Perhaps it would help them to understand something about how we see the world." Yet even as I thought that, I knew we are so diverse, we couldn't even begin to speak with one voice.

I tried to help them recognize their own context and step into a different one. "Here in Afghanistan, I hear the words *Allahu Akbar*, 'God is greatest,' five times a day, often from three loudspeakers at a time. To me, as a foreign resident in Afghanistan, I understand that those words are calling people to prayer. I watch the men walk to the mosques and see the women roll out their prayer mats. I recognize those words as a call to prayer."

My two students agreed. Shafiqa, the one who dreamed of university teaching, said, "Yes, those are beautiful words."

Then I turned to the American context. "Most Americans don't hear the call to prayer five times a day. When they hear *Allahu Akbar,* they don't think of prayer."

Shafiqa was engaged. "What do they think of?"

I responded simply. "Violence."

Both girls were absolutely shocked. They couldn't imagine such a reaction. "Why? Why?"

"In America, we hear those words on the news or in movies when they are shouted by some attacker before he blows himself up or flies a plane into a building or when he's sentenced to jail for planning an attack against Americans."

The girls tried to shake off that idea. They explained that the words must be associated with the call to prayer before anything else.

I told them I would like that, but that as long as the statement is most heard in violence, it will not call to mind devotion to peaceful worship.

Shafiqa tapped the carpet in front of her knee, looked back up at me, and launched into a brief explanation of jihad, "holy war," or the struggle to defend Islam. She said that when a man practices jihad, he must declare those words to dedicate his actions to Allah.

I pulled my knees up and rocked backward. Even Shafiqa had connected violent attacks with jihad. I had not made that connection in our conversation, but I followed her lead. "When must one practice jihad?"

Shafiqa articulated her position, convinced of her rightness, with the impassive voice of an unthreatened conscience. She told me Afghans must fight in the name of Allah when their country is invaded by foreigners or when Allah himself or the Glorious Quran are insulted. When she was satisfied with her answer, she waited for me to acknowledge the rightness of her position.

I remembered the young student's speech against satellite television. I wondered if this university student would justify jihad to keep the influence of satellite TV out. I asked my next question cautiously. "Should Afghans fight jihad when their culture is influenced by a foreign culture?"

Shafiqa didn't pause. "Yes, of course. Any invasion by an infidel culture must be fought against. It cannot be allowed. This is a Muslim culture, and any non-Islamic influence is an invasion."

I understood. My presence, the Internet, international trade, television and radio, books and magazines—any influence from non-Muslim nations could be targeted as threats to Islam and must be defended against.

I tried to explain that as a Jesus follower, I look to God to protect me from temptation and show me what's good and what isn't. When I see or hear things, I must consider those things and pray. I try to understand what Jesus taught or showed and how what I've seen compares. If I hear something I know isn't true, I reject it. If I see something that's true, I accept it. I trust the Spirit of God to protect my faith, not my society.

Shafiqa didn't accept that approach. For her, it was the responsibility of the community of Islam to protect Muslims from non-Islamic influence. That protection could include war.

I looked at my two English students, just girls, really, convinced that somehow their country could live in the world, enjoy the benefits of the world, and yet simultaneously seal themselves against any influence that tempts their people to consider stepping outside of the strong framework of Afghan Islam. In the end, I explained that this support of violent resistance to outside influence encourages some Westerners, perhaps many, to view Afghan Islam as a religion of war.

Shafiqa mulled over my response and said only, "I will learn English, and I will teach infidels to be Muslims."

I told her that in my culture, she is completely free to do exactly that. We believe that each person must be allowed to make her own choices. After all, each individual will stand alone before God on judgment day.

Shafiqa was satisfied with her plan and her position; her conscience remained untroubled. I doubted if she even recognized our profound differences.

I welcome an understanding of the profound differences between these two cultures. For me, the perspectives and ideas provide opportunities for me to consider, pray, and grow. I trust my God and my faith. If either cannot withstand the deepest questions, then neither is true. My faith has grown stronger in Afghanistan because of the influence of my Afghan neighbors and because of the questions they've asked and the teachings they've put before me. I could not share in the lives of Afghans if I feared their voices in my own life and beliefs.

I was the stranger, the outsider, the foreigner. For the most part, my neighbors welcomed me. We drank tea and shared our lives. We influenced one another. I always knew that while most people welcomed me and many would take what they could from me, some would mark me as a threat and seek to kill me.

Once my neighbor's husband called me to his house. I sat down with the man, his wife, and about a half a dozen children. The wife served her husband and me cups of tea and trays of treats. Clearly, the husband had something important to tell me, but in Afghanistan you can't just jump into business straightaway. We spent considerable time, perhaps even forty minutes, talking about my family in America, his relatives in Europe, and their son in Iran who they thought was taking his own wife. We talked about the weather and how floods from the year before had destroyed some farmland and orchards. We talked about the price of fuel imported from other countries and one of the local bread sellers who had been arrested for selling lightweight bread. I knew none of that was important. Still, I chatted along until the man was ready.

Finally my friend's husband reached his purpose. "You must be very careful. You must not trust anyone."

I heard depth in his warning and knew the required response. "Thank you, my neighbor. I will be very careful. I will not trust anyone."

He went on. "Some mullahs have come to our mosque. They are not from here. All of the men in the neighborhood went to the mosque for a meeting." He paused.

I nodded. Obviously, there was a very serious problem. I tried to calm my racing heart and listened to what my neighbor was trying to tell me.

"The outside mullahs wanted us to give you to them. If we would not give you to them, then they wanted us to throw rockets at your house."

The situation was grave, indeed. I had heard of other meetings at our local mosque. Once some outsiders came and argued with our neighbors about girls going to school. They wanted our neighbors to take all the girls out of school, put gloves and socks on their women, and send the foreigners away. Our neighbors had refused. After that some people in our community received night letters warning them that if they sent their daughters to school, they were not Muslims. Some families pulled their girls out of school, but most remained defiant.

I asked the obvious, most frightening question as impassively as I could. "What did our neighbors say?"

A simple and emphatic *no* was about the only response that could assuage my fears. That had not been the case.

"The visitors said we were not Muslims if we allowed you to live here. There was a great argument that lasted many hours. I only stayed because you are my neighbor and my guest."

I realized how great a service this man had done for me.

"The men at the mosque argued about what to do. They were

not in agreement. They're watching you very closely. You must be very, very careful. You must not trust anyone."

Some people believe that the government rules Afghanistan, but that's simply not true. On the street level, the mullahs rule. "What did the mullah from the mosque say?"

The man took a sip of his tea and tapped his fingers on the carpet. The situation was uncomfortable. The opinion of the local mullah was, indeed, the most significant. "The mullah said we must watch you. We must watch your staff and especially your Afghan staff. We must see if they are changing religion. If you are bad people, we must kill you."

The message was disturbingly clear. I worried about my staff, both foreign and national. If we were tried, the hearing would occur at the mosque and we would not be able to defend ourselves. If they determined that we were a source of temptation, a threat to Islam, we would be condemned. Again I struggled to calm my heart and focused on understanding as much of the mullah's position as I could. "What else did the mullah say?"

"He told the strangers that we will not give you to them nor will we throw rockets at you. You are our neighbors and our guests. That's what the mullah said. But they will watch you."

"Thank you."

We changed the subject to something lighter. When it was time for me to leave, I said my good-byes, kissed the wife and children, and went my way.

Many of my friends in America ask me how I can live in Afghanistan. They hear stories of gun battles, rockets, and roadside bombs. They read of injuries and deaths. They know I have no rifle, no body armor, and no real defense. I tell them I can only live if I'm welcomed by my neighbors. When my neighbors cease to welcome me, I can no longer live in such a dangerous country.

After my conversation with this neighbor, I went to my Afghan staff and explained the situation. They were sad and obviously frightened. We recognized the precariousness of our position. We talked about how we could clarify our work for our neighbors so that everyone understood what we were doing. Then my staff told me that people had already started asking them very specific questions. Neighbors questioned them about where we got our money. Our staff explained that we didn't work for the government of the United States, and our neighbors had been relieved. They asked about the status of our various projects and called relatives and friends in our project areas to verify what we said. I hadn't realized any of that had been going on.

There was one more piece of information that troubled me even more deeply. Our neighbors asked my Afghan staff members if they still prayed namaz. We all knew the gravity of that question. If my staff weren't praying namaz, they had converted. No one could be allowed to think that any of our staff members had converted. That would surely mean our death.

My neighbors did watch us. Of course, they knew that we, the foreigners in my office, were all Christians. That wasn't the question. The real question was, what was our influence? Was our staff converting to Christianity? Were we tempting our neighbors to change their religion? Were we a threat to Islam? The men in the mosque valued our projects and for the most part liked us. We were helping their families and communities. We followed the rules of their culture and didn't offend. Still, they knew it was their responsibility to protect the community from any non-Islamic influence or temptation, and they took that responsibility very seriously.

A few weeks later I met an Afghan professional woman, Nagina, who worked with a group of foreigners engaged in delivering maternal health education in a distant area of the country. Nagina and I drank tea and talked about Islam and Christianity, Jesus and the Prophet Mohammed. We talked about war and peace and our common humanity. I told her about my neighbor's warning message.

Nagina worked with foreigners and respected them. She considered some friends. She also loved Islam and the Prophet of Islam. She loved the Holy Quran and knew some of its translation. She considered Islam wholly good and was firm in her opinion: "Islam is the way of peace. You are our guest. You are here to help us. We cannot kill you. Islam is peace."

A month later one of Nagina's foreign coworkers, a young woman she loved and admired, was brutally killed in the mountains of Afghanistan. The woman had been a part of a medical team providing mobile clinics for villagers who were too far away, too remote from any hospital, to see an Afghan doctor. Over a several-week trip, her team had provided medical care to hundreds of Afghan men, women, and children. The work they had been doing had been both difficult and generous. And what was the response? Just as that team was leaving the mountain area, a group of armed men swept down and murdered them. Their crime? They were infidels in the midst of Muslims, influencers who could not be tolerated.

I didn't see Nagina after that event, but I heard she grieved deeply. I heard she wondered out loud if that foreign woman she'd talked to only once, over a cup of tea, had been right after all.

The truth is, we Jesus-followers must look to God to protect us from temptation. We have not been given permission to build protective walls around our neighbors nor to silence those who speak with voices different from our own. We are not permitted to destroy those who tempt us to think or behave in ways that contradict God's teachings. We are responsible for how we respond to temptations. We are to guard our hearts and actions. We must recognize that sin comes from within us and not from the society around us. Each of us is to listen and consider the examples we see, measure those examples and teachings by what we understand our God to say, and choose for ourselves the paths we should walk.

Once again my Afghan neighbors and I stood on opposite sides of a deep chasm. Over time I learned how differently we approach the process of even considering other ideas and ways of thinking.

understanding the journey

In America, we have this cultural idea that learning about other philosophies and religions is a good thing to do. Many students take comparative religion courses in college. A customer can walk into almost any large bookstore and find English translations of the Holy Quran and other books about Islam. This seems normal to us. However, it's not normal in Afghanistan.

I've walked into dozens of bookstores in Afghanistan, in the capital and out in the smaller cities. They typically carry a full selection of school textbooks, English language and computer books, abbreviated English literature books, multi-language dictionaries, and a wide array of Islamic books. Often their stock includes books about famous Muslim prophets and imams, but never a Bible or New Testament. These latter books are available, but only underground. They certainly can't be purchased in a public bookstore. How could they be? The community must be protected from any influence that might tempt them away from Islam.

The Holy Quran is available everywhere, but it is only meant to be read in its original Arabic form. Anything else is considered a commentary rather than a real translation. I've met Afghans who have Arabic Holy Qurans with Farsi translations interlaced or printed on the adjoining page. These books are available at even small-town bookstores, but Bibles are not. In fact, possession of a Dari Bible by any Afghan is considered a crime.

Once another foreign worker brought a copy of the book of Psalms in English with a Farsi translation on the adjoining page. She had bought the book in the West and brought it with her to Afghanistan. She thought she could use it to learn to read the beautiful Farsi script. Farsi, the language of Iran, is something of a higher form of Dari but similar enough. That foreigner wanted to find a local woman to help her learn to read the Psalms.

She took the book to her office and showed it to some Afghan women staff members. These were professional women, educated and earning salaries. They were sitting in a closed room, safely tucked behind a high wall. Yet the women gasped at the sight of the translation and begged the woman to put the book away in case someone saw it. No one would help her learn to read it.

I had a copy of the Dari New Testament that I read almost every day for practice. This was most helpful because I knew the stories and teachings in English. When I got lost in the Dari, I could look up the corresponding English text in my Bible and figure out what I was reading. After a while, I became adept at reading and added documents and a children's encyclopedia to my repertoire. Some of my closest Afghan staff members saw my Dari New Testament, but for the most part I kept it hidden.

I had heard a story of a foreign man who had given away a copy of the Dari New Testament to an Afghan man. The story was both interesting and intimidating. The Afghan man had approached the foreigner and asked for a copy of our holy book. He had asked several times. Finally the foreigner found a copy of the book and gave it to the man.

They were caught. The situation became public knowledge. Government officials seized the book. Some members of the community rose up and demanded the execution of the foreigner. The government ordered the foreigner to leave immediately, which he did. His work in the country was finished. I took the incident as a warning.

One day that story entered our office conversation. I took the opportunity to understand why it had been such a big deal. After all, for Westerners, reading books about things we don't understand is generally respected.

We were sitting around the *desterkhan*, our plastic lunch cloth, eating tiny sweet plums collected from our fruit trees. Those plums were amazing, soft, the size of quarters. We had collected the plums in a tin bucket and rinsed them with icy water from a deep well—no iodine, no chlorine. We scooped piles of plums out of the bucket and put them in bowls. We pinched the thin purple skin with our teeth, sucked out the sweet meat and juice, and then dropped the skin with the stone still tucked inside into another bowl. Our fingertips and nails were stained a deep reddish purple. Those plums were a special treat.

The empty lunch dishes were already piled on a large silver tray and pushed into a corner. It was an oppressively hot day, and we had given up on tea and were drinking clear water drawn cold from the well and stored in baked clay urns.

Several weeks before, when the summer heat arrived in force, we had moved our lunch gathering to the coolest room in our mud-brick office building. Outside, dark green canvas awnings blocked most of the sun, and woven screens nailed across the windows cut the light into bright shafts that cast stripes across the walls and floor. Lightweight purple and blue curtains, drawn closed, shifted in the slight afternoon breeze. We sat on thin, solid-colored brown cotton mats, leaned against the cool wall, fanned ourselves with bright pink plastic fans, and ate our sweet plums slowly, with deep satisfaction. In the midday heat, none of us had the energy for an animated discussion. We drifted slowly, patiently through the topic.

I explained to my staff that in America, we can walk into any bookstore and buy a copy of the Holy Quran. We can carry it with us and read it as we choose. I told them that I myself had received a copy of the Holy Quran about fifteen years earlier from an American coworker. The coworker had been a Nation of Islam Muslim and had wanted me to understand his faith. The book was in English so I read most of it.

What I didn't tell them was what I'd actually thought of the book. The Holy Quran isn't an easy read. It doesn't follow a narrative format and, even as a compendium, doesn't tell an unfolding story. Some of it flat-out contradicts the teachings and narratives of the Bible. Plus there are passages that call for my dismemberment and execution. Eventually I lost interest and put it down. Later I received a thin book that contained a chapter-by-chapter summary of the Quran. I did read that.

That day as we ate our plums, Ahmad, one of my Afghan coworkers, decided it was time I converted. He was a graduate of Sharia law school and was absolutely convinced he knew the truth. He tried to explain why I should convert. By then he had worked for me for several months and knew my faith. He was sure I was wrong and, anyway, there are rules. All of Afghanistan is Muslim. If I was going to live there, speak the language, and share their salt, then I must adhere to their laws. I must convert.

Ahmad told me that if I knew what Islam teaches, then I would immediately convert. After all, Islam is the truth. It's the whole, complete, and final truth. He said he recognized me as a good person who obeys God, but that I was living in error. I was not submitted to

God. I must listen to him, obey, and respond accordingly.

I told Ahmad the obvious, that it was I who was living in a completely Muslim country and that everywhere I went, people were telling and showing me what Islam is. Every week, my Afghan neighbors told me about their Prophet and their religion. They shared stories about the life of their Prophet, proud of his submission to God, his strength and intelligence. They showed me the rules of Islam reflected in their lives. They urged me to become just like them, to believe what they believed and to do as they did. And I had listened.

Ahmad responded, "Then you know the truth. You must convert."

I told Ahmad that he had nothing I wanted. I did not expect him to be pleased with my response. He wasn't, but he remained somewhat patient.

He said I wasn't converting because I hadn't seen the truth he was offering.

I allowed him space to justify his demand, then told him a story. "Sometimes I go to the bazaar to look for fabric. I walk into one shop and then another. I look at everything they have and even talk with the storekeepers. Then I walk past the rest of the shops and look at their fabric from the street. I see quickly if they have anything different because all the fabrics are on display and there are no front walls or doors to the stores. But the shopkeepers do not let me pass in peace. They call out in English, 'Hello, mister. What do you want?'"

At that everyone around the *desterkhan* laughed. They knew that *mister* is not the English word for a woman. There were four of us that day, two women and two men, one foreigner and three Afghans.

"I tell the shopkeepers that they have nothing I want, and, Ahmad, neither do you."

My other Afghan coworkers smiled. The story I had chosen was clever. My message was plain.

Ahmad argued, "Clearly you haven't seen this product. You should look. You will find what you need." He had entered the story and was satisfied to carry it forward as our metaphor.

I responded, "Sometimes I go into a store. I tell the shopkeeper I'm looking for a particular color. Perhaps I'm looking for dark blue cotton with a simple pattern. Perhaps the shopkeeper responds by pulling out a bolt of green and pink polyester with plastic chips glued in for sparkle. He says, 'Look, this is very beautiful.' And I respond, 'Perhaps for you,' and I walk away."

My woman coworker pulled her scarf up over her mouth and laughed so hard her belly shook. That is exactly what happens to us in the bazaar.

Ahmad was not amused. My message was far too plain. My story moved him from earnest intensity to near rage. It took the strong counsel of another male coworker to convince him to calm down.

I told my coworkers I had also read a great many books about Islam and that I regularly read websites to understand more thoroughly what it is my neighbors believed and why. I told them this approach is respected in America. We believe it's good to understand other people, what they believe, and why. Finally I asked, "Why is it wrong for an Afghan to possess a Bible?"

Ahmad explained the Afghan perspective. He said that if a man receives a copy of the Holy Bible, then he has already converted to Christianity.

That surprised me. Once again, I found that I looked at things through very different, Western eyes.

I told my coworkers that although I had read much about Islam and had even possessed a copy of the Holy Quran, I had never converted. I explained that, in our culture, we read these kinds of books to learn and understand. We want to know what others believe and why. We may also consider the applicability of what we read or hear for our own lives. We learn different ideas and teachings. We consider and decide for ourselves what we believe.

Ahmad rejected that approach entirely. He was without doubt.

He repeated himself, "If a Muslim possesses a copy of the Bible, then he has already converted to Christianity. Conversion is a crime that requires punishment. The convert must be killed."

I was more interested in the journey of conversion than the passing of sentence. I already knew that Islam teaches that Muslim apostates must be killed. I wanted to understand why possessing or reading a Bible was so condemned. I asked Ahmad if it's possible for a Christian to possess a copy of the Holy Quran in Afghanistan.

He said it was possible, but it would indicate that the person had converted to Islam.

I was taken aback by that notion, and it helped me understand his judgment on those who had Bibles in Dari.

In Afghanistan I occasionally visited bookstores to buy stationery supplies, English language books, or very simple Dari books. Sometimes I tried to search out colorful children's books, but they were hard to come by. When I wanted copies of Dari religious books, I sent an Afghan to buy them for me. I never wanted to misrepresent myself to a storekeeper or anyone else. That was the right thing to do. If I did try to buy a Holy Quran, the storekeeper would have assumed I was a Muslim.

I asked Ahmad, "Wouldn't someone read the Holy Quran before converting to Islam?" That's what made sense to me. It's effectively what I had done, except with the Bible.

For Ahmad, that approach was completely backward. He explained the appropriate starting point in a Muslim convert's faith journey this way: "First a person must declare the statement of faith in Arabic."

I knew that was step one, but it also seemed step last to me. It's not a step of consideration, but rather of decision. As soon as a non-Muslim declares the Muslim statement of faith in Arabic, they immediately become a Muslim. It's a done deal.

Throughout my time in Afghanistan, many different people had tried to get me to declare that Muslim statement of faith. Once, while I was in a government office trying to collect stamps and signatures for a project, one of the government officials demanded I repeat the statement. The office was full of desks, chairs, and even a couch with its springs fully sprung. Every sitting space and even the doorway was filled with Afghans—every space except my own. They watched the situation unfold. I was definitely outnumbered, plus I needed the stamp and signature to go on with my business.

The government official sat behind a large desk with a blank computer monitor and dusty putty-colored keyboard stamped "USAID" for the United States Agency for International Development. Behind him stood a bookcase of blue binders representing each registered organization in his country. A cigarette dangled from his lips. He held my papers and said, "Just repeat after me. It's easy. You can do this." Then he declared the statement of faith. He did it over and over.

At the time I sat on a low couch, my knees together, my hands wrapped around a plastic folder, sweat dripping beneath my long coat. I kept telling the official I couldn't do it or he would think I had become a Muslim—and I was not a Muslim.

The official just smiled, held my papers in the air, and repeated, "You should become a Muslim. Repeat this . . ."

The room grew tense. We were headed for a showdown. A couple of the younger men with their stylish Western clothes offered diversions, but it didn't help. The two other women in the room demanded I come to their houses for Eid-e-Ramadan, the celebration after the monthlong fast. Still the official continued.

Finally I found a way out with humor. I offered up a self-deprecating joke, and it worked. The room broke into laughter. The official stiffened but then relaxed and gave up his efforts. He signed, stamped my documents, and sent me—still a Christian—on my way.

I asked Ahmad what happens after a person declares the statement of faith.

He replied, "Then he is taught how to pray namaz."

In all my years in Afghanistan, no one had tried to teach me how to pray namaz. I finally understood why. Only a convert should pray namaz, not someone who's merely interested in Islam.

Namaz is the ritualistic five-times-a-day prayers required of every Muslim. Shiites pray the same number of prayers but pray them only three times a day. Namaz is only prayed in Arabic. I've often asked Afghans what they're actually saying when they pray namaz. I've heard no end of diverse and interesting responses. Most of the women I've talked to in Afghanistan have no idea what they're saying. Some of the men do, but others clearly don't. I imagine that if I learned to pray namaz in Arabic, I probably wouldn't learn what those words meant either. I would be praying words I didn't understand. To me, the most important conversations I could ever have are those I share with God. It seems to me that I ought to mean what I say.

The idea of praying words people don't understand made perfect sense to Ahmad. He told me that just praying the words was significant regardless of whether the person speaking them understood them or not. He said that, of course, it's better if the person understands the words, but if they don't it really doesn't matter.

I asked what happens after the person learns to pray namaz. I was trying to understand the process and where the acquisition of the holy book fits.

My coworker continued his explanation. "Then the man goes to the mosque. He performs the ceremonial washing and prays namaz. After he has done that, he is given his own copy of the Holy Quran as a gift."

I understood. People don't even go to the mosque until after they've converted. So the order was clear: Say the creed, learn namaz, go to the mosque and pray namaz, get a Holy Quran.

I was intrigued. We have such a different way of doing things. Our churches are completely open; anyone can go. Bibles are readily available, and anyone can purchase and read one. We expect people to know and accept the most basic foundations of Christianity—Christ, His death for our sins, and His resurrection—before they embrace Christianity.

We also recognize that someone can possess a copy of the Bible and even attend church yet still not be a Christian, just as someone could possess a copy of the Holy Quran and not be a Muslim. Followers of Jesus understand that conversion is a matter of the heart. Real conversion follows revelation. It cannot be reduced to a declaration followed by indoctrination.

Ahmad completely rejected that perspective. "If a man possesses a copy of the Bible, then he has obviously become a Christian. If he was a Muslim, then he has broken the law and must be killed."

Once again I stood on the edge of a gulf, a wide chasm separating another aspect of my perspective from that of my Afghan neighbors.

I've always been careful not to repeat the Muslim statement of faith in Arabic. I haven't even written it here in English. I certainly don't believe that just by repeating the words I will have embraced the Muslim faith, but I don't want to misrepresent myself. I don't want to put on any kind of display that would be so totally incongruous with what I really believe.

There are many Westerners who find beauty in the Muslim liturgy, and I can certainly understand that. I've listened to the call to prayer from the mosques, heard the Holy Quran chanted, and watched my friends pray namaz. It is beautiful. There is an elegance and unity in the sight of a thousand men interrupting their day to kneel and pray side by side, heel to forehead, every motion the same. I once watched a man stretch out a prayer mat on a domed rock overhanging a tumbling mountain river and kneel beneath the darkening evening sky. Yes, there is a beauty in the ritual. The beauty of the ritual, however, has never been enough for me.

That hot afternoon, over a bucket of sweet plums, I learned some important things from my coworkers. I learned their understanding of conversion and where prayer, the Bible, the Holy Quran, and the mosque fit into the process. That understanding helped me answer other questions Afghans posed to me.

At one time a piece of fascinating video recorded in Kabul was broadcast on Afghan television. The film had been taken with a cell phone and depicted Afghan men with Dari Bibles singing songs to God in Dari and being baptized. I wish I'd seen the film, but I never did.

The release of the film sparked riots and demonstrations all over Afghanistan, including in my small town. My coworkers and I stayed locked within our homes until the storm passed. When it finally did, we went back to work.

About a week after the last demonstration I was at a national NGO office trying to get a contract for a partnering project signed. When I arrived the office sitting room was full of women, and I took my place beside them on a cotton mat on the floor. A cup of tea was brought to me, and I settled in to wait. I didn't know most of the women but still fell into conversation with them.

One woman in particular was very interested in me. It turned out she was the head of some aspect of girls education in town. I'm not exactly sure what her role was, nor did I ask for her name. Women's names are private, and unless someone is a good friend, I don't ask for it.

This woman considered me for a long time and finally asked a question that baffled me: "Does someone take a bath to become a Christian?"

I had forgotten the film and didn't know where her question came from. A bath? Real baths, with submersion into water, are uncommon in Afghanistan. Most people bathe with a bucket. Some pay for hot showers in the local bathing house.

I asked the educator to explain what she meant. I thought perhaps she was using a word or phrase that I didn't understand. That's when she described the film, and I understood the question.

We have a word in English that we use for baptism, but there is no corresponding understanding in Afghan culture. There are two possible words to use, but most people don't understand what they mean. This very educated woman had translated baptism into taking a bath, so as we spoke, we continued using that word.

The room was full of people, and I wasn't sure how much of an answer I should give or what approach I should take. I prayed as I listened to the woman.

Finally she asked a question I thought I could answer: "What must a person do to become a Christian?"

I didn't think for a minute that she wanted to convert. That was not the point of the question. She was trying to understand a religion different from her own, and I respected her for it. She knew next to nothing about Christianity. She had only seen a confusing fragment of film.

The room fell into silence as I gave this answer: "Usually, a person first learns about the Honorable Jesus Messiah, who He is and why He came."

One of the women in the room interrupted, displaying her knowledge. "The Honorable Jesus is a prophet from God."

"Yes, He was born of the Spirit of God by the Virgin Mary. You know that."

They all agreed.

I went on. "The Bible says that Jesus is the Son of God because He was born of the Spirit of God. God is His father."

The women watched me carefully. I had just said something that's very difficult for Afghans to understand. Still, I continued. "He was born of the Virgin Mary, therefore, the Bible says He is the Son of Man. He is the Son of Man and the Son of God." I had used the word that's normally translated *humankind* for the word *man*. If I had said that Jesus was born of a man, they would have thought Jesus had a human father.

To the women, my statement was interesting, something they had never heard before. They wanted to know how we could call Jesus both the Son of God and the Son of Man.

I reminded them that He was born both by the Spirit of God and by the body of the Virgin Mary just as the Holy Quran says. He is the Son of God by the Spirit, not by a body.

The women accepted that response, and I went on. "A person learns who Jesus is, that He came from God and that He took all of our sins and gave His own life as a sacrifice in our place."

The educator interrupted. "A person hears these things and takes a bath? Then they are Christian?"

"Not quite. A person must receive faith from God that the Honorable Jesus is who the Holy Bible says He is and did what the Holy Bible says He did. Faith is a gift of God. If a person does not receive that faith, they cannot become a Christian, even if they take a bath."

Now this was an astonishing statement. After all, one becomes a Muslim by stating the Muslim creed, the statement of faith. It's an act of the will. I had to explain the idea of faith coming from God several times before my listeners fully understood what I meant.

The educator asked again, "So a person receives this faith and then takes a bath?"

"No. First, a person must act on their faith. That's when they become a Christian, not when they take a bath."

"What does that mean?"

I used the analogy of *Eid-e-Qorbon*. That's when Muslim families all over Afghanistan lay hands on an animal and slaughter it in offering to God. They do this in memory of the sacrifice God provided to Abraham in place of his son, whom they believe to be Ishmael.

I said, "It's like Eid-e-Qorbon. At Eid, the head of the family lays hands on the Qorbon sacrifice and offers prayers for the entire family. Jesus is like the sheep of the Eid sacrifice. We give our sins to Jesus. We do this by repenting and then confessing our sins and asking Jesus to take them. The Bible says that if we do this, Jesus takes the punishment for our sins and we are made clean."

The women in the room listened and obviously thought about what I said.

I went on. "This is a conversation, a prayer between God and the person. A person can pray by themselves or with other people. It doesn't matter, because the important part is between the person and God. That's when a person becomes a Christian. The person admits that Jesus is both their Savior and their highest and most important teacher. They may do this in private, and they usually do."

The women watched me. Finally the educator summarized: "So first a person must receive faith from God and then must give oneself to God?"

I smiled. She had used a word that describes a person putting themselves into another's hands. It depicts the lesser submitting themselves completely to the greater. I affirmed her interpretation and added a bit more clarity. "Yes. It is a private matter between the person and God. Others may be present, but the conversion must come from the heart."

"Then they take a bath?"

"Yes, then they take a bath."

"So what does the bath mean?"

"When a person becomes a Christian, they become part of the family of the Honorable Jesus. Usually they find a group of Christians and enter into community with them. Then they ask to be baptized. That's what the bath is. They only do that once. I was baptized in a very large ocean by the leader of my church. When we are baptized, we declare publicly that we are followers of the Honorable Jesus Messiah."

The educator was still considering the film. Finally she asked, "So the men on TV who took the bath were already Christians?"

"Yes. The bath does not make someone a Christian; it shows that he has become a Christian."

The women were amazed. I had provided such new information, and yet what I had said made sense. Eventually one of the women brought me back to their own well-defined ground. She asked, "Why don't you pray namaz?"

I smiled. "The Honorable Jesus didn't pray namaz. He doesn't tell me to pray namaz. I am a follower of Jesus, so I don't pray namaz."

They agreed that they were followers of Mohammed and therefore must pray namaz.

They were trying to understand what it means to live as a Christian. For them, being a Muslim means praying namaz, fasting during Ramadan, and going on a pilgrimage to Mecca if they have opportunity. Most women don't give the required alms to the local mosque, but their husbands do. They all make the statement of faith. These are the foundations that define what it means for them to be Muslim.

I tried to answer the question that seemed to puzzle them. "Being a follower of the Honorable Jesus means we continue to read the Holy Bible, we pray, and we learn to live as our Teacher Jesus teaches us to live."

The women found that a satisfactory answer.

Eventually I accomplished my business in that office; we signed our contract and I left. I never saw any of those women again, but I was intrigued by our conversation. It pointed out the widely differing understanding of what it means to become a Muslim and what it means to become a Christian.

I've been privileged to learn to share our faith stories. I wasn't satisfied, though, with my response to their question about namaz and what it means to live as a Christian. It would take more work to find a way to respond well to that question in the context of Afghanistan.

HOW DO WE LEARN
TO LIVE OUR FAITH?

One lovely spring day I drove alone across open country with a taxi driver I barely knew. Since he had been recommended by someone I trusted, I counted on him keeping me safe. The territory we traveled had already shifted into disorder, and I understood I would need someone who knew the road and the various local militias who ruled it. This driver had that knowledge.

Every few miles along the road there were roadblocks, some legal and some illegal. The main police roadblocks usually included some kind of a small concrete barracks with a wide, roofless porch. The police officers lived in the barracks when they were on duty. Usually, in the summer, there were men sleeping outside on cotton mats or metal beds. In the winter, they huddled inside. The barracks was almost always perched on the edge of a hillside so that the police could look down at the road.

At each legal checkpoint, the men had cut the asphalt road surface and installed a wide metal caterpillar track from a conquered tank. This rough speed bump slowed traffic to a near stop. There we usually saw two or three uniformed officers standing around on the edge of the road with Russian Kalashnikov assault rifles dangling from their fingertips. These were the real police. They would stop us, inquire as to our destination and origin, look inside our car, and wave us on.

Illegal and informal roadblocks were ad hoc. Usually they included a vehicle parked sideways across the middle of the road to force traffic around the edge, where six or eight men stood, some uniformed, others without uniforms. These men also dangled Kalashnikovs, and these were the ones that made me nervous. A traveler could never know for sure if they were actual police, legally empowered militias, or some local criminal gang.

Police, militias, and illegal gangs must be viewed with suspicion and treated with care. The police force in Afghanistan is riddled with corruption. It's impossible to distinguish the law-abiding from the bribe-demanding until an encounter turns sour.

The legally empowered militias are a resurrection of the warlord and private army system that ruled Afghanistan during the days of the brother-war—the civil war that swept the country after the Russians left. The Western forces, in partnership with the Afghan government, rearmed the local militias in our area in the hope that they would fight the Taliban. They did fight the Taliban, but they also exercised their power to their advantage, regardless of the law. Some, if not all, of these militias were deeply corrupt. They took what they wanted, and there was little authority to control them.

The illegal gangs were simply criminals, members of the local community protected by local elders and empowered by their possession of handguns, Kalashnikovs, mines, and small bombs.

It was always difficult to tell the difference between the police, the local militias, and the illegal gangs. Police and army uniforms in Afghanistan are easy to obtain and temporary roadblocks simple to establish.

For me, the greatest danger on the road was kidnapping. Roadside bombs were always a threat, but they didn't come with a roadblock. Once a roadside bomb damaged a German convoy less than twenty minutes after I'd driven past the spot where the device had been activated. Really, I didn't worry about that risk. I figured if I hit an IED, an improvised explosive device in a regular vehicle, we'd all die pretty quickly. There was nothing we could do to avoid a hidden roadside bomb—nothing that would ensure our survival if we hit one. Kidnapping was another matter. I might have to live through that.

In Afghanistan, kidnapping is the third most lucrative economic activity, just behind opium and stealing or embezzling foreign development money. Locals, especially the children of wealthy men, are kidnapped and sold back to their families for hefty ransoms. Foreigners are more rarely kidnapped, but also more highly prized. We could be sold back to our families, or we could be traded to the Taliban to be used as political pawns. Americans could be rescued by force and might even live through the experience. Then again, we might not. We might just disappear. I knew I was considered a valuable asset worth the effort and risk of acquisition. That reality made traveling on an open road an anxiety-producing experience.

That day the road we traveled passed through thinly populated land punctuated by checkpoints, both legal and illegal. I had hired my chosen driver specifically because he knew the legal checkpoints and could differentiate among the real police, militias, and criminals. I counted on him not to sell me to some random gang on the side of the road.

It was early spring, and the land was simply beautiful, carpeted in brilliant green that appeared lush and soft in the distance but sparse and brittle in the foreground. It was a treat after the previous brown fall and winter. On one side of the road, the mountains rose with startling abruptness, their faces scooped into wavelike rhythms crisscrossed by goat and sheep trails. On the other side, the land stretched out nearly flat into the distance. I could see freshly tilled and half-tilled fields and clusters of men, wielding locally made shovels, bending their backs beneath the morning sun.

The shovel and the Kalashnikov will forever be the iconic images that depict Afghanistan for me. Each day I saw men with shovels, and each day I saw men with Kalashnikovs. Those Kalashnikovs are the ubiquitous Russian-made assault rifles that every Afghan family seems to own. Afghan men handle both the shovel and the Kalashnikov carelessly, tossing them over their shoulders or swinging them absently from their fingertips. The shovels didn't give me pause. The Kalashnikovs did. I've often wondered if they knew where the rifles' safety switches were or even if those Russian Kalashnikovs *have* safety switches. They certainly kept the weapons fully loaded even as they tapped the muzzles absently against their thighs or shins.

Every few kilometers I saw another village, a group of homes tucked away in the crease of the hillside or bundled around walls on wide open fields. I had never been to those villages, but my driver knew them all. He reported the ethnicity and history of each as we traveled along. He related the major battles, though he didn't need to. I could see the graves of fallen warriors marked with colorful, if tattered, pennants fluttering from poles. Those pennants signaled the graves of martyrs.

In one location, we passed through two distinctly separate scattered clusters of villages distanced across a river. My driver told me that one was Hazara and the other Pashtun, two very different Afghan tribes. He told me that for years during the brother-war, armies of mujahedin stationed themselves on either side of the river and threw rockets at one another. No one won, but everyone suffered. Between the villages, all along the river, were graveyards marked with pennants. It was a colorful but haunting display.

At one point we rounded the side of a steep hill, and my driver jammed on the brakes. We slid nearly sideways across about thirty yards of dust and gravel, found good asphalt, and straightened. I gasped. My driver laughed, but I could tell he wasn't pleased. He owned a dark blue Toyota Corolla, four-door with a trunk—a fine car for which he was deeply in debt. Used Corollas are the most popular and prized vehicles next to Land Rovers in Afghanistan. He certainly didn't want to lose his.

He told me the road must have washed out in the recent floods but that I shouldn't worry. It was a good car, and he was a good driver. He reminded me that I was his responsibility and he would not allow me to be hurt. I knew he believed that and counted on it.

Then he asked a startling, completely out-of-context question: "If, for example, a Muslim wanted to become a Christian, what must he do?"

I trusted him not to sell me, but I didn't trust him enough for this conversation. Was he setting a trap? Was he a spy for the government? Was his question sincere or simple curiosity? I considered my position and the vulnerability of my journey. I considered the driver and the Afghan who had recommended him to me. I prayed, took a deep breath, and decided to answer him.

"If a person wants to become a follower of Jesus, he must understand that Jesus died for his sins. He must confess his sins and ask God to forgive him. Then he must follow Jesus as his teacher and his master."

The driver explained to me that if, for example, a Muslim chose to become a Christian, he would not be able to tell anyone or he would be killed.

Of course I understood.

Then he asked, "If, for example, a man became a Christian and his neighbors discovered it, would you be able to help him get out of Afghanistan?"

The truth is, I probably could, although I didn't know how. It's not something I'd ever done, and in those days it was difficult for Afghans to get entry to countries that used to offer asylum. I had no idea how to navigate the emigration and immigration systems. I also didn't know what my driver was angling for. Was he just fishing for a ticket out of Afghanistan? Did he think feigning conversion and provoking persecution would open the door? Other Afghans had done this, and I didn't want to encourage this man to believe such a dangerous dream. I told him I didn't know how an Afghan Christian could escape the country.

My driver accepted my lack of knowledge and went on with his questions. "If, for example, a man became a Christian, how would he live?"

That question baffled me. At first I thought he was asking about livelihood, work and food. Was he looking for a job? That certainly wasn't unusual. There's another myth in Afghanistan: that foreign Christians will give jobs to Afghans who claim Christianity. If he wanted to feign Christianity for a good job, he was going to be disappointed. I explored his intentions, and he helped me understand.

"A Muslim must pray namaz every day, five times a day. He must go to mosque at least on Friday for the afternoon prayers. He must fast during Ramadan. He must give money to the mullah whenever he's asked. These are things he must do."

Ah, context. I was beginning to understand.

"If, for example, a man became a Christian, what must he do?"

I loved his repetition of the phrase "If, for example." We were clearly having a significant conversation but without anyone declaring anything incriminatory. He would walk away with new knowledge but no admission of his own journey and I would be innocent of proselytizing. I played along.

The driver was looking for a list of things that one must do and not do as a follower of Jesus. He wanted a set of laws, rules, and behaviors. We don't really have such a list, but there are things that a follower of Jesus usually does. I tried to make my response simple and clear. "If, for example, a person becomes a follower of Jesus, he will read his Bible and try to do what it says. He will pray, worship, help other people, and gather together with other Jesus followers to learn truth and celebrate."

The driver was fascinated. He asked a dozen or more follow-up questions, and I did the best I could to respond.

At one point the driver focused on the "read the Bible and try to obey" part. He said to me, "Here, in Afghanistan, the mullah tells a person what to believe and how to live. Who tells a Christian what to believe and how to live?"

That was certainly a contextualized question, one I had never heard an Afghan put so succinctly. I answered immediately, "Jesus" and shrugged. There really was no other answer.

The man looked at me in his rearview mirror and smiled.

I realized I hadn't even used a culturally appropriate title for Jesus. I added a few words, referring to the New Testament: "The *Injil* tells us about the Honorable Jesus. It tells who He is, what He did, and what He taught. His followers read those words and learn from Jesus Messiah Himself."

I thought about the mullahs in Afghanistan, the Arabic language of the Holy Quran, the methods Afghans use to train people in their faith and the nature of churches and mosques.

In Afghanistan, there are no visible churches and no recognizable pastors. There are certainly Afghan Christians, but they're hidden. And of course there are foreign Christians.

In our town, there were just a few foreign Christians. Most

weeks we gathered for worship, prayer, and Scripture study. Often one of us would bring a short message, about twenty minutes long. Sometimes we'd listen to a teaching CD. Usually we'd talk about what we'd heard. We celebrated communion together and prayed for one another. There were only a few of us, sometimes just two. Sometimes, if we had visitors and everyone was in town, our gatherings swelled to eighteen.

We met in one another's homes, with no separate building, of course, and no paid staff. We just met as a group of believers coming together to celebrate our shared faith. It was our church. Each of us considered it important to gather. It's refreshing to be with people who believe pretty much the same things. Still, we were a diverse lot. We came from different countries and different Christian backgrounds. We learned to respect one another's faith journeys and our unique interpretations and application of Scripture. We were too few to divide into denominations.

We were also deeply committed to one another. When one needed help, the help was provided. Once I needed to evacuate my house under kidnapping threat. One of the foreigners in my community simply called and said that he was coming to get me and I would stay with his family until the threat passed. Another foreigner's child tore off the tip of her finger in a play-yard accident. Immediately the only foreign doctor in our small community answered the call to help. Yet another time I didn't receive my living expenses from America on time. I borrowed money from another family in our community without the slightest shame or embarrassment. Our lives in Afghanistan were precarious, and we needed one another. We learned from one another, encouraged one another, and helped one another from the foundation of our shared faith.

I was pretty sure there was no such Afghan community of Jesus-followers in our town for my Afghan driver to join. There were Afghan followers of Jesus, but they feared exposure far too much to come together. There were no Afghan pastors. Obviously, I couldn't advise my driver to visit a church or join a neighborhood Bible study group. That kind of thing seems normal in the West but makes no sense in Afghanistan. As I thought about my driver's question, "Who tells a Christian what to believe and how to live?", I knew the most important answer wasn't found in church. It's found in Jesus Himself.

I drew from my experience and practice and told him, "Every day I read the Bible. Every day I worship God, and every day I pray. I ask God to teach me how to live, and He does."

My driver nodded, then turned his eyes from the rearview back to the road. Our conversation continued.

Several months later I visited his wife in their home. In the interim she and I had become friends. When her husband entered and found me drinking tea with his wife, he pulled down a cloth-wrapped manila envelope, slid out a stack of loose pages, and showed them to me. It was the entire gospel of Matthew printed on white computer paper. Clearly he prized it. I asked where he got it, and he said someone had printed it for him from the Internet. We talked about the stories it contained, and he put his treasure away. He had dropped his hypothetical disclaimer, "If, for example . . ." but still didn't admit to any emerging faith. I didn't ask. I allowed whatever God was doing in his heart to remain his own private journey.

After that trip, I thought a lot about the question, "Who can tell a person how to live?" I realized that, although I had some understanding of how Muslims learn their religion, my picture was incomplete. That set me on yet another quest to understand.

Every day, six days a week, I watched the children walk to the neighborhood mosque with their Holy Qurans wrapped in colorful fabric and held carefully above their waists. I didn't know what the children were learning in the mosque, so I began asking my neighbors about religious education in my town. I thought that mothers would be the best source since they're the ones responsible for small children, and I sought them out.

The first thing I learned was that our town was nearly one hundred percent Sunni Muslim. It was small and religiously homogenous. It did include different tribes, each with its nuanced customs. Still, there was one standard way to educate children, and all children were expected to participate. Attending the local public school was optional; attending the mosque was not.

In Afghanistan parents can send their children to school or not as they see fit. Children can choose not to go to school, and no one will make them. Often teachers are relieved when children disappear from their classes. Many of the classrooms contain up to fifty students, with only one teacher. There are nowhere near enough schools for all the students, and in the outlying areas there aren't enough teachers.

It's a different scenario for the *madrasas*, the Islamic schools that teach, primarily, religion. Madrasas function within the neighborhood mosques. In town, there are mosques every few blocks. The mosques are experiencing a renaissance. Someone discovered that many of the mosques in Afghanistan weren't actually facing Mecca, and many others are either damaged from age or from war. Afghans are tearing down old mosques and building new, bigger, more beautiful mosques in their places. Schools may hold their classes in crowded tents. There's no local money for new school buildings. Mosques are different.

Every village in Afghanistan has a mosque, but they don't all have mullahs. In some areas, one mullah serves three or four villages. Most mullahs were outsiders, men from other communities who had been trained in Afghan or Pakistani madrasas.

Parents send their children to the neighborhood mosque when they're quite small, usually five to seven years of age, to begin their religious education. The children attend about an hour each day, the boys and girls practicing separately. They start by learning the Arabic alphabet.

I've interviewed dozens of literacy students and been impressed by how many of them, from all over Afghanistan, had gone to the local mullah to learn the Arabic alphabet. It made a difference when it came to learning how to read and write in Dari. The Arabic alphabet is very similar to the Dari alphabet, so if a person learned the Arabic alphabet as a small child, he or she was more prepared to learn to read than her neighbor who had never been to the mosque.

In my town, virtually all children went to the mosque to learn the alphabet. I asked a woman what happens if a child misses a day. She told me that if a child starts missing classes at the mosque, the mullah will find the child and punish him. The mullah may even berate the father for the child's absence. Madrasa education at this level is compulsory.

In the villages, the approach to children's education is more lax, usually because there is only one mullah for several villages.

Eventually, a child begins reciting the actual Holy Quran in its Arabic form. Those were the children I saw walking up and down the street with their brightly wrapped books clutched safely against their chests.

I've walked past mosques in the summertime, looked through the gate, and seen the children sitting on raised, carpet-covered platforms outside the mosque building, rocking back and forth over their books, chanting the text. I've also seen adults rock back and forth in that same way when they read in Dari.

The children learn to recite the Holy Quran through practice. The mullah walks through their ranks and corrects their pronunciation as the children read along. At this point, the children don't learn the meaning of the passages. They only learn to recite the text.

When a child has completed reciting the Holy Quran in Arabic, they receive the title *Hatme-Quran*, or one who has finished reading. It's an important distinction and marks the end of religious education for many boys and most girls. A few students will continue their studies. These are the older boys and occasionally older girls who actually begin to learn the translations of some of the passages in the Quran. They also read commentaries and study tracts from whatever collection of Hadith their group has embraced.

If a girl continues learning, she typically sits under the teaching of a neighborhood woman mullah. These women aren't actually mosque-mullahs, but they have religious education. I've known many such women mullahs who taught girls in their homes. Sometimes Afghan women called me a "Jesus-mullah." I never liked the title but recognized it as a term of respect.

The son of a friend of mine was studying at the advanced level. One day I asked him to show me how he reads the Holy Quran. He pulled the book out, gently unwrapped it, kissed it, and then touched it to his forehead. He unfolded a wooden book stand and placed the book carefully on top. Then he began reading. When he finished, he smiled with deep satisfaction, with the kind of pride one sees in a child's face when he feels he has accomplished something wonderful.

I told him his reading was beautiful and remarked on how it must be a blessing to be able to do it. He beamed. Then I asked what the passage meant. Immediately his face darkened. He rebuked me. "The blessing is in reading the words and hearing the words read. You have heard these words read and therefore you have received *sawab.*" His mother nodded her proud agreement. Apparently, I had missed the point.

I had sought to understand how Afghans learn the tenets of their faith and how to live it out. I realized that the source, for most Afghans, wasn't the Holy Quran or even the commentaries or Hadith. The source for most was the neighborhood mullah himself.

That explained why, when I spoke to Afghans, they would describe laws and rules rather than refer to specific Quranic texts. We often had lopsided conversations. I would say, "The Honorable Jesus said this . . . or did this . . ." and my neighbors would say, "In Islam a man must . . ."

I have read the entire Bible, many times over. In Afghanistan I get a great deal of credit for having done this. Not only do I read the Bible, but I know what it says and can explain its teachings in Dari. Again, I get credit. Of course that credit is assigned by my neighbors based on what they can understand of my knowledge.

Once Faiz Mohammed, an Afghan man, asked me how many verses of the Bible I had memorized. I was dumbstruck by the question but not tempted to try to count. I do have a great many verses memorized, but I've never intentionally worked at it and I've certainly never counted them. Faiz Mohammed was able to tell me, with obvious pride, how many *ayats*, or verses from the Holy Quran, he had successfully memorized.

Then Faiz Mohammed told me about an Islamic teacher he greatly admired. This imam appeared weekly on Afghan television. Faiz Mohammed told me the imam had memorized the entire Holy Quran and so he was a great man indeed. Faiz Mohammed asked how many verses of my Bible the leader of my church in America had memorized.

I told Faiz Mohammed that when a pastor becomes ordained in America the people who decide if he can be a pastor don't ask him how many verses he has memorized.

Faiz Mohammed found that confusing, nonsensical. Since then I've asked his question of several pastors in the States, to see if any of them had ever kept track of their Scripture memorization. They've invariably looked at me like I was some odd creature. Many Christians practice Scripture memorization, but I've never met one who kept a tally.

I responded to Faiz Mohammed's question with this story: "One day when the Teacher Jesus was on earth, He taught a very large group of people about what it means to live righteously, the way God meant us to live. At the end of His teaching, He told them a parable: 'A person who hears these words of mine and does them is like a very smart man who built his house on rock.'"

In my part of Afghanistan, all people build on rock. If they didn't, their houses would twist, shift, and fall. Donkeys pull carts full of large boulders down unpaved streets. Men take the boulders and pound them with sledgehammers until they split. They dig deep trenches the size of the building and neatly interlock the split boulders. That becomes the foundation.

"The Teacher Jesus said, 'A man who hears these words of mine and does them is like a very smart man who built his house on rock. The winter and spring rains fall, the ground turns to mud, the wind blows but the house stands.' Why?"

Faiz Mohammed knew the answer. "Because he has built on rock."

"Yes. The rock is solid, and the house doesn't move when the storms come."

Faiz Mohammed nodded. That was simply common sense.

I went on. "Then, the teacher said, 'The man who hears what I teach but doesn't do it is like a man who builds his house on dirt. The dirt is soft, and when the rain comes and the wind blows, the house falls down and all his work is lost.'"

Faiz Mohammed nodded and smiled. The story had spoken. He knew that I had responded to his question, not with the answer he'd requested, but with what the Teacher Jesus had said was more important: understanding and obedience. It's Jesus who tells a Christian what to believe and how to live.

Then I turned the question back to Faiz Mohammed. "If we hear the teachings of God in a language we don't understand, have we heard?"

Faiz Mohammed bristled. I had made my point, but now I was making another. He found his defense. "Of course it would be best if everyone could read and understand the Holy Quran and the teachings of the Hadith, but this country is backward and not everyone can understand."

I recalled the question the driver had asked me between the checkpoints on the road. I rephrased it for Faiz Mohammed. "So how does an Afghan learn to live a righteous life?"

He gave the obvious answer: "A person must obey the mullahs. The mullahs will teach him how to live, and he must obey."

"How does he know that what the mullahs teach him is what is actually in the Holy Quran or in the Hadith?"

"That's the mullah's responsibility. The man must obey."

"And the woman? She can't go to the mosque to learn, can she?"

"Of course not. Women don't go to the mosque. She must learn from her husband, her father, her brother, or her son."

Faiz Mohammed did understand some of the Holy Quran. He had studied and learned quite a bit. Still, by his own admission, he didn't understand much of it. I've always been amazed by the fact that so many Afghans spend so much time reading a book they don't understand.

I thought it would help if I told Faiz Mohammed the story about the Reformation in Christianity. Afghans are surprised to hear that for a long time the Bible was only available in a language local people didn't understand. I told him about the men who translated the Bible into the languages of the people and how some of them were killed because they had done so. Afghans understand that, but they are surprised to hear that it happened to us.

Faiz Mohammed told me his story. "A few years ago, there was a man in Afghanistan who translated the Holy Quran into Dari. He printed copies, and he and a friend distributed them across the country.

They were not allowed to do that. It's sin. They were arrested and put in jail."

I remembered the story, but when I'd heard it I hadn't understood it. Before and immediately after the men were arrested, there were protests all over the country. Afghans shouted for the men's execution. I hadn't comprehended their crime. After all, they were Muslims. The way Faiz Mohammed explained it surprised me. He said the men had translated and printed a Dari version of the Holy Quran, but it had not included the Arabic version interlaced with the Dari. Therefore they had committed a crime. Also, they were not authorized to do the translation. Only appropriately authorized Muslim scholars or mullahs are permitted to even write verses of the Holy Quran.

I thought about a particularly difficult season in my life when I had written Bible verses on Post-it notes and tagged them all over my apartment and car. Each day, everywhere I went, I saw the verses and was reminded of who God is. I needed that during those dark days. Those little scraps of truth encouraged me.

If I had wanted to write verses from the Holy Quran, I would have had to pay a local mullah to write them down for me.

Many Afghans do that. There are mullahs all over town who write out verses for a fee. If anyone, a man or a woman, has a problem or concern, he can go to one of these mullahs. If an infant is sick or colicky, the mother will go to the mullah, pay him, and ask for a charm. The mullah may require her to do something—drink or eat something specific or perform some act. He will also write down a verse in Arabic on a scrap of paper. The paper will be folded neatly into a little cloth packet, usually shaped like a triangle and pinned to the baby's clothes. It's like a talisman that protects the carrier or represents the answer to his or her petition.

We have a completely different view of the Bible in our culture. Church secretaries mount letter tiles to spell out verses on signs.

Painters letter verses on billboards. Artists add verses to their calendars, websites, or paintings. Some people even append verses at the bottoms of their e-mails, and virtually all of our Bible study materials come with verses typed directly into the booklets in the language we speak and read. For us, it's the meaning of the verses that makes all the difference. We read to *understand*. We look for truth to speak to us, to guide, strengthen, and encourage us.

Here's the source of the tension, the challenge my very presence in their community brought to the conservative Afghans around me. My driver had asked how a Jesus follower learns what to believe and how to live, and I had opened a book not printed on paper but stored in my heart and mind. I had also brought my Jesus-following self with all the work I did and the attitudes with which I did it.

In Afghanistan the mullahs have a lock on theology and law. They define the rules, and Afghans are meant to follow them without expressing doubt or hiding disobedience. Ahmad had inadvertently revealed the threat I carried inherently when he said, "If a Muslim possesses a copy of the Bible, then he has already converted to Christianity." My neighbors, coworkers, and friends did possess a copy of the Bible. They possessed it in me.

Most Afghans can't get a hold of a printed Bible or even a New Testament. They're illegal and difficult to acquire. Plus, most Afghans either can't read at all or read at such a low level that a printed Bible would be useless to them. But those Afghans who have chosen to share their lives with me have "read" the Bible in my life and in the stories I've shared. Through our conversations, the perspectives we traded, I introduced my neighbors to Jesus. I told them His teaching and His examples. I revealed what I believe and allowed them to see how I lived. Some watched, listened, and turned away. Others who saw Jesus in my life and my stories found Him beautiful and drew His teachings into their hearts, minds, and lives. And I certainly wasn't the only foreign Christian living in Afghanistan.

Afghans meet Christian foreigners in their workplaces, their universities, and their homes. We attend their weddings and funerals. We sit at their *desterkhans*, drink their tea, and eat their salt. We become human. We break down the wall of separation and enter their world. We speak their language, wear their clothes, and begin to understand their culture. We live in their neighborhoods in houses we've rented from them. We have no guns, no tall watchtowers, and no concertina wire to protect ourselves. We ride in their taxis, their minibuses, and their rickshaws. We buy our bread from the corner baker, and our food—fruits, vegetables, meats, rice, everything—from their local bazaars.

Our very presence challenges the power of the mullahs and the worldview of our neighbors. It's one thing to hate and reject the voiceless, faceless masses of pig-eating, alcohol-drinking sons of Satan from the other side of the world—mythic caricatures interpreted by the mullahs through history and religion. But we Christian foreigners are flesh and blood with eyes and voices, laughter and tears, stories and faith. When Afghans meet us, see our lives, hear our stories, and recognize our humanness, conflicting worldviews collide. The safe box of well-defined ideological fortress-orthodoxy trembles, walls collapse, and doors open.

It's easy to sneer at a stranger you've never met; it's safe to categorize an entire ethnic group, race, or religion from the other side of the world. The book of their lives, their faith, and love remains closed. Groupthink breeds ignorance, and ignorance breeds control. But then the Christian foreigners come.

Afghanistan is full of foreigners—private contractors, NGO workers, educators, medical practitioners, diplomats, and soldiers. The vast majority of these foreigners live behind concertina wire and batteries of armed guards. Many who do go out into Afghan communities ride in convoys of armored vehicles. For our Afghan neighbors, those weapon-protected and weapon-yielding foreigners, even as they kick down doors or sit with village elders, are not quite human. They don't have their own voices. They speak through translators, if they converse at all. One soldier looks like any other.

But there are other foreigners, hundreds, perhaps thousands of individuals and families who have entered the world of our Afghan neighbors and invited them into their own world. These are doctors, nurses, and midwives who daily do everything they can to alleviate the suffering of very poor Afghan families. They treat their patients with honor and compassion. Foreign teachers and trainers face corruption, threats, and accusations to bring quality courses to hungry young Afghans seeking to better themselves and their country. Foreign development workers partner with local Afghan NGOs and community leaders to deliver training, literacy, health education, and a hundred other small and large programs designed to build the capacity of local Afghans.

Many of these foreigners, like me, have stepped out of the faceless, distant, long since categorized "other" and crossed the divide to become something closer—"our foreigner," claimed by our neighbors and the people we serve. We've shared our tea, our salt, and our stories.

Our presence, actions, and stories threaten the control of the mullahs. That's why the mullahs and the men argue in the mosques over whether or not to allow us to be there. That's why the Taliban post night letters directing our neighbors to kill, kidnap, or evict us.

Every week I stumbled into conversations full of questions and opened a "book" tucked away within me. My neighbors gave me rules, and I gave them Jesus. Together we explored His teachings and got to know Him through the things He said and the works He did. For a Jesus-follower, Christianity is all about knowing and following Christ. He tells us what to believe and how to live.

Jesus said that life starts with love for God and love for our neighbors. That's the foundation. Everything we do should flow from love. When Afghans asked me how a Christian lives, they were looking for rules—how do we gain credit for heaven, how many verses do we memorize, what is our declaration of faith? I learned that each question my friends put to me came from a context a chasm away.

One of the most common questions Afghans asked was about prayer. It's such a foundational part of both their faith and practice and mine. Once again my Afghan neighbors had a structure and well-defined rules for prayer that I have never embraced. For me, prayer, like all other aspects of faith, flows to and from love.

HOW should we pray?

Every culture has its markers, the tags people use to declare themselves to one another. In the West, a Christian might attach a metallic fish shape to his car. A Jew might wear a Hebrew letter chi or a star of David on a necklace. A Muslim woman might wear a scarf. Each of these markers indicates to which group the bearer belongs. But what markers or behaviors identify an individual as actually having faith or as being sincerely religious?

In America a person might ask me if I go to church each week. My response identifies me as "religious." In Afghanistan, the test or evidence of submission to God is prayer. Often one of the first questions Afghans asked me, after they'd determined my marital status, was, "Do you pray *namaz*?"

For Afghan Muslims, there are two types of prayer, *namaz* and *dua*. Namaz, known as *Salah* in Arabic, are the prayers Muslims are required to pray five times a day. Namaz is formulaic or liturgical and is only prayed in Arabic. All Afghan adults and older children are required to pray namaz.

Dua is informal prayer spoken by the individual Afghan either in Arabic or in his or her own language. *Dua* is good but optional.

One day at our office we welcomed a new Afghan woman as a part-time worker. On her first day, she rose from our lunch gathering and sought a place to pray. She didn't have her prayer mat with her, so I gave her a clean piece of cloth to use; then I showed her the direction of Mecca and provided her with an empty room. Each day for several days she pulled that clean piece of cloth from the bin I'd stored it in for her, spread it out in the empty room, and prayed namaz. It took her about ten minutes to step through her prayers; then she was back to work.

Also each day a couple of my male coworkers left our office immediately after lunch, walked down to the neighborhood mosque, and prayed namaz. They were usually gone from the office about fifteen minutes. Occasionally I saw men roll out their mats and pray on the street. At the Kabul airport, I often saw Afghan men unfold square cloth *desmals*, or neck scarves, spread them out next to the wall in the waiting room, and step through their prayers.

For my neighbors, these prayer practices evidenced genuine faith. Of the five pillars of Islam, praying namaz daily is the most visible. It's easy to see if someone is praying namaz. It's a clear marker.

I found the liturgy of Islamic prayer practice beautiful in the same way that I find the prayer practices of the ancient Catholic monks and the abbeys and cloisters in which they prayed beautiful. And yet I can't imagine embracing such practices.

In Afghanistan, my neighbors, both men and women, often asked if I prayed namaz. My prayer practice was an important marker to them. I always responded that I did pray but that I didn't pray namaz. That answer never fit their framework. To admit to praying and yet to say I didn't pray namaz made no sense to my neighbors. They invariably wanted to know, "Why not?"

One afternoon while I was waiting in the office of a national

NGO that provided training for women, a group of Afghan women gathered around me and pressed the question of prayer.

By then I had found a comfortable response. "You are followers of the Prophet Mohammed, therefore you must pray namaz. I am a follower of the Honorable Jesus. He did not teach us to pray namaz, nor did He pray namaz, therefore, I don't pray namaz."

That answer elicited both surprise and confusion. The notion that Jesus didn't follow Muslim practices as taught by the Prophet Mohammed was a new concept. After all, Jesus was righteous and a great prophet of God. Righteous people obey the teachings and follow the practices of the Prophet Mohammed. Therefore Jesus must have obeyed all the practices that Mohammed taught, right? Here was another chasm between our perceptions.

The women challenged me. "Do you pray?"

"Yes, of course."

"How do you know what to pray?"

I've always considered that an excellent question, yet it also reveals a vast difference in our understanding of prayer. For my Afghan neighbors, namaz is a beautiful ritual that must be practiced consistently. For me, as a follower of Christ, prayer is an intimate conversation with the God of the universe. I've never felt completely satisfied with my answer to this question. After all, if I asked a woman what she speaks to her best friend about, she'd be overwhelmed by the length of the topic list. Women talk about everything.

I told the women I'd just met, "I pray what's on my heart. I pray for my family and my work. I pray for you and your family and for peace in Afghanistan."

That explanation only deepened their confusion. I had had this conversation often enough to recognize the disconnect my prayer practices illumined. Afghans know I should pray namaz and I'm condemned if I don't. Yet I did pray and even prayed for them. That's a beautiful and honorable thing. I broke the rules yet showed myself to be spiritual or religious. It is difficult to comprehend different faith practices in a country with only one religion.

One of the women asked the next obvious question: "How often do you pray?"

She was looking for a specific number of prayers and corresponding times of the day, but our prayer practices, as followers of Jesus, are not prescribed. If I told her that I prayed, read Scripture, and worshiped each morning, she would translate that practice into a rule or law that all Christians must follow. I didn't want to give her that assumption, so I replied, "I pray anytime, all the time, whenever I want, whenever I can."

There's a story that the Prophet Mohammed went to heaven and met with one of the old prophets. He told the prophet that praying all the time was just too much. He negotiated an agreement to allow the Muslims to pray just five times a day. When I tell Afghans that I pray all the time—when I'm sitting in my house, when I'm walking down the street, and even when I'm sitting in their houses, they translate my words and try to understand them in the context of their experience.

Afghan Muslims must walk through a ceremonial cleansing process before they can pray namaz. Then they must find a clean piece of cloth, roll it out on the floor, and speak the specific words that they've learned for namaz. With this context, the idea that I pray whenever I want makes no sense.

I tried to explain to the women what Jesus taught His students about how to pray. "When the Honorable Jesus was on earth, teaching people the way to God and healing people, His students came to Him and asked Him to teach them to pray."

The women leaned in and paid attention.

"The Honorable Jesus said, you should pray like this, 'Our father who is in heaven, holy is Your name.'"

This very first sentence always provoked immediate interruption. That day was no exception. One of the women rebuked me sharply.

"You can't call Allah 'father.' Allah is Almighty. He has no partner. He has no children. He neither begets nor is begotten." This was always a sticking point. "Do you really believe Jesus is the Son of God?"

If I answered that question directly, the women would assume that I believe that God took on a physical form, had sexual relations with Mary, and conceived a son. That's not a notion I've ever believed, and I didn't want them to think I did.

Over time I've learned an explanation that seemed both comprehensible and satisfying to my neighbors. I gave it. "God is spirit. Your Holy Quran says that God, who is spirit, breathed and the Virgin Mary became pregnant with the Prophet Jesus."

The women agreed.

I continued. "It's written in the Holy Bible that Jesus is the Son of God because He was conceived of the Holy Spirit of God. He has no human father. Maryam was a virgin. It is also written that Jesus is the Son of Man because He was conceived by the Virgin Mary. Jesus is not the Son of God according to flesh, but according to Spirit."

Usually, that's an acceptable response that makes sense. That day my response elicited another question: "How can you believe there are two gods?"

Most Afghans who have learned anything about Christianity have been taught that we believe in three gods. Some say we believe in God the Father, God the Son, and God the Virgin Mary. Others believe we worship God the Father, God the Son, and God the Angel Gabriel. Afghans believe that God is spirit, but I've never met any who have heard the term *Holy Spirit*.

I once read an old Arab Christian explanation of the Trinity that I liked better than any I'd heard before. I've used it over and over in Afghanistan and found it effective. I shared the analogy with the women. "I do not believe in two gods or three gods. God is one. I worship God the Father, God the Son, and God the Holy Spirit—one God." Even I understand that's a difficult concept.

I continued. "God the Father is like the sun that sits in the midday sky. The sun is so strong that if we stare at it, we will go blind. It's so far away that we can't get to it. If we did get to it, we would be destroyed because it burns with such a great fire. We cannot come near the sun in the midday sky. God the Son is the light of the world, just as your Holy Quran says. We need the light of the sun to live. Without it, no plants would grow. It would be forever night, and our lives would be spent in darkness. God Jesus is like the light that comes from the sun in the sky. And God the Holy Spirit is like the warmth that the sun provides. Without it, the earth would be covered with ice and we would die. The sun, the light it shines, and the warmth it gives are all one thing; they cannot be separated. You cannot have light or warmth without the sun in the sky. You cannot take a sword and separate the light from the sun or the warmth from the light. The three are one, and yet they are different."

There are no perfect and complete analogies to describe the Trinity. God is a mystery beyond our ability to comprehend, and yet those of us who follow Jesus recognize the Trinity, God who is three in one. Usually, the sun analogy genuinely helps my Afghan neighbors comprehend what I believe. At the very least, it helps them understand what I don't believe.

Jesus' introduction to prayer is also difficult because Muslims consider themselves slaves of God, not children. I tried to explain to the women in that office why Jesus told us to address God as Father: "The Prophet Jesus said that anyone who receives Him can be called a child of God, born of the Spirit of God."

One of the women responded immediately, "No, that's not possible. Allah has no children."

I tried again. "The Prophet Jesus, whom God sent to earth, said that those who receive Him are born of the Spirit and by the Spirit of God become children of God."

Muslim means "submitted to Allah." If there is one word that describes Islam it must be *submitted*. The community does not view it-self as a family with Allah as their father. That would be blasphemy. Allah is too great, too far away, too transcendent to be viewed as a father. My understanding of the loving fatherhood of God is absolute blasphemy to my Afghan neighbors. Once again, we stood on two sides of a chasm. We saw God very differently, and that difference in-fluenced how we prayed and how we viewed prayer.

I didn't get very far with the women in that office. They had never seen me before; we had never talked. They had no under-standing of how I viewed our relationship with God, and, perhaps most importantly, they had never seen me pray.

Once, when the husband of one of my friends challenged me on the subject of God as our father, I shared one of Jesus' teach-ings with him. At the time, he was rocking his small daughter in his arms. I asked, "Do you love your daughter?" I knew that he did.

"Yes, of course. She's my daughter."

"Do you think you are greater than God?"

Blasphemy! "No, of course not. Allah Akbar, Allah is greatest."

"Do you think that you, as a man, are able to love your daugh-ter more than God is able to love you?"

My friend's husband stumbled in his answer. This was not a question of law, but a question of something much deeper.

Usually when Afghans talk to me about faith, they focus on the outward differences, the rules. They investigate my adherence to the laws of Allah and invariably find me lacking. "You let your hair show from under your scarf. You eat pork. You don't pray namaz." For me, these are the wrong discussion topics. It's our different un-derstandings of the nature and character of God that frame our very different faith practices and worldviews.

I asked the man the same question that Jesus asked a group of men when he was teaching. I changed the gender of the child involved because he was rocking his daughter and not his son. "If your daughter asks you for a fish, would you give her a snake?"

In Afghanistan, we're all afraid of snakes. Once there was a dark gray one about three-and-a-half-feet long in my *aouli*. My dogs killed it, but we had to dispose of the carcass. What does one do with a snake? In the end one of my staff members carried it on a shovel to the street and buried it outside the wall. Some men walking by came near to see what the man was doing. When they saw the snake, they ran away even though it was dead. Afghans don't like snakes.

Fish, on the other hand, are expensive and tasty. In the mountains, we eat small river fish deep fried or baked stiff over kebab coals. It's a treat we look forward to when we travel. I had asked the man, "If your daughter asks you for a fish, would you give her a snake?"

"Of course not. She's my daughter." He looked down at the small child in his arms and smiled. He did love her very much.

"You're a good father."

"I try to be." He smiled at the child again.

I went on. "If your daughter asks you for an egg, would you give her a scorpion?"

The man shuddered. No Afghan father would give his beloved daughter a scorpion. Scorpions are to be feared. They're plentiful, and their sting is intensely painful.

"Do you really think you are able to love your child more than God is able to love you?"

The man looked down at his sleeping daughter, curled safely in his arms. In a flash, he saw God in a way he had never seen Him before. A whole new possibility opened before him. How could he ever assume he could be greater than God in any way, including as a father?

I went on. "If your beloved daughter wants something, do you want her to ask you for it?"

His child was old enough to talk but had yet to learn to make sentences. She had mastered favorite nouns for sweets, cookies, cake, juice. Her father loved to fulfill her requests. I knew this, of course.

He explained the things she liked to ask for. It was his pleasure to come home with some treat buried in one of his many vest pockets. The little girl expected those treats and searched her father's pockets until she found what was obviously hers. It was a favorite game, and they both delighted in it.

I continued with my story. "You do love your daughter, and that's a beautiful thing. But God loves your daughter more than you ever could. He loves you. When the Honorable Jesus was on earth, He asked a group of men the same questions I asked you. Then, He said, 'If you, who are evil, know how to give good gifts to your children, how much more does God, who is our father in heaven, know how to give good gifts to us?'"

This astounding comparison thoroughly caught my friend's attention.

"The Teacher Jesus told us to pray for the things that we need. He told us that God hears us. God is wiser than a man. He knows what's good for us and what isn't, just like you know what's good for your baby girl and what isn't. If she asks you for something that's not good for her, you won't give it to her, will you?"

"No, of course not." His daughter was particularly fond of the leftovers his wife threw in their dog's bowl. Despite the child's frequent insistence, he wouldn't allow her to eat it. Of course he wouldn't fulfill her every request. He loved her too much for that.

"God is even greater than you. He wants us to ask for the things we need and trust Him to give us what's good for us."

Over time this family developed the practice of praying for the things they wanted and needed. They had learned that God loves them, and now they pray freely. The last time I saw them, they prayed for me.

One day a woman friend told me that her hip and knee were extremely painful. She wasn't looking for help; she was just complaining. Considering the absence of chairs and Western-style toilets, it was a significant problem.

I said to her, "My friend, you know I'm a follower of the Prophet Jesus."

By then she was used to me talking about Jesus and asking questions about her faith and culture.

"The Prophet Jesus healed people. He healed blind people, and they saw again. He healed sick people, and they became well. He even healed two people who were dead, and they came back to life."

My friend had heard some of those stories.

"The Prophet Jesus said that we can pray and ask Him to heal people. Can I pray for your hip and knee?"

My friend immediately agreed.

I'd learned how much Afghans value prayer. Many times I'd prayed for the needs of Afghans I'd met along my journey there. Often a woman would tell me that her husband or son had no work, and I would offer to pray right then and there. Usually I was pretty sure they wanted me to provide a job, but they were always obviously grateful when I offered to pray and then even more after I did so. Afghans believe, with greater faith than I usually see in America, that God answers our prayers. If I prayed for a sick or crippled child, they expected the child to be healed. If the child did get better, they credited it to my prayers and told everyone about the gift.

I also learned to pray for meals. The Afghan custom is to pray after the meal. Those post-meal prayers are formulaic and prayed in Arabic. Most families didn't bother with them. I continued my habit of praying before the meal, but I adjusted it to the Afghan style. That is, I learned to lift my hands and keep my eyes open. I learned to seal the prayer by passing my hands over my face. I also developed the practice of speaking God's blessing over people and their families.

These different types of prayers were well received by my Afghan neighbors. It was another way of expressing God's love to them.

Unfortunately for me, praying in a second language did not come easily. The language of prayer must be learned. How do we address God when we pray? How do we express our requests? How do we close or end our prayers? For me, learning to pray in Dari required serious study. It took time with different language helpers and dozens of questions presented to Afghan men and women. And it took practice. I've stumbled through a great many prayers. I could've prayed in English, but then those for whom I was praying would have had to guess what I was saying. Sometimes that would have made them uncomfortable. They wouldn't have known what I had asked for. So I worked hard to develop my own prayer language. I learned the vocabulary and structure of petition and blessing. I learned to close my prayers, "In the name of the Honorable Jesus Messiah, my Savior." I learned and practiced until praying in Dari flowed from my heart.

But on that day when my friend's hip and knee were causing her pain, I didn't yet have many words but I had faith. I reached over, laid my hand on her hip, and prayed a simple prayer: "God Almighty, Father in Heaven, You sent Jesus as Healer. Your will is to heal. Please heal my friend's pain. In the name of the Honorable Jesus Messiah, my Savior." Then I laid my hand on her knee and prayed again.

Immediately the pain was gone. She stretched her legs in front of her and folded them again. She stood up and sat down. She was delighted. After that, whenever she was with me in the company of other Afghan women, she told them they should ask me to pray because God answers my prayers. Often they did, and I found myself praying for everything from closed wombs to the legal return of family land. Most of the time I never discovered the outcome of those prayers.

One chilly spring day a foreign friend and I were sitting in a bright, beautifully decorated room. It was the home of a successful but not wealthy family. The walls were creamy yellow, probably painted just before the winter. Thickly flowing yellow curtains framed the wide window, and thin white sheers blocked the view. There were even curtain rods, thick and metal knobbed, something lacking in most homes where thin printed cotton fabric was nailed directly to the window frame or suspended on elastic cord.

The red carpet beneath us was machine made but thick and shiny. The *toshaks*, the cotton floor mats we sat on, were covered with new swirling red and gold cloth. The pillows behind us were thick, oversized, and wrapped in last year's newest fabric, a sort of cream and burgundy wavy striped pattern. Their size was noteworthy, not the usual smaller pillows that only provided support up to the middle of the back. These pillows were huge. Not one part of my shoulders touched the cold wall.

We had finished a sumptuous lunch of steaming rice cooked with spices and oil, carrot strips, and raisins, and topped with pressure-cooked lamb. The girls of the household had taken the *desterkhan* and the used dishes away. Our host had distributed soft, thick Chinese blankets, one for every two members of our little gathering. We stretched the blankets across our folded legs and pulled them up against our chests. Then we relaxed into conversation.

The group still with us included two older married women, two daughters-in-law, four adult girls, and two small children. One of the older married women, a woman of about fifty, was the female head of the household and our host. She had nine children and several daughters and two sons who were already married. One daughter-in-law had already given her two grandchildren, both of whom graced us with their presence. The youngest was still in diapers. I had been in so many homes where toddlers wandered about diaperless, and wetting when and where they wanted, that I was grateful for those diapers. I recognized the diapers as another sign of financial prosperity. The older boy was about four and apparently did as he wished. Their mother sat with us, but as a daughter-in-law she said little, deferring to her mother-in-law and aunt. The aunt was nearly sixty and was visiting from a distant town. She wore enough gold and makeup to mark her as well-to-do, also. The four adult girls were the daughters of our host. All were educated. Two studied at the university, and the other two expected to go.

During the meal we had talked about the conditions up in the mountains, the early marriage age of girls, and my office's work to provide communities with maternal health training. We had talked about corruption in the country, the bribes that had to be paid to get my host's children into university, and the appalling state of the police and judicial systems. We had talked about the long years of war and the losses our host's family had suffered. We had talked about sick relatives, floods, and failed crops.

Most of our conversation involved the two older married women—that is, our host and her visiting sister, the aunt. The older daughters engaged occasionally. The daughters-in-law said little.

It had been one of the older daughters who had first asked if my friend and I prayed namaz. That was near the beginning of our visit, just after I had prayed a blessing on the household and given thanks to God for the meal. At the time, I had provided a brief explanation but promised more later if they wanted it.

The aunt brought the subject back. By then we were warm under our soft blankets and well satisfied with our meal, so I leaned back and tried to explain.

"I am a follower of the Honorable Jesus Messiah. When He taught us to pray, He said to pray this way: 'Our father who is in heaven, holy is Your name. Your kingdom come, Your will be done on earth as it is in heaven.' You have asked how I pray. Often I pray that people would do the good works of God here in Afghanistan. I pray that people would stop doing things that are evil. For example, I pray that government officials would stop taking bribes but instead serve the people honestly. I pray for the peace of Afghanistan. I pray and ask God to heal people who are sick like your small nephew who has become crippled. I pray for everyone to live in God's kingdom here on earth, to recognize God's rule and submit to it. If we live God's way, then we will do the will of God. We will love God, and we will love one another. Then we will have peace, and our lives will be good. I pray for these things."

The aunt's first response was simply, "Thank you."

She was thanking me for praying for God's blessings on Afghanistan. It's a strange and unusual thing for a non-Muslim foreigner to pray for Afghanistan and its people. My hosts were grateful.

I would have liked to go on to explain the rest of the prayer that Jesus taught us, but the phrase "the kingdom of God" was so completely new to my companions that they asked about it.

I wasn't surprised. When Jesus taught in first-century Judea, His listeners already seemed to have some understanding of the concept of the kingdom of God. They expected or at least hoped that the Messiah would restore God's kingdom and all would be well with the world. It seems clear from Jesus' teachings that the Jewish understanding at the time was deeply flawed, but at least the concept was there.

That's not true in Afghanistan. Even the phrase "kingdom of God" seems to be completely unknown. The "kingdom of God" is at the center of Jesus' teachings so I wanted to help my friends understand, but the kingdom is also a mystery and difficult for me to unpack. I tried. "The kingdom of God is the rule of God on earth. It's the will of God, the desire of God. When we do good works and live righteous and generous lives, we are doing the will of God. We are living in submission to His kingdom. That's what God wants. When we do bad works, we are listening to Satan and living in the kingdom of this world. God doesn't want that for us. God created His kingdom for us and us for His kingdom. God's kingdom is good."

For my hosts, submission to God is defined first by the five pillars of Islam. These are the creed, or Islamic statement of faith; namaz, the liturgical prayers undertaken five times a day; fasting, which involves abstaining from food and drink during daylight hours through the month of Ramadan; Hajj, or religious pilgrimage to Mecca; and *zakat*, the giving of alms. I had stretched the definition of God's will to apply to every act of our lives. Also, to my hosts, a person is either a Muslim, submitted to Allah, or not a Muslim. I had said that a person is submitted when they do the works of God. I had changed the conversation.

My hosts seemed to understand what I was trying to say. We went on to talk about God's rule, good and evil works, and what it means to be submitted to God. We talked about the day, someday, when all people would do what is just and righteous and loving. I told them the kingdom of God is about love. It's about loving God and loving one's neighbor. It's about living out that love and doing what is good and right. I told them I pray for the kingdom of God to come to Afghanistan and to America. They liked that. In the end, we had a beautiful, encouraging conversation.

Often I stood in our office and prayed for wisdom for our projects. Some of my Afghan staff would turn their faces away. To them, this kind of prayer was not appropriate. They believe that Allah does not engage himself in our lives at this level. Other members of my staff would join us. They saw God differently and liked praying for His blessings on the communities we served and the work we did.

Once while I was doing a business training project, I worked with an Afghan man to help him develop his business plan. When we finished the work, which had taken several months, I told him I was praying for God to give him wisdom with his future business and for

God to help him make good decisions. He asked why I would pray for something like that. I asked why not. He confided that he never prays for such things because Allah is not interested in these details. I told him that God tells us not to be anxious, but to pray about everything, including our work. I also told him we should do all our work for God, as though God is our boss. He liked those ideas and carried them away with him.

Some of my Afghan friends watched me pray for the details of our lives—for sickness, jobs, and everyday wisdom—and picked up the example. Those who did recognized that God loves them, and they felt welcome in His presence.

Often in Afghanistan I've heard people repeat the stories and Jesus-teachings I've shared with them. Most Afghans I've encountered, though not all, genuinely love the stories and teachings of Jesus. They see Jesus as wise and good. They admire Him and recognize truth in His teachings. Many learn from Him and are changed.

For a while there were a couple of *ambuks*, the two wives of one man, who frequently visited me. I knew they were looking for jobs for their sons and husband, but what could I do? I had no jobs to give them. When the *ambuks* came to my gate, I stopped what I was doing, made them tea, and served them treats. That's simply the way things are done.

They often had a long list of personal complaints and spent their time reiterating the litany of everything that was difficult about their lives and everything they disliked about their neighbors. Their visits were never fun. We didn't laugh. The conversation was invariably negative, and their attempts to manipulate me into giving them something were barely veiled.

One day the *ambuks* came seeking money so they could pay a bribe to one of their son's teachers. The boy was failing his classes but wanted to pass the grade. I explained that giving money to pay bribes was not something I could do. I told them that my holy book says that paying a bribe perverts justice and is not right. If I did it, my own hands would be dirty, and I didn't want that.

They were not satisfied with that response and launched into yet another extensive litany of their troubles and difficulties.

When their discourse had continued through two cups of tea, I'd had enough. I gave the women a challenge: "Listen, we all have problems. We all have difficulties. But it's not good to spend all our time looking at what's bad. Here's what we're going to do. We're going to go around this circle and we're going to thank God for the good things He's given us. Okay?"

The truth was, I couldn't emotionally afford to focus on all that was frustrating. I had my own list. I had to wear clothes I didn't like. I had to speak and understand a language that was obscure to me. I couldn't drive myself anywhere. I couldn't buy much of anything on my own. I couldn't go out to the street or shopping without being harassed. I couldn't eat the food I wanted. My house was either freezing or baking. I didn't have a shower. And if all that small stuff wasn't enough, there were men in the mosques frequently debating whether or not to kill me or drive me out. Clearly, I had my own list and I couldn't afford to focus on it.

I had developed this habit of intentionally practicing thanksgiving to keep my heart and mind sane. I would sit behind my window, eating my breakfast and drinking my morning coffee, look out onto my yard, and thank God for things He'd given me. Sometimes I was so weary and my heart so depressed that all I could do was thank Him for my dog, the fruit on the trees, and the turtle who ate what fell to the ground. Sometimes I did better. I could thank God for the bigger things—for His goodness, for the privilege of knowing Him in Afghanistan, for the joy of learning more about Him, for the friendships He had given me, for my safety, and for the people back home who loved me.

The best cure for complaining, even my own, was to refocus on what's good. That's what I tried to share with the *ambuks*. I felt sure that if they found the lightness, ease, and joy that thanksgiving brings, they would embrace the practice and give up their pattern of constantly complaining.

That day there were four of us in the room, the two *ambuks*, an Afghan friend of mine, and me. My other friend understood immediately what I was getting at. The *ambuks* didn't, and I had to explain myself several times. At first they argued that there was nothing good in their lives. I challenged them, "God has given you nothing?" They certainly couldn't say that! Eventually they gave in. It went something like this:

"I thank God we have a house and food to eat."

"I thank God my son is healthy and can go to school."

"I thank God there is no war in this town anymore."

"I thank God I have a healthy daughter and a new baby son."

"I thank God my husband is a good man."

"I thank God my mother is well."

On and on we continued until each of us was smiling. There's something simply good about giving thanks. It's good for our souls, for our spirits. It pulls us out of despair and reminds us that God is good.

I told the women that God tells us to give thanks at all times. They agreed, of course. They knew that was true. I told them giving thanks is one of the things we do when we pray. We thank God for the gifts He's given.

I challenged the *ambuks* to sit down together each day, share a cup of tea, and thank God for what He's given them just as we had done. Those *ambuks* shared a house and spent more than considerable time together. I encouraged them to spend a little of that time each afternoon, before they prepared the evening meal, giving thanks.

They agreed it had been a good experience and their hearts felt lighter, but they didn't continue the practice. They just added me to their list of complaints. After all, I hadn't done for them what they wanted. I had given them nothing they considered valuable.

It was my other friend who had sat with us that day who picked up the practice. Six months later she and I were together again eating a meal with a group of Afghan women. The women fell into complaining. I listened to the complaints, acknowledged the difficulties in their lives, then I suggested we spend a little time thanking God for all He's given us.

The women laughed. I was a foreigner. I couldn't possibly understand the trouble they'd seen. In many ways, they were right. Their burdens were heavy.

Then my Afghan friend stepped in. She told a story that made my heart swell. It went something like this: "I used to be very angry all the time. I didn't want to marry my husband, but my family forced me. Then I lost three babies in pregnancy, two boys and one girl. I fought with my husband all the time. He would do something or forget to do something, and I'd get angry. I would stay angry. Then our foreign friend here said I should stop and thank God for what He's given me. At first it didn't make sense. God knows what He's given me, and I do the things I should do. I pray namaz. I fast. I do what I can. But I thought, What can it hurt? I'll try it. So I started thanking God. I saw that even though I had lost three babies, I now have two healthy children, and I thanked God. Even though I didn't want to marry my husband, he really is a good man. He's patient and works hard. He's kind to me. Now every day I try to stop and thank God for what He's given me. I'm not angry anymore. I used to be angry all the time, but I'm not anymore. My husband and I are happier together. We used to fight. Now we almost never do. We laugh more, and our children are happier."

The Afghan women in the room sat in silence. Here was truth wrapped in a gentle and beautiful experience. They stopped mocking me and genuinely considered the words of their neighbor. It's one thing for the foreigner to think she has anything to be thankful for. She's wealthy. She's free. She hasn't lived through thirty-plus years of war. She never even had to marry. What does she know of troubles? But here is one of us—an Afghan woman who's seen the same kinds of troubles we have. The women listened. A handful of seeds tumbled onto their hearts.

I don't know if the women thought about my friend's story after we left. I don't know if the story helped them. But I know this: When two cultures come into contact, they're both changed, and sometimes those changes are good. When we see or hear an idea or thought that's good and right, it resonates in our hearts. It's as though something within us recognizes goodness and truth and embraces it. We taste and see that it's good. Then we long for more.

My Afghan neighbors constantly asked me about prayer. For both of us, prayer really was a daily practice but something we viewed and did differently. My neighbors understood rules, the protocols for approaching the greatest, most powerful being in the universe, and they endeavored to follow those rules. They viewed prayer as the marker that identified a person as spiritual or religious. They looked into my life, expecting to see a form of prayer they could recognize. Instead, they saw a completely different attitude toward God and a prayer practice that reflected that attitude.

I knew that for my neighbors to make sense out of my prayer life, they would have to grasp something of my understanding of God. They would have to see God as Father—near, loving, and powerful, One who desires intimacy with His children, One who loves us and blesses us at every turn. I knew I would have to change the definition of submission from following prayer rules to living generous and loving lives.

HOW should we fast?

"Daanetana waz konen."

"What?"

"Open your mouth."

"Why?"

"Are you fasting?"

I was standing in a small, wood-framed room crowded with Afghan women. Both the front and back doors were covered with cheap canvas sheets. A single lightbulb hung naked from the ceiling. There were no thermoses of tea, clear glass cups, or plates of treats. We were in the middle of Ramadan, and everyone was fasting. I wasn't.

My bag sat uninspected on the metal table. Instead, the guard demanded to look into my mouth. It wasn't the first time someone had made that demand, but I still found it rude.

The woman opened her own mouth wide and drew so close to me that I could smell her dark breath. In a flash I saw her yellow teeth, the gaps where two or three had been removed, and a very dry tongue. She was fasting.

"Open your mouth," she demanded, and again I refused.

I had come to one of the government offices in downtown Kabul to collect some necessary stamps and signatures for a project my NGO wanted to start. Every project required stamps and signatures from someone in the government. The collection of these stamps and signatures was never without challenges.

That day I had taken a taxi from one side of the city to the area where the Afghan government offices are located. I got out of the taxi two blocks from the ministry and walked the rest of the way. The road in front of the ministry was closed for security. When I arrived at the gate, the male guards signed me in and then waved me through a doorway into a wooden shed. Inside the wooden shed were seven women, some standing and some sitting. I had greeted them in nearly perfect Dari and dropped my bag on the table to be inspected. The guard rose. She was thirtysomething, dark-haired with a loose black scarf with silver trim. She wore a modified police uniform. Instead of slacks, she wore a long skirt with lightweight pants underneath. Her jacket was the police officer's jacket, and I imagine she was quite hot in the early morning summer weather. I had greeted her with a smile and offered my hand. Instead she demanded to look into my mouth. I was tired, impatient, and not in the least bit amused.

"Why?"

"Are you fasting?"

"No, of course not."

"Why not?"

"I'm a follower of the Honorable Jesus Messiah. I am not a Muslim."

One of the other women in the room assessed the situation correctly. "Right, it doesn't matter if she's fasting. She won't get any *sawab* (reward from Allah). She's not a Muslim."

The rest of the women discussed that fact for several minutes. Some said I should fast even though I'm not a Muslim because it was Ramadan and I was living in Afghanistan. Others said that was silly. My fast would have no value, so what would be the point? Eventually they reached a conclusion: I should convert to Islam and then fast.

They asked me the follow-up question I always expect when the subject of fasting comes up: "Do you fast at all?"

Generally, Afghans assume that I never fast. They're mistaken. I responded to the women's question. "Of course, but I don't fast like you do." I needed a stamp and signature from the ministry and didn't want to get into a lengthy discussion about fasting, so before they could ask the next question, I smiled and wished them the blessing of their fast.

That seemed to satisfy them. They shifted gears and invited me to their home for Eid-e-Ramadan, the celebration after the month of fasting. Of course, those weren't real invitations, but they were being polite and I accepted graciously.

The woman guard waved me through the checkpoint. She never did look inside my bag for bombs, nor did she check my body for guns. Bombs and guns were, apparently, not so important as the inside of my mouth.

Every Muslim must fast for the thirty days of Ramadan. Like namaz, the five-times-a-day prayer, fasting during Ramadan isn't negotiable. It's an absolute requirement for every Muslim. I could be naïve and say that every Afghan fasts faithfully during Ramadan, but I don't think that's true.

I've talked to Afghans who've told me that maybe seventy percent of the people in Afghanistan who are supposed to fast actually do. Others have told me that perhaps only thirty percent actually fast. I'm certainly not going to judge. I do know that when people don't fast, they hide it. I've never met anyone—except Afghan Jesus-followers—who have admitted to violating the Ramadan fast. It's just not allowed.

I've asked a great many Afghans why they fast during Ramadan. I've heard only three different responses. The first, of course, is because fasting is required.

"Why do you fast during Ramadan?"

"Because it's Ramadan." Implied is, "That's really a stupid question."

The foundational reason for fasting during Ramadan is because it's the commandment of Allah. In fact, this fast is one of the five pillars of Islam. Every Muslim must fast during Ramadan, and many Afghans, like the guard, are diligent to make sure their family members, neighbors, and coworkers all obey the commandment.

I tried again. "What benefit do you get from fasting?"

That question usually brought a stock response, "We fast to receive *sawab*."

Sawab is credit for heaven. It's good works for which one expects to receive reward. Afghans believe that Allah will weigh a person's good works in a scale against their bad works. If people have enough good works, they'll go to paradise. If they don't, they'll go to hell temporarily until their punishment is complete. Then they can go to paradise.

The third response is usually more thoughtful: "During Ramadan, while we're fasting, we draw near to Allah and he hears our prayers." Men will often add, "During Ramadan, we go to the mosque every day and recite the Holy Quran. There's *sawab* in reading. Some men will recite the entire Holy Quran before the end of the month of Ramadan. There's great *sawab* in that."

It's that response that moves the conversation from obedience to Sharia law to a more nuanced, spiritual discussion. It's also usually at that point in the conversation where I affirm my neighbor's fast and speak a prayer asking God to receive my neighbor's prayers and worship. My neighbors always welcome those words of affirmation and blessing.

I'm told Afghans follow the same fasting rules as Muslims all over the world, but the practices around the fast vary from culture to culture.

In Afghanistan, the women of the household wake up first, often between three and three-thirty in the morning. They prepare the morning meal that must be enjoyed before the first call to prayer. Sometimes they serve leftovers from the night before. Other times, depending on the family, they prepare the morning meal from scratch. The point is for everyone to eat a full meal before the pre-dawn call to prayer. That's when eating and drinking must stop for the day.

The fast encompasses everything that's ingested—liquid, food, smoke, and even spit. From the morning call to prayer onward, Afghans are meant to abstain completely from any and all of these things.

Every year Ramadan moves ten days forward on the Western calendar. When Ramadan falls during winter, it's not so difficult. The fast only requires abstention during daylight hours, and really only one meal is skipped. In the wintertime, the days are short and cold, so the fast isn't so arduous. In the summertime, though, the days are long and extraordinarily hot. That makes the fast exceedingly difficult.

During Ramadan, Afghan men tend to work only in the mornings. Offices close in the early afternoon. Many men will simply nap the afternoon away. For women, of course, the rhythm is different. They try to do as much of the housework as possible early in the mornings while they have strength and the air is cool. The women must prepare food for the children who are too young to fast and for those women who are ceremonially unclean and are therefore barred from fasting. In the middle of the afternoon, they start preparing the large evening meal. That meal should be served as soon as the evening call to prayer releases the community from the day's fast.

During the last two weeks of Ramadan, the women prepare their families and homes for Eid-e-Ramadan, the end-of-fast celebrations. If it's possible, everyone in the family should have a new set of clothes, one nice outfit they can wear for the three days of Eid-e-Ramadan visits. Sometimes women will sew these outfits themselves on hand-cranked household sewing machines. Sometimes the men will purchase the clothes in the bazaar.

Houses must be cleaned from top to bottom. The process is called *khana-kashi*, which means "pulling everything out of the house." The women drag raw cotton *toshaks* and carpets out into their *aoulis*. They beat the dust out of them with long, thin sticks. They scrub the insides of their houses from floor to ceiling. If there's money, their husbands make arrangements to have the rooms painted. Whether there's money or not, the women remove the curtains, wash them, hang them to dry, iron them, and return them to their windows. All of this work is particularly difficult for the women while they're fasting, especially if Ramadan occurs during the worst heat of the summer. Still it has to be done. I've seen women exhausted and weary from the effort, but I've never heard any complaints about it. Eid-e-Ramadan is an exciting time, and everyone looks forward to it.

Afghans tell me that during the first week of the Ramadan fast, everyone is hungry and thirsty. From my perspective, everyone's a bit short-tempered, also. I try to avoid Afghans during that first week. My friends tell me that by the middle of the second week, everyone's accustomed to fasting and it's easy after that. There's a great communal spirit in the fast, full of strong encouragement. It's a shared experience that draws Afghans together.

When I was in their country, I often heard Afghans talk about the importance of not gaining weight during the fast. Afghans aren't supposed to experience a material or physical benefit during their season of self-denial. They're meant to receive spiritual benefits.

I did see people gain weight. It's almost inevitable. If you eat two huge meals a day, one in the morning and one in the evening, you're likely to gain weight, particularly if the evening meal is followed by sleep.

Small children don't fast. I've never been clear about what age a child should be when he or she starts fasting. I've asked, but the responses differed, and most of my friends hedged. My sense is that it depends on the child. Once a child starts fasting, he or she must fast every year thereafter, so it's an important transition.

In Afghanistan, pregnant and lactating women generally fast. I've never met one who didn't try. I don't think it's good for their babies, but considering that most Afghan women are either pregnant or nursing for much of their adult lives, it's necessary. Apparently there are defined rules for how many days a person must fast after Ramadan to make up for days lost from not fasting during Ramadan. The rules seem to differ from tribe to tribe. It may depend on what the local mullah teaches. Regardless of the specific equation, all missed days must be made up.

A woman is not permitted to fast during her monthly menstruation. During that time, she's ceremonially unclean, and her fast doesn't count. I think the women at the government checkpoint who demanded to see my tongue used the concept of uncleanness to decide that even if I fasted, it wouldn't be accepted. I'm unclean because I'm not Muslim. Therefore, even if I fast, it's not acceptable. The challenge for women is that they have to make up all the days they miss. I've met very old women in their country who were still fasting outside of Ramadan to make up for days they thought they'd missed as younger women. There's a mathematical equation, and Allah is the mathematician. No one can know until they reach his judgment whether they have enough *sawab* or not.

Eid-e-Ramadan is the celebration that follows the month of fasting. Afghans go house to house, visiting neighbors and relatives. It's a wonderful social time but also a huge amount of work for the women who have to prepare the home and serve the guests. Plus, it's expensive.

Afghans have something of a folk hero called "Mullah Nasruddin." Mullah Nasruddin is both a foolish and clever character. He does and says things that are nonsensical. There are hundreds and hundreds of Mullah Nasruddin jokes; one addresses Eid-e-Ramadan. In the joke, Mullah Nasruddin visits a distant village. He sees that everyone is wearing fine clothes and the homes are welcoming strangers and feeding them wonderful treats. Mullah Nasruddin sees all of this, and announces that every day should be Eid-e-Ramadan. That's the joke. When Afghans tell this, they laugh and groan. Eid is wonderful, but it's a huge amount of work and expense. Can you imagine trying to put on a Christmas dinner or Thanksgiving feast every day? Still, Eid is a wonderful cultural practice, full of joy and celebration.

During Ramadan, the subject of the fast is foremost on everyone's mind. That makes it the number one conversation subject.

In general, my Afghan neighbors assumed I didn't fast during Ramadan. When I visited my neighbors or friends during the fast, they invariably served me tea and treats even though they were fasting. They told me they would get even greater *sawab* for providing this service. I often tried to refuse, but it was always a battle.

Even though they didn't expect me to obey the Ramadan fast, they still asked about fasting. Initially, I didn't know how to respond. I first arrived in Afghanistan right in the middle of Ramadan. Everyone I met wanted to know if I fasted, how, and why. In those days, I had virtually no language skills and did my talking through translators. That's a challenging limitation. I couldn't really hear the words people were speaking and align them to the speaker's body language or facial expressions. It was frustrating and exhausting to genuinely understand what people were communicating to me. I had no idea what kind of response would be culturally appropriate. In the beginning, I turned to other foreigners for help with that question.

I asked a Christian friend of mine who'd been in the country for several years how he responded when asked. He said, "I just tell them we fast, but it's a private matter."

I thought that was an unsatisfactory response.

He reminded me what Jesus taught about fasting: "And when you fast, do not look gloomy like the hypocrites, for they disfigure their faces that their fasting may be seen by others. Truly, I say to you, they have received their reward."

Jesus does tell us we shouldn't use our fast to gain public respect or affirmation. But I knew that revealing my own fasting practices wasn't going to earn me great public respect in a land of thirty-day fasts. Besides, what's really important is what the Bible teaches about fasting. That was the real question.

That first year in Afghanistan, I followed my friend's example. I told my neighbors I did fast, but that fasting was a private matter. They were always surprised to hear that I fasted, but I didn't think they really believed it.

By the second year, I had enough language to respond for myself, but I still stumbled through my responses. I told people that I fasted and tried to describe the kinds of fasts that I undertook and my reasons for fasting. Often they were impressed, but I still wasn't satisfied with my responses. I realized I really didn't understand what the Bible teaches about fasting. That drove me back into the book. By the third year, I was ready.

I told my neighbors what Jesus said about fasting, that it's part of a private conversation between an individual and God. I told them that when we fast, we deny ourselves something, maybe food, and instead turn our attention to prayer or giving. I explained that sometimes I fasted as an act of worship, sometimes to seek God's specific direction in my life, and sometimes just to refocus my heart on God.

Then I tried to share stories of different prophets who fasted and why they fasted. Afghans recognize more than 4,000 prophets, from

Adam to the Prophet Mohammed, and count them all as significant. I told some of their stories. I told them about the prophet Moses, who fasted for forty days when the tribe of Israel had disobeyed God. Moses sought forgiveness for the people. I told them about the prophet David, who fasted when his newborn son was sick. He wanted God to heal his son. He also fasted when the King of Israel was killed. That was a fast to express his grief. I shared the story of the prophet Daniel, who fasted from tasty food when he was enslaved. He did that to express his faithfulness to God. I also told them about the time the prophet Daniel fasted as part of a season of prayer and how God answered that prayer by showing him a vision. I told them about a man who fasted and prayed because he wanted to know the way of salvation. I told them God answered that prayer and sent another prophet to show that man the way of righteousness. I told them about Jesus, who fasted for forty days in the wilderness and defeated the temptations of Satan.

Then I told my Afghan friends about my fasts. I told them about fasting during the forty days of Lent. Usually I give up something or add something to focus on Jesus, His crucifixion, and resurrection. When it's been possible, I've observed a complete food fast from the Thursday before Good Friday, Maundy Thursday, to Easter Sunday. I explained that I fasted before I made big decisions. I told them that I fasted before I decided to move to Afghanistan.

I was intentionally changing the conversation from a discussion about rules and a prescribed form to talking about fasting as a spiritual exercise meant to bring us into a deeper relationship with the God who loves us. Often these were difficult conversations full of unique vocabulary, complex language tenses, and very foreign concepts, but they were also rich conversations full of deep spiritual meaning.

Each Afghan enters the season of Ramadan within the context of his or her own life. One comes to the fast with grief from having lost a loved one. Another comes with a need for healing or deliverance.

Yet another comes with an ache to know more deeply the God they worship. So when I shared about the prophets and my experiences, some of my friends found their own hopes and desires affirmed. Our conversations encouraged their fasts and gave them space to express more personal spiritual desires and motivations in it. As for me, I learned a great deal through the process, and my own understanding and practice of fasting grew and deepened. I was grateful for the opportunity.

Afghans aren't meant to receive any tangible benefit through their fast. I understood that and saw it as another opportunity to discuss a different purpose for fasting. At our office, we provided a very good lunch for all of our staff, both Afghan and foreign. That lunch was one of the benefits of the job. During Ramadan, the foreigners ate lunch, but the Afghans didn't. That meant that Afghans were sacrificing a significant part of their salary. I decided to offer them a deal.

I had copied out a section of the Bible, Isaiah 58:6–11, to share with my staff. In that passage, God teaches the idea of fasting to benefit other people. That was the idea I wanted to present to my Afghan staff members. I knew better than to bring the entire Bible in Dari into my office. That would've been scandalous. I also knew I would never be able to memorize that passage in Dari. I could barely read it. Before I presented the idea to my staff, I took the passage to my language helper and practiced reading it until I could make my way smoothly through the difficult language of the Old Testament and the right-to-left Farsi script in which it was written. Two weeks before Ramadan began, I was ready.

We were sitting in our office enjoying a wonderful lunch. That day there were only Afghans present. All the foreigners except me were out of town. When we had finished our main meal and were happily carving the skin off Afghan apples, I began, "You know Ramadan is coming, and I understand that you will not be eating lunch here at the office. Is that right?"

My staff agreed. There were both men and women in the room, and I knew that on some days my women staff would eat, but I would not bring that up in the presence of the men. That was shameful. We would have that conversation privately.

I went on. "I understand that you should not gain a benefit from your fast. Is that right?"

They agreed. They understood I was talking about material benefit. One of the men explained that the fast is meant to be self-denial and that no man should get fat through Ramadan.

I nodded and continued. "I don't think our office should gain a benefit through your fast, either. It's your fast, the service you give to God. However, if you don't eat lunch at the office, our office will save money. We would use that money for other needs, but you wouldn't get it."

One of my staff members immediately began negotiating. "That's very good. You could give us the money the office saves during the fast. It would be a good thing."

I smiled and responded, "But then you would gain benefit from your fast. You would get extra money. If you do that, God will not accept your fast, right?"

The man who had tried to negotiate immediately saw his mistake. No, they could not receive a bonus for their fast. Perhaps if I hadn't pointed that out, they could have received the bonus, but since I had deferred to their own law, there was no way they could receive it.

Anyway, I had a different idea. "I want to read you something God said about the fast. It comes through the prophet Isaiah. It's very difficult, so please be patient with me."

The men and women nodded and I began, "In the name of God." I knew that phrase was required before I read the Scriptures. Usually Afghans use a phrase in Arabic, but I spoke in Dari. Still, I had dedicated the reading to God, and that was good.

Then I read, slowly and carefully, "Is not this the fast that I choose: to loose the bonds of wickedness, to undo the straps of the yoke, to let the oppressed go free, and to break every yoke? Is it not to share your bread with the hungry and bring the homeless poor into your house; when you see the naked, to cover him, and not to hide yourself from your own flesh? Then shall your light break forth like the dawn, and your healing shall spring up speedily, your righteousness shall go before you; the glory of the Lord shall be your rear guard. Then you shall call, and the Lord will answer; you shall cry, and He will say, 'Here I am.' If you take away the yoke from your midst, the pointing of the finger, and speaking wickedness, if you pour yourself out for the hungry and satisfy the desire of the afflicted, then shall your light rise in the darkness and your gloom be as the noonday. And the Lord will guide you continually and satisfy your desire in scorched places and make your bones strong; and you shall be like a watered garden, like a spring of water, whose waters do not fail."

My staff loved the words. They had listened to them intently and had even passed their hands over their faces as if sealing a prayer when I finished reading. Then each of the men offered their own response.

One said, "During Ramadan, we bring *zakat* to the mosque. That money is used to help the poor." Giving *zakat* is another one of the pillars of Islam. In Afghanistan, *zakat*, or alms, are given during Ramadan.

Another man shared a story he had heard: "There is a very wealthy man who lives in one of the other neighborhoods. Last year he slaughtered two cows and prepared a meal for the poor people in his neighborhood. He's a very good man and will receive great *sawab* for that."

Other stories followed, so I waited and listened. Finally their attention returned to me. They knew that I had something to offer them but couldn't imagine what it was.

I tried to explain. "I know that none of you are rich like the man who could slaughter two cows for his neighbors."

The men nodded. The women just waited; they neither gave *zakat* nor bought cows for neighbors.

"I also understand that if a man is in debt, he cannot give *zakat*. Is that correct?"

The men said he could give *zakat* but should pay off his debt first. I didn't add that I knew all of my male staff members were in debt.

"None of us are rich people with servants working in our fields. Therefore we don't have any servants to oppress. We don't have any power to help Afghans who are oppressed."

Again the men agreed, and the women watched.

"I do think we can help the poor, though."

The men immediately objected. If they were going to help the poor, they thought they would do it through giving *zakat*, and since they were all in debt they weren't going to do that. They saw themselves as too poor to help anyone else.

I presented my idea. "God says that when we fast, it would be good to take what we don't eat and give to the poor."

This was a new concept, and my staff members were intrigued.

I presented them with my offer. "Here's what I propose. I will save the money that the office doesn't spend on lunch for you during Ramadan. At the end of Ramadan, I will add up that money and tell you how much there is. Then you can choose one family to help, but you must agree on which family you want to help. You must decide as a group. Then you can give the money you didn't use for your lunches to that family."

The room exploded into conflicting conversations. The women were immediately delighted. Each knew a family to help. Some of the men thought it was a great idea, too. They had neighbor families they wanted to help. Unfortunately, each staff member had a different family in mind. One of the men was convinced that I should divide the money and give each person, individually, the money for what they didn't eat and let them give it away. I had it in my mind that I wanted my staff to work together, so I stuck to my idea.

Eventually, they said they would agree on one family to help since they had almost six weeks to make the decision. In the end, though, they didn't succeed with that part. They never did agree on a family to help.

Still, I was pleased to have changed the focus from following rules and gaining credit for self-denial to actually helping someone else, which, anyway, was the purpose of our NGO office in Afghanistan.

During each year in Afghanistan, even when it wasn't Ramadan, I often sat down with women who were fasting. Women have to make up the days of fasting they'd missed during Ramadan. They also fasted to fulfill vows, so it wasn't unusual for me to walk into a gathering and find a woman fasting.

One day a foreign friend and I visited a group of friends in a neighborhood outside of the city. We had caught a line taxi and traveled over bumpy, unpaved roads to the dusty *aouli*. When we entered the gate, we walked up an outside staircase to an upper room. There we sat down with three women—two grandmothers, a grown daughter, and her baby. The daughter immediately brought us tea, a bowl of candy, and a bowl of almonds. She poured herself a cup of tea but didn't serve the grandmothers. I begged them to drink with us, but they refused and then admitted they were fasting. It wasn't Ramadan, so I asked the obvious question, "Why are you fasting?" I thought perhaps they were fulfilling some kind of vow. I was wrong.

One of the grandmothers, Lilamah, explained. "We're making up fasting days for being *be-namaz*."

Be-namaz is the word used to describe the week when a woman is ceremonially unclean. She can neither fast nor pray during those days because Allah won't accept her devotion. The two grandmothers were very close friends of mine, so I smiled and teased them, "Grand-mother-jan, I think you are too old to be *be-namaz.*"

The room broke into laughter. Both grandmothers readily agreed. They were long past menopause. Once a woman becomes old, she has no excuse for not fasting. I knew that.

Again Lilamah offered an explanation. "You're right, you're right. We are no longer ever *be-namaz.*"

We laughed again. These are things that people don't discuss. They're shameful, but we were women friends and therefore safe.

Lilamah continued. "But we were young once and without doubt missed days of fasting. We have to make them up."

I was fascinated. "How many days have you missed? How many days do you need to make up?"

Both grandmothers laughed. Lilamah explained, "We have no idea, but we have to make sure. If we haven't made up all of the days, then we won't have enough *sawab* to get into Paradise."

"How do you know when you have enough *sawab?*"

Again they laughed. "We never know until we get there. We can't know. That's why we have to fast."

That led to an explanation of how many days of fasting must be made up for each day missed. These women were taking out insur-ance. They needed to make sure they had fasted all the required num-ber of days. They told me that if they didn't fast enough, Allah would be angry with them—and no one wants that.

I was intrigued. I asked, "So you're fasting so Allah won't be angry with you?"

"Yes, of course. We need to make sure we have enough *sawab.*"

Two conversations continued simultaneously. My Afghan friends explained the law and what had to be done to fulfill it. My foreign friend and I talked about love. For a while, the two conversations were interlaced.

I said to Lilamah, "But God loves you."

She said, *"Inshallah,"* which literally means "God willing" but also implies, "I hope so."

While we were talking, the seven-year-old daughter of the young mother came into the room. The mother, Shahira, had been sitting on her knees between the grandmothers and the doorway. The young daughter came in, sat down on the floor in front of her, and leaned back into Shahira's lap. Shahira absently stroked her daughter's hair and kissed her. It was a lovely sight. I had an idea.

When the women had finished explaining the nuances of the law, I asked, "Does God love you only when you're good and do the things you're supposed to do?"

Shahira immediately responded, "Yes. God hates us when we're bad."

The grandmothers agreed.

I changed the focus to them. "Do you only love your children when they're good and do the things they're supposed to do?"

At that, they were not agreed.

Shahira responded first. She nodded and said, "Only when they're good. When they disobey, we hate them." Shahira was still a very young mother with only small children.

The grandmothers shook their heads. Lilamah offered her words but this time with a sigh. "No, we always love our children. We can't help it. They're our children."

The grandmothers and Shahira debated the question for a couple of minutes. The truth is that when we've lived long enough, we know the pain and disappointment of loving people who go the wrong way, get themselves lost, and do things that destroy themselves or others. I counted on the grandmothers to have lived that long. I wasn't disappointed. Shahira listened and eventually saw their point. She hadn't experienced it, but she recognized it as a possibility.

We were still talking about fasting and why we choose to do it.

I had told them that when we fast, we shouldn't do it because we're afraid of being punished if we don't, but we should fast as a gift we bring to God, who loves us. I used Shahira and her young daughter as my example.

"Shahira, do you love your daughter?" She was still absently stroking her daughter's hair and kissing her.

"Yes, of course."

"Do you like it that she came in, sat down, and put her head in your lap?"

Shahira smiled, looked down at the child with eyes full of love, and nodded.

The grandmothers also looked at the child, their grandchild, their faces full of love and pride.

"How would you feel if your daughter wouldn't come to you? Or if she came to you afraid you were going to hit her? Or if she only came because you made her?"

The women smiled and nodded. They understood what I was getting at. No parent wants her child to come to her begrudgingly or full of fear. We want our children and our grandchildren to know we love them and delight in them.

"That's what God wants. He loves us and wants us to come to Him not because we have to, but because we *want* to."

Our wonderful discussion weaved around this topic for about twenty more minutes. We had shifted from a discussion of the law to a discussion of how beautiful God is, how much He loves us, and how much we love Him. My foreign friend and I affirmed the fast of these precious grandmothers. We affirmed their desire to fast for God. My Afghan friends began to see their fast as a gift rather than an obligation or debt. We prayed for them, that God would accept their fast and their prayers, and they were grateful.

In the end, I asked Lilamah again, "Do you believe God loves you?"

She smiled. "Yes, God loves me." At that, she passed her hands over her face as though sealing a prayer. It had been a beautiful day.

So often in Afghanistan I found myself in conversations or situations I really didn't know how to respond to. The problems and challenges Afghans face every day are so different from our own. Their worldview is startling, initially even incomprehensible, and it affects so much of what they believe and do. Yet despite the chasm that often separates us, we are precious individuals on our own journeys with God, trying to understand Him better and live lives that reflect who we know Him to be. In this journey, we can encourage one another and often did.

During my time in Afghanistan, my neighbors and I talked about prayer and fasting. These are both such important activities for all who love God. We learned from one another. We also talked about how to live with open hands, how to give to our neighbors and help those in need. Sometimes even figuring out how to give is difficult, but God calls us to love our neighbors whether they're Afghan or much like us.

HOW DO WE LIVE
with open Hands?

Afghanistan is a poor and struggling nation. Afghans don't suffer from the mass starvation that sometimes sweeps through parts of Africa, but malnutrition and hunger are rampant. Many families lack fuel to stay warm against the bitter winter cold. Internal refugees surge from one part of the country to another, depending on who's at war with whom. Medical care is improving but still limited in access and quality.

Foreigners in Afghanistan have a well-earned reputation for doing good. We build the roads and bridges, schools and clinics, deliver emergency food, and underwrite the cost of the government, police, and army. Afghans look to us as providers, so when local Afghans met me, they wanted to know what office I worked for and what kinds of projects I did. That's what they expected, and they were right. Locals were satisfied with the answers I gave to these questions. To Afghans, I was the good kind of foreigner who came to help people, but there were always more requests for help than I and others like me were capable of providing for. I struggled over the years to learn what it means to live with open hands in a place where the needs were far too great.

Sometimes random Afghans would walk up to me on the street, step directly before me, and ask for some specific medical advice or treatment. I'm a foreigner, after all, don't I know about medicine? No, I don't. I'm a project manager. That's my experience. I've never studied medicine, at least not until I went to Afghanistan. Since then I've studied a great deal and have learned more than I ever wanted about sickness and death, but I'm no doctor. Sometimes that didn't really matter.

Once I squeezed into the crowded backseat of a minibus bumping over a rock-hard dirt road out to a village beyond the city limits. I had wedged in beside an old woman and her grandson. The grandson was about ten years old, and the old woman immediately pushed him onto my lap. At the next stop, a youngish woman pushed in on the other side of me. Her young teen daughter made her seat on both our laps. It was deep summer and well over 110 degrees. I could barely breathe. Suddenly, the old woman beside me clapped the back of my head and in a hoarse voice demanded, "Give me good drugs."

"What?" I nearly cracked up laughing. "What?"

She repeated, "Give me good drugs. You must have good drugs. Give me good drugs."

The entire backseat of the minivan smiled, although no one could move enough to watch us. We were wedged in tight like potatoes piled into a truck. "Are you sick? What kind of drugs do you need?"

"I'm old. Of course I'm sick. Give me good drugs."

At this, everyone in the back of the minivan laughed. I had no idea how to respond. The truth is that in Afghanistan most drugs, even those sold in pharmacies with prescriptions, are counterfeit.

Many items come with recognizable Western labels but certainly weren't produced to Western specification. Every product is a knock-off. Even the health and beauty products are counterfeit. I once purchased Pantene shampoo, and it came out blue—obviously not the real deal. I actually did own a private stash of "good drugs"—not much, but some. I brought the most necessary medicines with me—paracetamol, ibuprofen, ciprofloxacin for evil stomach attacks, and malaria medicine. I was pretty sure I didn't have whatever this lady wanted, and I certainly didn't have medicines with me. Still, I often ran into people with serious medical ailments and was able to provide a way for them to get treatment at the CURE hospital in Kabul. I didn't want to shut this lady down too quickly.

"Missus, is there something wrong with you?"

She clapped the back of my head again and roared. "I told you, I'm old. Don't you have any good drugs?"

"What do you want drugs for?"

"I don't care, whatever you've got!"

At this everyone in the minivan, including the men wedged into the front seat, cracked up laughing. I smiled, too. "I'm sorry Missus, I don't have any good drugs. I don't have any drugs. I'm not a doctor."

The old woman smacked the back of my head for a third time and said, "Bah! What good are you then?" The minivan rocked with laughter.

Sometimes the requests were deadly serious. Once a friend came to me on behalf of his seven-month-old niece. The girl's tiny stomach was distended as though she were starving, but she wasn't. She had fever and would barely eat. The family had taken her to both the private and public hospitals in our town, to no avail. They had piles of medical reports—X-rays, lab reports, and even a supermarket-sized plastic bag full of various drugs—all representing a variety of misdiagnoses.

My friend came and asked if I could help. I was glad to do it. It's a deep privilege to be able to help another person, especially when helping results in a life saved. I had some money from friends in the States and a foreign doctor friend at CURE hospital in Kabul. I sent the baby and her family to Kabul for tests and treatment. The trip alone was financially out of their reach. They'd already borrowed what they could for the local doctors and treatments. CURE provides its services at deep discount, with the costs underwritten by generous foreigners. The family was hopeful, grateful, and frightened. They'd already tried every available Afghan option. To them, the foreigners were their last hope.

At the CURE International Hospital, doctors welcomed the family. They examined the baby and recognized tuberculosis in her abdomen. In Afghanistan, many families feed newborns unclean cow's butter or milk until their mother's own milk comes in. It's a persistent and unhealthy tradition that's only slowly changing. The CURE doctors in Kabul treated the baby for tuberculosis, and now she's completely well, a growing little girl. If we hadn't sent her, she would have died. Sometimes we try and can help.

Sometimes we try but can't help.

One afternoon I was sitting with a foreign coworker and some Afghan friends in the small home of an Afghan refugee returnee. We had been drinking tea, laughing, and teasing one another when a stranger entered the room. She was a small, half-toothless, wiry woman wrapped in the ground-length black scarf of a refugee returnee from Iran. Under the huge scarf, she carried a bundle wound inside a thick Chinese blanket. She didn't say *Salaam* to us. She sat down on the floor and set the bundle between my foreign coworker and me.

Our host didn't know the woman well. She was a neighbor, but they had never been to each other's houses. They had no social relationship, and my host was taken aback to see the stranger in her house.

The woman waved away the tea that was immediately served her. This wasn't a social visit, and the stranger had broken all the social rules. Even I knew that wasn't a good sign.

My coworker unwrapped the bundle the stranger had set between us. We saw the face first, narrow and hollow. A baby's eyes looked back at us, huge, haunting, far too knowing. I shuddered. The blanket trembled in my coworker's fingers.

She asked, "How old is this child?"

"Maybe nine months," the stranger replied.

The little girl's head was huge, but her body was thin and long. Her elbows and knees pressed through their enveloping skin. Her belly was swollen and dropped off suddenly to fatless legs. Her hands and feet caught my attention. They were far too long for her tiny body—long, bony, and dexterous. The child caught my finger and held it with surprising force. Her eyes found mine, then my coworker's, and then mine again. This child was starving to death.

My coworker directed the questions. "What's wrong with her?"

"She doesn't nurse."

"Has she ever nursed?"

"No."

"Did you try to nurse her immediately after she was born?"

"Yes."

"How many days?"

"Three, when my milk came in."

"Did your milk come in?"

"Yes, but there was never enough, and then it dried up. She wouldn't drink."

Many Afghans believe that the mother's first milk, the colostrum, is unclean. The common practice is to feed newborns unpasteurized cow's butter from the mother's fingers. It satisfies the hunger of the infant but exposes him or her to infection. That's why my friend's baby niece had tuberculosis. If the cow is sick, the baby dies. Slowly, now, Afghans are learning that the colostrum is important, that it's full of fantastic antibodies the child will need to grow strong. But change is slow.

My foreign friend went on with her questions. "Did you give her butter when she was first born?"

"She was hungry."

"What do you feed her now?"

"Powder."

Powdered formula is available in little shops all over town. It's expensive but sometimes helpful, especially if the mother's milk doesn't come in.

"Can you show me?"

The woman immediately disappeared, leaving the starving child half-wrapped in her blanket, one hand wrapped around my finger and the other wrapped around my coworker's, her eyes moving carefully between the two of us.

Our host tried to help us understand the story, but it was clear from her tone that she was more disgusted than empathetic. She didn't know the woman personally, but she knew of the situation from talk in the neighborhood. The family was very poor. This was the fifth or sixth child. They had been back and forth to the hospital, but every time they returned, the child just got sicker. They couldn't afford to keep taking the child to the hospital. The other children were hungry, and there wasn't enough money. There was never enough money. The family was very poor.

My coworker and I struggled. Our emotions were torn. This child, this beautiful little girl, was dying. We talked between ourselves about causes and options. We wanted to do something.

The mother of the starving child returned with a can of powdered formula in her hand. My coworker asked her to show us how she fed the child. One of my host's small daughters was sent off to bring back a cup of hot water and a spoon. The girl returned and the mother scooped a nearly level spoonful of formula and mixed it into three quarters of a cup of hot water. Then she took the child in her arms, cradled her, and tried to slip the mixed formula into the child's mouth.

The child swallowed greedily and then took a second and third spoonful. But by the fourth, she was tired and wouldn't eat any more.

The mother was exasperated. "You see, she won't eat. She refuses to eat."

The other Afghan women in the room were silent. It was clear they didn't like this woman.

My friend picked up the can of formula and patiently explained to the stranger how to use it. One level spoonful was not enough.

The woman balked. "The formula's too expensive."

It felt like all the women in the room were sighing. I searched their averted faces but saw only sorrow and disgust. Babies in Afghanistan are precious—beautiful, hard-won gifts of the God of the universe. They are also vulnerable. Too many die too soon. Every family has a story.

My coworker, an experienced nurse, started over with the mother and again emphasized the importance of using the right amount of formula. She explained that since the child was already starving, she would need to eat only a few spoonfuls perhaps every twenty minutes.

The mother rejected my coworker's advice, which would involve such time-consuming and expensive care. "I have other children. I can't do this."

The conversation that ensued broke our hearts.

The stranger explained herself. "We've done everything we can for this child. We've taken her to the doctor. We've taken her to the hospital. We've paid for everything. We have other children. What can we do?"

My coworker and I listened very, very intently. This woman's words "What can we do?" sounded to our hearts like "What can we do to get rid of this problem?" The woman no longer believed her child could survive, and yet she had brought her to us, the foreigners. Why?

We called a local foreign doctor to get his advice. He told us to bring the baby to the nutrition unit at the hospital and she might—she *might*—survive. We told the mother.

But she wasn't interested. "We can't pay for anything. We have other children. Our family is hungry. What can we do?"

My friend and I immediately told the mother we would cover the expenses—the taxi, the hospital, the medicine, the food, even any necessary bribes. We figured that if the child lived, it would probably cost us between $40 to $100, but certainly no more. We'd pay it.

My coworker told the woman, as clearly as she could, "We will pay for all of it. We will pay as long as it takes, and then we will give you your daughter back. Are you agreed?"

The stranger hesitated. Everyone else in the room scowled. It was obvious we'd hit a wall we couldn't see. I took a guess. I ordered the mother to go home and discuss the offer with her husband. Only he would have the authority to decide. Healthcare is in the power of the men of the family, not the women. I reminded the woman that we would pay for absolutely everything. We would try to save her child.

The woman got up, wrapped herself in her long, black refugee returnee scarf, and shuffled out of the gate.

My Afghan host exploded. "She's not going to ask her husband. She doesn't care if this child lives. She doesn't want this child."

The other women in the room agreed and had nothing but unkind things to say about the woman.

I didn't know how to react—what to say or what to do. I had looked into that beautiful little girl's eyes. She'd held my hand. I couldn't just walk away. We had to try.

My coworker felt the same. She added more powdered formula

to the cup, stirred it, cradled the tiny infant in her arms, and patiently fed her. The whole time we talked to the child, sang to her, stroked her skin, prayed for her, and loved her as best as we could. She watched us, hollow-cheeked, silent, and wide-eyed.

Our Afghan friends wouldn't touch her, couldn't. "She'll die. Maybe today. Maybe tomorrow." They wouldn't look at her. Babies are precious in Afghanistan, and loss is far too common. Every family I've spoken with has grieved the death of a treasured child. My friends didn't want to love this child. They knew she would die.

My coworker and I still had hope. We counted on the nutrition unit and the care we knew we could provide. We just needed permission to try.

The mother returned. She didn't even look at the child. She scooped her up without seeing her, wrapped her in the thick Chinese blanket, and said, "My husband said no." She grabbed the can of powdered formula and walked out.

The little girl died two days later. Our host and our other friends from that community didn't send over fruit or sit with the mother to grieve her loss. They wouldn't honor her that way. None of us had any way to interpret the experience. None of us understood why the mother had brought her starving child to the foreigners and then rejected what assistance we could provide. Perhaps she had expected us to give the child a magic shot that would cure everything. Perhaps she thought we would have medicine in our pockets that would make all the difference. Who knows? Our Afghan friends certainly didn't. They couldn't understand why the mother would refuse to allow these foreigners to take a dying child to the local Afghan hospital and pay for her treatment. In the end, they just said, "She has other children, and they're all hungry."

Sometimes in Afghanistan I could help. Sometimes I couldn't. Sometimes my heart hurt so much I didn't want to face another need.

When I first came to Afghanistan, I was overwhelmed and confused by the requests for help. Strangers would knock on my gate looking for medical care, jobs, or loans. People would accost me on the street and ask for medicine or show me the ailment of a child and expect me to recognize it and know the solution. Often people asked me for food or blankets. In the beginning, I had no way to understand when I should help and when I shouldn't. Jesus tells us to help those who ask, but I knew that if I helped indiscriminately I wouldn't serve those in genuine need and I would spend my limited resources on those who really didn't need them.

I learned quickly that everyone had a story and that many who had access to foreigners would leverage that access for their own benefit, regardless of the needs of their neighbors. I learned that some people would lie and I wouldn't know it. Still others would look to me as the real satisfier of their needs, a role only God should hold. I needed help.

I spent about a year praying and considering the situation. I read books about poverty, its causes, and solutions. I talked to my foreign friends who were wrestling with the same issue. I talked to my Afghan friends until I thought I understood the cultural guidelines for help and responsibility. Finally I resolved to help only individual Afghans in partnership with other Afghans who were not their direct family members. If an Afghan wanted to partner with me to help a needy neighbor, they would contribute and I would give a lot more, and the two of us would provide the assistance.

The plan worked magnificently. It honored and empowered local Afghans to meet the needs of their neighbors, and it allowed me to recognize who was viewed as actually needy.

Over time I developed wonderful giving relationships with different Afghans. One such woman, Nooria, was a great source of wisdom and partnership. She was a widow with grown sons and had returned from nearly twenty years as a refugee in Iran. Somehow her family had managed to acquire a piece of property on the outside edge of the city and had built a small house in a neighborhood full of other returnees. I quickly learned that Nooria knew everyone in her neighborhood and cared deeply about the people around her.

Once another member of that neighborhood came to me with a very sad story. It was deep in the winter, the most brutal winter we had experienced there. The family—a grandmother, mother, and seven small children—were huddled together in a half-built house without doors or glass on the windows. The winter moved in with bitterness and took the life of the grandmother. The father had disappeared more than a year before. He'd gone to Iran to seek work and apparently found it, but he hadn't sent any money home. The mother and her seven small children were only able to live in their house because the grandmother was with them. Two adult women is enough, but one isn't. When the grandmother died, the young mother was forced to leave her husband's property and move. She was desperately poor, and no one could imagine taking in her and her seven children. She had no relatives nearby and couldn't return to Iran.

The elders of the community took up a collection in the neighborhood and brought bags of flour, rice, and beans to the young mother. A local Afghan asked me if I would help, too, so I did.

While I was in the neighborhood delivering the food, a gray-bearded man came to me. He pointed out a house around another corner and said, "They need help. Will you help them too?"

I made a mental note of the father's name and the location of their *aouli* and then went to visit Nooria for advice. I felt sure she would know what to do.

We drank our customary cups of tea in Nooria's long, narrow living room. I looked at the posters of Mecca, Najaf, and Karbala as we talked. Nooria's family were Shiites, poor, but deeply religious. All of the children—three daughters and two sons—were educated. The two sons had attended university, one of the daughters was in university, and at least one other was expected to go. Only Nooria was illiterate. She had been born in a village in the Hazarajat part of the country. There were no schools for girls in her village, and education wasn't viewed as important. After she married, she and her husband fled to Iran to escape the war that had reached their remote village.

The first time I met her I recognized Nooria's compassion and wisdom. She was a woman who helped where she could. Sometimes she would send her daughter to a neighbor's house with a tray full of steaming plates of *palao*, a baked dish with rice, meat, and herbs. Other times, she would send over a few clumps of coal when she saw a family's smokestack go clear in the worst of winter. I trusted her.

Nooria knew I'd helped the woman whose husband had abandoned her and whose mother had died in the cold. She affirmed my gift, and she said everyone in the neighborhood had compassion for the woman. She was an honorable mother who worked hard to raise her children. She even made a little money cleaning lentils for pennies. Nooria was grateful that I'd helped.

Then I asked about the family around the corner that the bearded man had interceded for.

Nooria answered immediately, "No, no. You mustn't help them."

The strength of her response surprised me. "Why not?"

Nooria poured another cup of tea and explained. "The husband of that woman went to Iran three years ago. He didn't send back any help while he was there. He just disappeared. His two older sons found work in the bazaar delivering loads in wheelbarrows. The woman worked cleaning lentils. It wasn't enough. The neighbors had to help. Three years, three years." She was emphatic. "He brought his wife and children here from Iran, built a house, and left them alone. Now he is back in Afghanistan. He must work and feed his family. This is his job."

I understood and thanked Nooria for her advice.

I've learned that it takes a great deal of wisdom to help the poor in Afghanistan. I thought, when I first arrived, that it would be easy, that I would know who to help and who not to help. But that wasn't true. I learned to rely on my Afghan neighbors and friends. If they believed in helping someone and were willing to give something from what little they had, then I could be pretty sure we should help the family too. If they didn't want to give a little something, then I knew I shouldn't either.

Sometimes my Afghan friends gave food, like a bag of macaroni or a bottle of cooking oil. Sometimes they gave their work.

Each winter for several winters we distributed blankets. I skipped the process of going to the male neighborhood elders and turned directly to my women friends. Afghanistan is unfortunately corrupt. When there are public distributions, the neighborhood elders compile the lists of beneficiaries and the neighborhood women complain. They say the list is always stacked with relatives of the elder, not those who are really in need. I never had enough blankets to give so carelessly, so I partnered with the women I trusted.

My office driver and I packed Afghan-made blankets into the office Range Rover and drove from neighborhood to neighborhood through ice, snow, and bitter cold. At each neighborhood, my friends dispatched their sons to unload just ten or twelve blankets and then sent the boys door-to-door with one or two blankets for each of the poorest families in the neighborhood.

I loved to work that way. Months or years later I might meet someone who received one of those blankets. They were always desperately poor and needy. Most of my friends had not only chosen well, they'd been blessed with the opportunity to help.

When I left that town, my office hosted a farewell luncheon. We were an integrated office, so we sat together, men and women, at lunch. The women sat at one end of the *desterkhan*, and the men sat at the other. We foreign women sat between the Afghan men and Afghan women. The foreign men sat at the head of the *desterkhan*, the places of highest honor.

When the meal was over, it was time for the good-bye speeches. There's a formula, a cultural pattern, and we followed it. Each of the men spoke, starting with the foreign men. The first was a Westerner, who thanked me for my hard work, my positive attitude, and my willingness to jump in and get things done. These are attributes we Westerners respect, and their words affirm my efforts.

The next man to speak was an Afghan. His perspective was completely different. What he said stuck with me forever. He said, "You came here to work and to do projects. You did them very well. That was your work. But you also fed our widows and our orphans. You didn't have to. You went out when it was hot after you worked all day and delivered food to our neighbors who were hungry. You went out when it was cold and delivered blankets to our poor relatives. You fed our widows and our orphans. Thank you."

I was stunned. I had no idea how much my Afghan coworkers valued my stumbling efforts at living with open hands.

Often Afghans asked why I came to their country. Some believed my salary was paid by the US government. Others thought I was a spy. Some believed I earned a huge salary. Others assumed I came to earn credit with God. None of these ideas were true.

One of my coworkers said, "I have an uncle who lives in America. He says no one would give up living in America to come to Afghanistan. There must be a reason you are here." He was looking for something nefarious, something sneaky.

After one of my trips home, I brought back a large poster of the Pennsylvania countryside near where I live. It depicts beautiful green hills, fields, woods, and farms. I nailed it to the wall in the living room of our guesthouse. The first person to ask about it was our cook, who used the kitchen in the guesthouse to cook for the office. She looked at the poster. "Is that your home?"

"Yes."

She studied it carefully. Then she said, "If that were my home, I would never leave it."

Once a foreign friend brought her longtime Afghan friend back to America to attend her wedding. The Afghan woman had been working with foreigners for more than ten years and thought she knew something about us. Her experience, in just one week in America, proved she had been completely wrong. In some ways, she was shamed. She stayed in an American home with a normal American kitchen, bathroom, shower, central heating, and air-conditioning. She drove on American roads with lines, traffic lights, and stop signs that people actually paid attention to. She walked in American malls and sat in American restaurants. In the end, she returned to Afghanistan with a shocked appreciation for the distance we foreigners have come.

Again and again I was asked, "Why have you come to Afghanistan?"

How I answered that question often depended on how much time I had and how well I knew the people who were asking. Usually my response was brief: "Because God tells us to love our neighbors, and you are my neighbor."

Afghans don't consider Americans their neighbors. We are foreigners, far away, rich, and clearly not Muslims. Afghans have cultural rules regarding who should help whom. These are defined by family relationship, physical neighborhood, tribe, and religion. But cultural rules are human constructs overlaid on top of the human spirit. The human spirit is made by God and has its own God-created life. The joy a person finds in helping another, in giving to a genuine need, is a God-created joy. The desire to be generous breathes beneath the surface of cultural rules and religious laws.

I often asked my Afghan friends and neighbors directly if they wanted to help someone. Sometimes they spent months collecting their coins, then said, "We're ready." More often they resisted, hesitated, or refused.

One day I was sitting with the two wives of one husband, their daughter-in-law, and several children and toddlers. The women lived two gates up the street from an Afghan orphanage. The orphanage housed about thirty boys and fed and educated another sixty boys and girls who lived in the town. I asked my friends if they'd ever considered helping the orphans.

The younger wife responded, "No, we don't have a relationship with those orphans. We don't visit them, and they don't visit us. Why should we help them?"

I laughed at her, but gently. "How could you have a visiting relationship with those boys? They're boys and not your family. Of course you have no reason to visit them, and they have no reason to visit you. Still, they're orphans. Afghan orphans. Would you consider helping them?" I put my neighbor on the spot.

The younger wife evaded, "We're poor. How can we help them?"

That was the question I really wanted. I smiled and shared a story. "One day the Honorable Jesus Messiah was standing in the house of God in Jerusalem with His students. People came into the temple to give money to the poor."

My friend recognized the context. In Afghanistan, men carry money for the poor to the mosque during funerals or on special Muslim holidays. Giving it is required of all Muslims who aren't in debt. I was stretching *zakat* to include helping the orphans.

I went on. "While the Teacher and His students were in the house of God, a very rich man came in to give. A group of people came with him. They were dressed in expensive clothes. Everyone, including the Honorable Jesus and His students, watched. The man walked up to the jar where the money was collected and threw his gift in. He had a lot of coins, so it made a lot of noise."

I picked up all the wrapped hard candy from the glass bowl in front of me and poured it back in, slowly, with a flourish. Then I scooped up the candy two more times and made more noise. We all laughed.

I continued with the story. "Everyone said, 'Oh, what a good man. That is a very good man. Did you see that good man?' And the rich man with his rich friends walked out of the house of God."

I sat up straight and mimicked a very proud, very fat person making a show of himself. We laughed again.

"Then, a small widow woman shuffled into the house of God." I bent forward and tried to make myself small and shy. "She walked up to the jar and gently slid two little coins in."

I took two pieces of hard candy I'd hidden in my hand and quietly put them back into the bowl.

"The widow woman turned and walked away. Then the Teacher Jesus Messiah looked at His students. He asked, 'Did you hear that person's gift, how beautiful it was?' But the students were still watching the rich man with his friends. They said, 'Oh yes, he's a good man. He's a very good man.' The Teacher Jesus Messiah said, 'Not him—the old widow woman. Did you hear her gift? It was beautiful.' His students looked around, 'Where? Who?' The Teacher Jesus showed them the widow walking quietly away. His students said, 'Her? She's poor.' The Teacher Jesus said, 'Her gift was the best of all. She's poor. She doesn't have much, but what she had she gave. That rich man, he only gave a little. He has much more. She gave all she could. Her gift was more beautiful.'"

My friends loved the story, but I wanted more than to entertain.

I put myself in the shoes of the rich man. I offered my friends a deal. "If you give what you can, I'll give more, but God will still call your gift more beautiful, because you don't have much." I smiled.

My friends smiled too. The younger wife nodded her agreement. She had to ask her husband, but he agreed. In the end, we packed up hygiene kits for the boys who lived in the orphanage, thirty kits. My friend provided a bar of soap for each child. It wasn't much, but it was what she could give. I provided towels, toothpaste, toothbrushes, and clothes-washing powder. We packed each child's gift into a colorful bag sewn by a group of older women in America and carried our gifts to the boys.

I convinced my friend to come with us for the distribution. She came, she watched, and she wept as her young son gave each orphan boy his bag. The orphan boys got hygiene kits, but my friend got something even better. She got the opportunity to help a stranger in need, and she loved it. Generosity is part of what we're made for. Beneath the overlay of cultural rules and religious laws is the God-created human spirit that longs to live as God created it.

One day while we were eating lunch, our staff celebrated the completion of a small project we had done for that same orphanage. We had built a mud platform and had set up a used German army tent for use as the children's lunchroom. The project had only cost about $750, but it provided good value for the orphans. My staff wanted to know where that money came from.

I told them this story. "There is a church in a very small town in America."

Immediately, they wanted to know what the church looked like. That particular church was a traditional, old, white-clapboard Baptist church on the top of a flat plateau of farmland in a semirural area in New Jersey. I described the building and the land around it. Then I went on. "Every week, the families go to church."

They stopped me again. "The families go to church? Together?" In Afghanistan, men go to mosques to pray and hold meetings where they debate issues and make decisions. They vote for village leaders and argue about politics and slipping social mores. In rural areas, women bring their children to the porch of the mosque to receive vaccines, but they never go into the mosque to pray or talk. In most places in Afghanistan, children take classes before or after school and during their school holidays. Boys and girls go separately. Afghan families don't *ever* attend the mosque together.

The question of family attendance led to a description of Sunday church. I described the inside of that church. I explained Sunday school classes where people come to learn what Jesus teaches. I described the sanctuary—benches, a pulpit, and an area for the choir and worship band. My staff members were surprised to hear that people sing in church. They were also surprised to hear that men and women sit together and usually their children sit with them.

I continued with my answer about the money. "In that church, each week, the families come. They go to Sunday school where they learn about Jesus. Every week the children bring coins, pocket money like the money Afghans give their children to buy kites, French fries, and sweets on the street. In Sunday school, they give some of that money. Every week each child gives something. Then when they've collected a lot of money, they send it to me to help the children in the orphanage."

My story was full of revelation for my staff. They already knew that private citizens in America gave the money that supported our office and our regular projects. But children? Children give?

One of our men, a maintenance man with rough hands, a huge heart, and his own children asked, "Why do they do that?"

I tried to answer. "Parents who follow the Honorable Jesus try to teach their children to follow the Honorable Jesus too. The Teacher Jesus said we should love God with everything He's given us and we should love our neighbors as ourselves. Many Jesus Messiah-following parents teach their children to love their neighbors far away by giving money to help them. So each week, the children come and give a little bit of money. They're not rich, and it's not much money. They have to save it until they have enough to send. They send it here because I told them about the orphanage. They like helping the children in the orphanage. They want to do it."

By then we were pulling bright orange rinds off our *kinos*, sweet oranges, and dropping them into little piles on our red-and-white plastic plates. My Afghan staff considered teaching children to give an amazingly good idea. Our maintenance man told us how people in Iran collect money to help the poor in that country. They agreed that Afghans should do this too. They said that if Afghans collected small amounts of money to help the orphans, the orphans wouldn't be so poor. I encouraged their thinking.

My Afghan staff decided we would try to collect money in the neighborhood for the orphanage. Our neighborhood wasn't poor, so we thought we might be able to do something in partnership with our neighbors' gifts. Our maintenance man made a deal with a local shopkeeper to do the collecting.

The orphanage still needed a carpet to put down on the platform we had built for them. Afghans don't sit directly on naked floors. They sit on carpets or mats. If there's no floor covering, they squat. The tent protected the children from the sun, but they still needed a carpet to sit on. We priced the carpet and found that it would cost about $120. We decided to try to raise $20 in the neighborhood and pay the other $100 ourselves as matching funds. Our maintenance man gave the local shopkeeper a small wooden lockbox, and the man agreed to explain the idea to everyone who came to his store. He would ask our neighbors to contribute. I was delighted, confident that would get the children their carpet and that our neighbors would enjoy helping.

It didn't work. After two weeks, the shopkeeper gave the box back, empty. He told us that our neighbors wouldn't contribute. Apparently every neighbor he spoke with had said that the orphans were not their responsibility. The government had to pay for them. They accused the person who ran the orphanage of stealing and lying. They wouldn't help.

My Afghan staff members were disappointed and not a little

embarrassed. How could children from a faraway town in America care more about children in Afghanistan than Afghans did? We talked about how important it is to love our neighbors, even those we don't know directly. My staff agreed with that teaching. We never did buy the carpet for the orphans, but one of my staff members did something truly amazing.

He took the wooden lockbox and nailed it to the wall just inside our gate. It was his job to answer the gate, so every time someone came, he asked them to put something in the box. He asked everyone, foreigners and Afghans alike. The amount of money in the box grew. Then, the rains came.

We heard news that several families in another town had lost their houses in a flood. That was need. My staff decided they would help. Our maintenance man opened the wooden box and pulled out the money. Unbeknownst to him, the box had filled with mud from the wall it had been nailed to. Patiently, he washed every Afghani and American bill and Afghani coin. Then he spread the money out on the floor in the room where we ate lunch. He lit the little sawdust heater to dry it. When the bills were stiff, he counted the money and was delighted to discover more than $100. He tucked the cash into an envelope, sealed it, and put it into the hands of an Afghan friend who delivered it to one of the families who had lost their house.

That money provided a month's food for the family. It replaced destroyed bags of rice and flour, salt and matches. The family, of course, was astonished and grateful, but it was the reaction of my staff that I loved the most. They were so proud of themselves, so grateful for the opportunity to give, so delighted to be able to help someone else in need. I watched and rejoiced.

My staff stepped into the heart of God when they collected that money, saw the need, and reached out to meet it. They experienced the beauty and joy of living the way we're meant to live. When we recognize that God loves all people and respond by loving God and our neighbors, not only with our hearts but also with our hands, we're the greatest beneficiaries.

Over the course of five years, I've had the privilege of providing Afghans with the opportunity to help others in their community. I watched them step into it and rejoice. For most who participated, the opportunities I provided were just what they were looking for— a way to do what they knew was good and right. I saw beautiful compassion expressed through words and sacrifice. None of my staff members, nor the neighbors with whom we worked, were rich. They didn't have nice houses, fancy telephones, or cars. They were average Afghans finding a way to live the way they knew they were meant to live. My part was to share the stories that resonated in their hearts and to provide opportunities and encouragement to do what they recognized was good and right. It was a beautiful thing to see my Afghan neighbors, friends, and staff lean into the heart of God—a beautiful, tender thing.

saying good-bye

My friends in America ask me what could possibly bring peace to Afghanistan. My American neighbors watch the Afghan situation on television and the Internet and struggle to understand. The things that happen in Afghanistan don't make sense to most of us. The culture is so different, the lives of the people incomprehensible. Most Westerners understand very little about Afghanistan and even less about the culture. Foreign military serving in the country only understand a little of the culture. They see it from a distance, separated by body armor, weapons, and lack of language.

Afghanistan is a complex country, and its problems run deep. It's hard to see the solutions, yet our sons and fathers, mothers and sisters, have given their money, their lives, their health, and even their limbs to bring peace to this war-torn nation. The world calls Afghanistan the "Graveyard of Empires," but in reality the graves in Afghanistan overwhelmingly bear the bones of Afghans themselves.

It's easy to see the manifestations of Afghanistan's troubles—war, bribery and theft, unemployment, ignorance, and oppression, but it's difficult to recognize why such national self-destruction continues.

We Westerners want to believe that if we can partner with Afghans to rebuild their infrastructure, create a space for legal businesses, build schools and hospitals, then somehow the country will find real peace. We assume that we powerful and wealthy outsiders can change the hearts and minds of a people by giving them stuff—electricity, roads, hospitals, schools, and even houses. Some Westerners believe Afghanistan will become a nation of peace and prosperity when the power of the Taliban is finally broken, as though the Taliban are the true and only source of evil, violence, and oppression. Others believe the government—including the police, army, and teachers—must stop taking bribes before the nation will heal itself. Still others look to the younger generation growing up in Afghan schools and attending Afghan universities to slowly change the culture.

All of the tangible gifts we bring are of value, and giving them to people who will never be able to pay us back is a good thing to do. But our military strength and humanitarian generosity cannot change the hearts of a people. We don't have that power.

The problems in Afghanistan run much deeper than the Taliban, corruption, or education issues. Those are only symptoms of a nation built on sand. Until Afghans change their way of thinking—the stories they tell about themselves, their neighbors, and their God—they will not change their country.

If the stories Afghans told me and one another were the only stories, I would certainly despair. If the stories I brought fell rejected into the Afghan dust, I would have no hope for our precious and beautiful Afghan neighbors. But that's not the case.

Many Afghans are hungry for change. They've seen the outcomes of their faith and the practices that define them. They've wondered how such a religious, God-obeying nation could descend into more than thirty years of war and self-destruction. They long for something better. The problem is that even Afghans don't know where to start. Even Afghans struggle to find the way of peace for their suffering families, communities, and nation.

Often I asked my Afghan friends if they had hope for the future. Most are trying to hold on to hope, but it's difficult. The daily news carries images of bombings, beheadings, corrupt officials, drugs, and a dozen other seemingly intractable problems. Every family carries its own horrors in stories told with hushed voices or hidden in shamed silence. Too many women enter marriage with tears in their eyes and fear in their hearts. Too many men know the bitterness of bribes given and justice perverted. Everyone has lost someone. Everyone has a story he or she struggles to make sense out of. The problems in Afghanistan run deep through Afghan hearts, families, and communities long before they manifest themselves in warlords and bombs.

My American friends ask me what I think will happen next. Do I have hope? Do I believe the lives of Afghans can change? Yes, I do have hope, but only because I know God loves the people of Afghanistan. God is not silent in His love. He is speaking to Afghans. He speaks through dreams and visions, through the stories of His children, and He whispers directly into the hearts of people He has loved from the foundation of the earth. God has given so many Afghans both a hunger for God and a longing for the love, joy, and peace that only His kingdom can provide.

The way of hope is the way of Jesus. His teachings show us the path. His stories make sense of the senseless. I've watched Afghans listen to the stories and words of Jesus and find wisdom, beauty, and truth in them. I've watched some Afghans appropriate those teachings into their own lives and reframe their own stories with beautiful outcomes.

The barrier, of course, is that the way of Jesus is not the way of Afghanistan. The teachings of Jesus challenge virtually every aspect of the culture, and many Afghans object vehemently to that kind of influence, regardless of its benefits.

My presence in Afghanistan, the work I did and the stories I shared, were like sweet-scented clean air to some, but destruction to others. Some embraced me and the stories I brought. Some rejected me. Others tried to redefine me as a way of interpreting my life.

One Afghan woman said to me, "Oh, you really are a Muslim; you just don't know it."

"No." I smiled. "I'm certainly not."

"But look! You speak our language and wear a headscarf."

"Yes, but I follow the teachings of the Honorable Jesus Messiah." That is the real difference.

We foreign aid workers, doctors, and educators who move into their communities shatter the stereotypes many Afghans have been taught to believe. We non-Muslims are supposed to be evil, and yet we cradle their dying children in our arms. We make arrangements for their sick to get medical care. We feed their widows and orphans. We give blankets against the cold, and in hundreds of other ways we demonstrate a different way to live. We tell a different story.

If, instead of loving my neighbors, I had brought lies and deceptions, corruption and immorality, I wouldn't have been considered a threat. I would have been held up as an example of what's evil and wrong in the world. But when I told Afghan Muslim people that God is good and God loves them, when I told them God forgives us and invites us to forgive others, when I told them God's kingdom was made for us and we were made for God's kingdom, and my stories resonated in their hearts, worldviews did change, attitudes shifted, and new actions followed.

That's the kind of influence conservative leaders in Afghanistan simply can't allow. They are the masters—the power-brokers, definers, and enforcers. We see the outcomes of their authority and shake our heads in dismay.

We read of the struggles of Afghan women and shudder. We pray for their deliverance and give money for programs to help them. There are laws designed to protect women in Afghanistan, but they're not enforced. Afghans don't accept those laws, regardless of the government's insistence. Until men and women view one another as precious children of the God they worship, there will be little improvement. Until men learn to love their wives as Christ loves His church—to walk with them and talk with them, to sacrifice themselves for them—there cannot be health in that most fundamental human relationship.

As long as Afghans understand God as a judge who only loves the obedient, they will never genuinely love one another. They'll never free one another to become the unique individuals God has created them to be. They'll certainly never love the unrelated neighbor or the non-Muslim stranger.

As long as Afghans hero-worship a warrior king who defined submission and required it at the edge of a sword, there cannot be peace in their country. As long as Afghans understand forgiveness as an option and retribution as a norm, the escalation of violence will continue.

When Afghan warriors slaughtered a medical team who had brought real health care to real Afghans, they neutralized the threat of outside ideas that came along with that desperately needed help. When the young student declared that anyone who watches satellite television is an infidel, she sought to set up thick walls of ignorance to protect people from being influenced. When another young student explained that Jihad must be fought against any influential non-Muslim culture, she articulated a desire that, taken to its conclusion, would leave Afghanistan in ignorance, violence, and oppression. That student believed that murder, maiming, and destruction are somehow better than trusting God to show us good and right ways to live. Such walls may keep me and others like me outside, but no one can keep the God who loves out of Afghanistan.

God loves our Afghan neighbors, and He will not be silent. It's His story that matters, that speaks truth into our hearts, that makes sense out of our realities and shows us the way to live.

As a follower of Jesus, I trust God to guide people into truth. I can't make someone accept one idea or reject another. Confirming truth in another's heart belongs to God alone. No human being has that power. If I have shared God's stories, His truth, His love, then I have scattered good seeds. If God is not speaking into a person's heart, then whatever good seeds I sow will fall onto concrete, but if God is speaking to a person and the story I share is truth, then the seed I scatter will find a home in his or her heart and will grow into something new in his or her life.

For some Afghans, different stories, like new ideas, are welcome as concepts to be evaluated, adapted, and appropriated or rejected. Many friends, neighbors, and coworkers embraced the stories I brought. Some found the sweetness of knowing God's love for them. Some found the freedom of forgiveness given to those who'd sinned against them. Others found the assurance of knowing their sins were forgiven. Some entered into the practice of thanksgiving and found their marriages healed. Others opened their hands to give and found themselves the greatest beneficiaries.

I consider myself privileged to have had the opportunity to journey into Afghanistan for those five years. I met a people I'd never known before, entered into their homes and lives, and found them as preciously human and beautiful as the friends I'd left behind in America. I was honored to share their salt and their stories, their laughter and their sorrows.

Afghans also helped me understand the teachings of Jesus more completely. The culture of Afghanistan today is much more similar to the first-century Judea of Jesus' day than my own Western culture is. The teachings and stories of the New Testament map almost exactly. The mullahs of today are more like the ancient Scribes and Pharisees than our pastors or priests. Sharia law is closer to the Law of Moses than the guiding principles Jesus taught us to understand and apply in the context of our ever-evolving culture. The agrarian society of Afghanistan, with its farmers and shepherds, grasps the stories of lost sheep and scattered seed far better than our post-industrial world.

I was often amazed when an Afghan heard a Jesus story for the first time and then told me what it means. Jesus spoke to a woman at a well, a woman who had had several husbands and was not married to her current partner. My Afghan women friends immediately saw the woman's shame. No woman in Afghanistan can arrange her own marriage. The woman at the well had been used by five men, and the last didn't even have the decency to marry her. The woman's question about where she should worship made sense. With her lack of honor and freedom, she couldn't have gone to Jerusalem or Mount Gerazim to worship. Stunningly, Jesus told her she could worship where she was, told her she was not cut off from God. He said worship isn't about form or place but about spirit and truth. For my Afghan friends living locked behind walls, huddled in teahouses or street corners, frightened of the neighborhood mullah, this is good news! Everything Jesus said and did is good news. It's no wonder so many listened to the stories and teachings of Jesus and were changed by them. How could we not be?

I learned to see the Jesus I love reflected in the context of my Afghan neighbors' culture and the simplicity of their questions. I was challenged to differentiate between my American culture and the teachings of Jesus. Sometimes I was driven back to the Bible to find answers to questions I'd never before considered. Often I was driven to prayer and sometimes to fasting. Through it all, I grew in my understanding of Jesus and of my own faith. I saw how wonderfully revolutionary Jesus really is and how amazingly beautiful.

This book is just a black-and-white sketch of a five-year journey into Afghanistan, but writing it has been a blessing. Even as I recorded these stories and shaped the chapters, I fell deeper in love with Jesus. I saw Him again in the context of my neighbors' lives and drew encouragement not only for myself but also for them. I listened to my Afghan neighbors again, and through the words of our conversations came to know them better and remembered why I love them so much.

You have joined me in the rickshaws and taxis, the bazaars, offices, and homes of many amazing and precious people. I hope you've enjoyed the journey. I hope you've met our distant neighbors and come to know them better. I hope you've seen their beauty. Afghans are wonderfully real people with real troubles, hopes, and dreams—they're precious men and women who are on a journey even as I am. This is a journey of faith.

My time in Afghanistan came to an abrupt end when security in our town disintegrated beyond what I could bear. Our neighbors still welcomed us and the local mosque had not decided to throw rockets, but illegal gangs and corrupt but empowered local militias had grown too strong, too quick to kidnap or kill. We foreigners could no longer ride in the rickshaws, walk down our tree-lined street, or drink tea in our neighbors' homes. We had to leave, and the parting was heartbreaking. I left behind my home, my fruit trees, and my garden, my dog, my friends, and the children who climbed in and out of my lap. I walked away from five years with a duffel bag, a backpack, and these stories. I will forever treasure the privilege of my journey in Afghanistan, the beloved people I met, and the stories we shared.

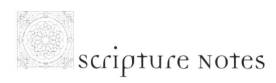 scripture notes

Chapter 2: Where It All Starts
Discussions about Scripture in this chapter derived from the account of creation in Genesis 1 and 2 and the fall in Genesis 3, and from the Ten Commandments in Exodus 20, especially the injunction against murder found in verse 13.

Chapter 3: Whose Example Do We Follow?
The account of God's creation of men and women, or of "arranging" the first marriage, appears in Genesis 2, and the reasoning about a man leaving his family of origin to make his own family appears in Genesis 2:24.

Even while hanging on the cross, Jesus provides for His widowed mother by making His close friend John a surrogate son to her, in John 19:27. This forms a great contrast to forced marriage for widows, a practice of Islam.

Chapter 4: Facing Hatred

The man quoting the Quran's instruction about destroying the Jews is translating and paraphrasing the Arabic text of the Hadith, Sahih al-Bukhari.

The biblical account of Abraham, Sarah, Hagar, Ishmael, and Isaac is found in Genesis, chapter 21, and establishes Ishmael (ostensibly the "father of the Muslim people") as the brother of Isaac (one of the patriarchs of the Jewish faith).

Jewish dietary laws are delineated in the laws of Moses, especially in Leviticus 11 and Deuteronomy 14.

The "two greatest commandments" appear in the various accounts of Jesus' teaching in the Gospels. See Matthew 22:36–39, Mark 12:29–31, and Luke 10:27. Jesus was elaborating on the Old Testament teaching of Deuteronomy 6:5.

The biblical injunction against murder appears in the Ten Commandments in Exodus 20:13 and Deuteronomy 5:17. Jesus elaborates on these by extending the guilt of murder to hatred in the heart in Matthew 5:21–22.

The story of Abraham's near-sacrifice of his son Isaac appears in Genesis 22.

Qur'an 3:45–51 Surah Ale-'Imran recounts the Islamic story of the annunciation. The angel Gabriel is not mentioned by name but credited with the message by Islamic tradition. The Bible's account of the annunciation can be found in Luke 2.

The story of the rich young ruler who wanted to "inherit eternal life," but went away without obeying Jesus, is found in Luke 18.

Chapter 5: Choosing Love

The plain statement that "God is love" appears in 1 John 4:8. The truth of this statement is described throughout all of Scripture.

Jesus' teaching to "Love your neighbor" appears repeatedly in the Gospels. See Matthew 22:36–39, Mark 12:29–31, and Luke 10:27.

First John 1:9 provides wonderful assurance of God's faithful forgiveness "when we confess our sins."

Chapter 6: Who Is God?

Find the truth that God is not just kind but that "God is love" in 1 John 4.

Psalm 139 expressively explains how uniquely and wonderfully God created each person.

My illustration about the bowls and Jesus becoming a bridge to carry me across to heaven, despite my sin, is grounded in the truths found in these Scriptures and others: John 3:16, Romans 5:8, Romans 6:23, and Ephesians 2:8–9.

First John 4:8 teaches that a person who does not show love to others does not know God.

Chapter 7: How Do We Respond to Evil Done to Us?

The words "Forgive us our trespasses as we forgive those who trespass against us" form part of the prayer Jesus taught His disciples to pray, found in Matthew 6:12 and Luke 11:4.

Matthew 5:42–44 includes Jesus' instructions to His followers to love their enemies.

The story of the servant who'd been forgiven so much and then failed to forgive another is found in Matthew 18:23–35.

Chapter 8: How Do We Respond to Insult?

Jesus' teaching to "turn the other cheek," rather than exacting an eye for an eye or a tooth for a tooth, is found in Matthew 5:38–39.

The account of Jesus being arrested, insulted, shamed, and beaten—and then praying for the forgiveness of His tormenters—can be read in Luke 23.

In Luke 9:51–56, Jesus rebukes James and John for wanting to punish the Samaritan village with fire from heaven.

Chapter 9: Who Can Judge?

Jesus teaches about the unwashed cup in Matthew 23:25–28. His promise to send His followers his Holy Spirit is recorded in John 14.

The injunction to "Judge not, and you will not be judged" is found in Matthew 7:1 and Luke 6:37.

Chapter 12: How Do We Learn to Live Our Faith?

Jesus' parable about the wise man who built his house on the rock is found in Matthew 7:24–25. I paraphrased the story to tell it to Faiz Mohammed.

Chapter 13: How Should We Pray?

In my conversations about Jesus teaching His students to pray, I paraphrased the words of Matthew 6:9–10.

Jesus describes the gifts of a good father to illustrate God's love for His children in Luke 11:11–13 and Matthew 7:9–10.

Scripture's teaching not to be anxious but to present our requests to God is stated simply in Philippians 4:6.

Chapter 14: How Should We Fast?

Jesus' words about fasting in private, which my friend quoted to me, are found in Matthew 6:16.

Chapter 15: How Do We Live with Open Hands?

The story of the Teacher Jesus Messiah affirming the small but beautiful donation of the widow can be found in Luke 21:1–4.

Chapter 16: Saying Good-bye

The story of Jesus meeting the Samaritan woman at the well is beautifully told in John 4.

acknowledgments

I've so enjoyed writing this book! The process allowed me once again to enter into Afghan homes and hear the voices of Afghan friends and strangers. In each chapter I welcome you into the world I walked in, loved, and sometimes wept in. These fragments of conversations that took place over the course of my five years in Afghanistan are true. Each person is real, and every setting is a place where I've walked and stood or sat.

As I read, my mind translates the pseudonyms back into real names. I automatically shuffle our conversations into the right rooms, but I've hidden these things from you, mixing the participants and locations to protect those involved. For example, I may have set a conversation in a yellow room when really the yellow room belongs with a different conversation. Or I put a conversation in an upper room instead of its actual basement location. But conversations that took place in homes are presented in homes. Conversations that took place in offices are presented in offices, and conversations that took place in rickshaws or taxis are all presented in those vehicles. Still, I've changed all the names and mixed the locations. I also mixed the times. Sometimes I changed seasons. I put a conversation about cloth-sellers into the season of plums when really that story belongs to a much colder season.

I did keep the general description of each participant. Those I designated as religious scholars are religious scholars. I identified people truthfully as men or women.

The point is to protect myself and everyone involved. Afghanistan is a dangerous country. My neighbors felt safe with me. They often shared openly, but that doesn't mean they wanted their Afghan neighbors to hear all their words. So I've protected those precious people who trusted me and welcomed me into their homes.

I recorded some of these real conversations on audio, wrote them up, and then destroyed the audio files at the request of the participants. Some stories were written up shortly after they occurred, and others are recorded from memory.

I thank all the Afghans who invited me into their homes and shared their lives with me. Without you, this book would be inconceivable. Thanks, too, to those special foreign friends who walked the dusty streets, stepped through the gates, and shared these conversations with me. I will forever treasure our friendship.

I'd like to thank my precious friends in the United States who prayed, supported, and encouraged me throughout the years of this journey. You have blessed me more than I'll ever be able to express. I'm especially thankful to special friends who carved out a home for me to rest in along the way.

I'm also grateful to each of you who encouraged this book, who reviewed the first draft, and who have celebrated its passage into being.

Most importantly, I'm grateful to You, my Lord Jesus, for inviting me to walk with You in the land of Afghanistan. What a privilege it's been! Thank You.

IN THE HEART OF A CHILD, ONE MOMENT CAN LAST FOREVER

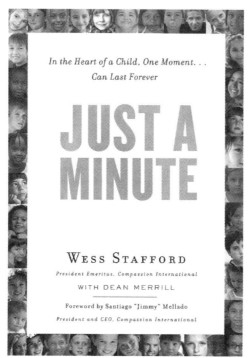

In the Heart of a Child, One Moment. . .
Can Last Forever

JUST A MINUTE

WESS STAFFORD

President Emeritus, Compassion International

WITH DEAN MERRILL

Foreword by Santiago "Jimmy" Mellado
President and CEO, Compassion International

978-0-8024-0966-9

All it takes is one moment out of your busy day, and you can be that someone in the life of the very next child who comes across your path. It may be your own son or daughter. Or perhaps it's the child down the street playing soccer. Or maybe it's the one having a meltdown in the grocery store.

Read on for story after powerful story of lives changed because someone took just a minute to really connect in the life of a child. Stay alert—you never know when your opportunity will come.